POSUTĀ
POSTER
POSUTĀ
POSTER
POSUTĀ
POSTER

ISBN 978-988-75666-6-3 Contemporary Poster Designs from Japan

Published and distributed by
viction workshop ltd.

viction:ary™

viction:workshop ltd.
Unit C, 7/F, Seabright Plaza,
9–23 Shell Street,
North Point, Hong Kong SAR
Url: www.victionary.com
Email: we@victionary.com

@victionworkshop
@victionworkshop
Bē @victionary
@victionary
小红书 @Victionary Book

Edited and produced by viction workshop ltd
Creative Direction: Victor Cheung
Design: Chris Chan, Scarlet Ng
Editorial: Ynes Filleul, YL Lim
Coordination: Katherine Wong
Production: Bryan Leung

Fourth Edition

ISBN 978-988-75666-6-3
Printed and bound in China

POSUTĀ POSTER POSUTĀ POSTER POSUTĀ POSTER

ISBN 978-988-75666-6-3 Contemporary Poster Designs from Japan

Foreword

Yudai
Osawa

Posters serve not only as a medium displayed in public places to be appreciated by a broad audience, but also as a means of fostering a sense of identity within a company when displayed internally, or even as a valuable commodity when sold. Additionally, with the widespread use of smartphones and the availability of high-quality digital signage, both print and digital posters are utilised in tandem.

Times are constantly changing, and designers must be attuned to the social climate in order to create designs that are responsive to current events. Lately, I have been closely following the trend of "non-print posters".

Non-print posters are primarily utilised on digital signage and social media banners, and can also incorporate video elements. Historically, video media has been reserved for TV ads. However, in response to the growing use of printed posters and digital signage, incorporating videos in posters is considered to be a more cost-effective and impactful way to communicate a message.

The media shift towards dynamic formats has led to a demand for still images to be just as dynamic. This demand extends beyond just the main visual, as logos and small accompanying graphics are now expected to feature dynamic elements as well. Consequently, many graphic designers are incorporating dynamic features into their existing style. Unlike traditional TV ads, the videos created by graphic designers often feature looping motions, with some parts remaining fixed and others moving cyclically. This dynamic visual system is also gaining recognition as an identity in its own right. Paradoxically, this also creates a relationship where dynamic elements complement the Corporate Identity (CI) and Visual Identity (VI) of a brand.

In light of these changes, the poster is increasingly becoming a central element in defining the identity of a project. Posters are shared as a representation of the project's identity and serve as a starting point for communication. As a result, there has been a growing trend towards developing CI and VI based on moving image posters.

New designs are often born out of new situations, and designs created under these circumstances, including posters, often feel more free than conventional designs. This newfound freedom may be attributed to the way that dynamic effects complement message conveyance. When dynamic elements are introduced into human cognition, the brain is able to compensate for information based on the premise of movement, even if the information is not animated. Ultimately, the incorporation of dynamic elements into posters and other design media provides a new avenue for creativity and communication, and opens up new possibilities for designers to explore.

As the nature of posters continues to evolve, it raises the question of what role posters will play in the future. While the traditional role of posters as a medium for public display is unlikely to disappear, the rise of digital media has introduced new possibilities for how posters can be used to communicate information and express identity. Ultimately, the future of posters is wide open, and it will be exciting to see how this medium evolves and develops in the years to come.

AFFORDANCE inc.

AFFORDANCE inc. was founded by Atsushi Hirano. The studio's work encompasses branding, corporate and visual identities, as well as signage and spatial design projects, with a focus on graphic design. It has received various awards over the years — a TDC Prize, JAGDA Newcomer Award, Minister of Economy, Trade and Industry Award, and SDA Award to name a few.

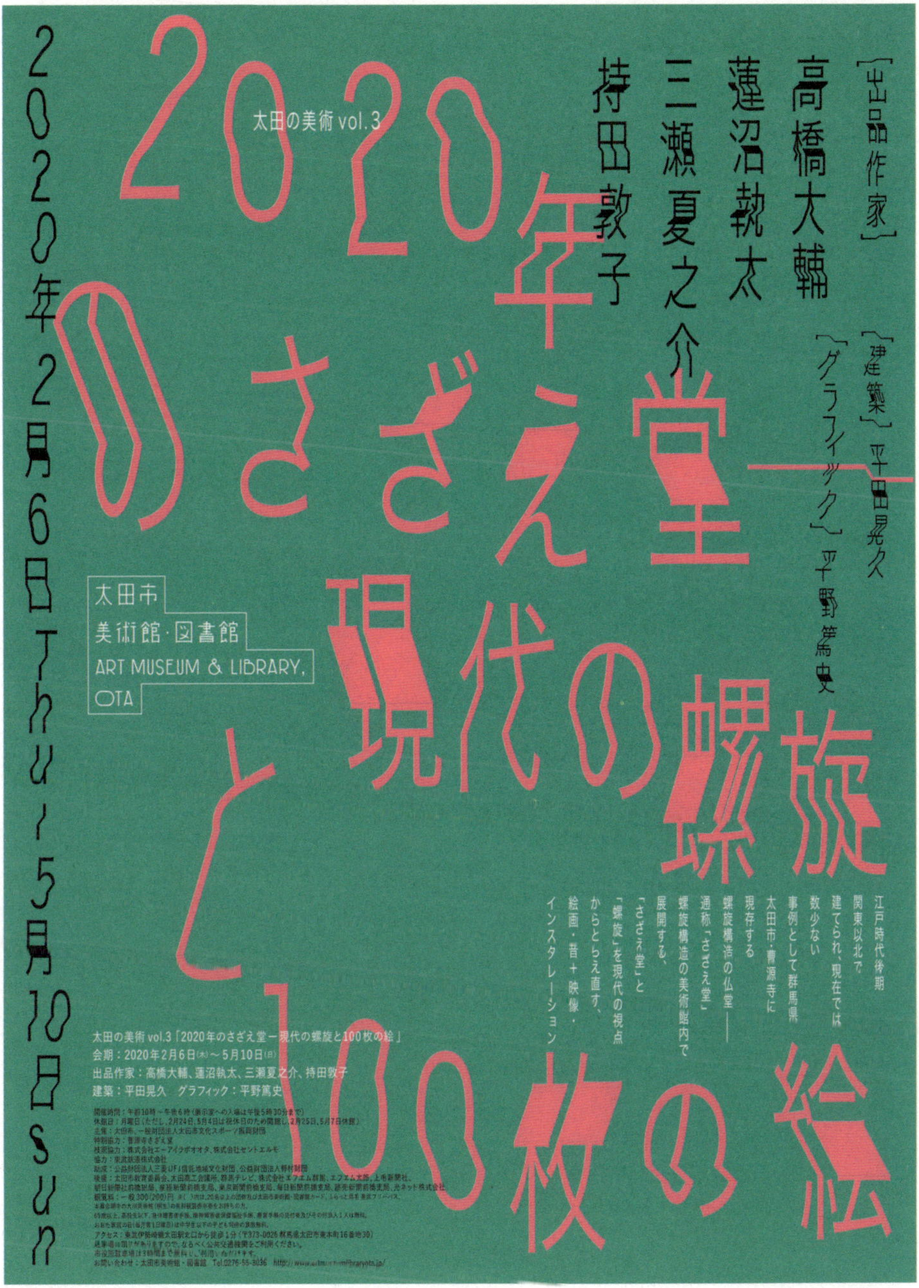
太田の美術 vol.3
2020年のさざえ堂
現代の螺旋と100枚の絵
〔出品作家〕
高橋大輔
蓮沼執太
三瀬夏之介
持田敦子
〔建築〕平田晃久
〔グラフィック〕平野篤史
2020年2月6日thu～5月10日sun
太田市
美術館・図書館
ART MUSEUM & LIBRARY, OTA
江戸時代後期
関東以北で
建てられ、現在では
数少ない
事例として群馬県
太田市・曹源寺に
現存する
螺旋構造の仏堂——
通称「さざえ堂」
螺旋構造の美術館内で
展開する、
「さざえ堂」と
「螺旋」を現代の視点
からとらえ直す、
絵画・音＋映像・
インスタレーション
太田の美術 vol.3「2020年のさざえ堂ー現代の螺旋と100枚の絵」
会期：2020年2月6日(木)～5月10日(日)
出品作家：高橋大輔、蓮沼執太、三瀬夏之介、持田敦子
建築：平田晃久　グラフィック：平野篤史
開館時間：午前10時～午後6時（展示室への入場は午後5時30分まで）
休館日：月曜日（ただし、2月24日、5月4日は祝休日のため開館し、2月25日、5月7日休館）
主催：太田市、一般財団法人太田市文化スポーツ振興財団
特別協力：曹源寺さざえ堂
技術協力：株式会社エーアイラボオオタ、株式会社セントエルモ
協力：東武鉄道株式会社
助成：公益財団法人三菱UFJ信託地域文化財団、公益財団法人野村財団
アクセス：東武伊勢崎線太田駅北口から徒歩1分（〒373-0026 群馬県太田市東本町16番地30）
お問い合わせ：太田市美術館・図書館　Tel.0276-55-3036

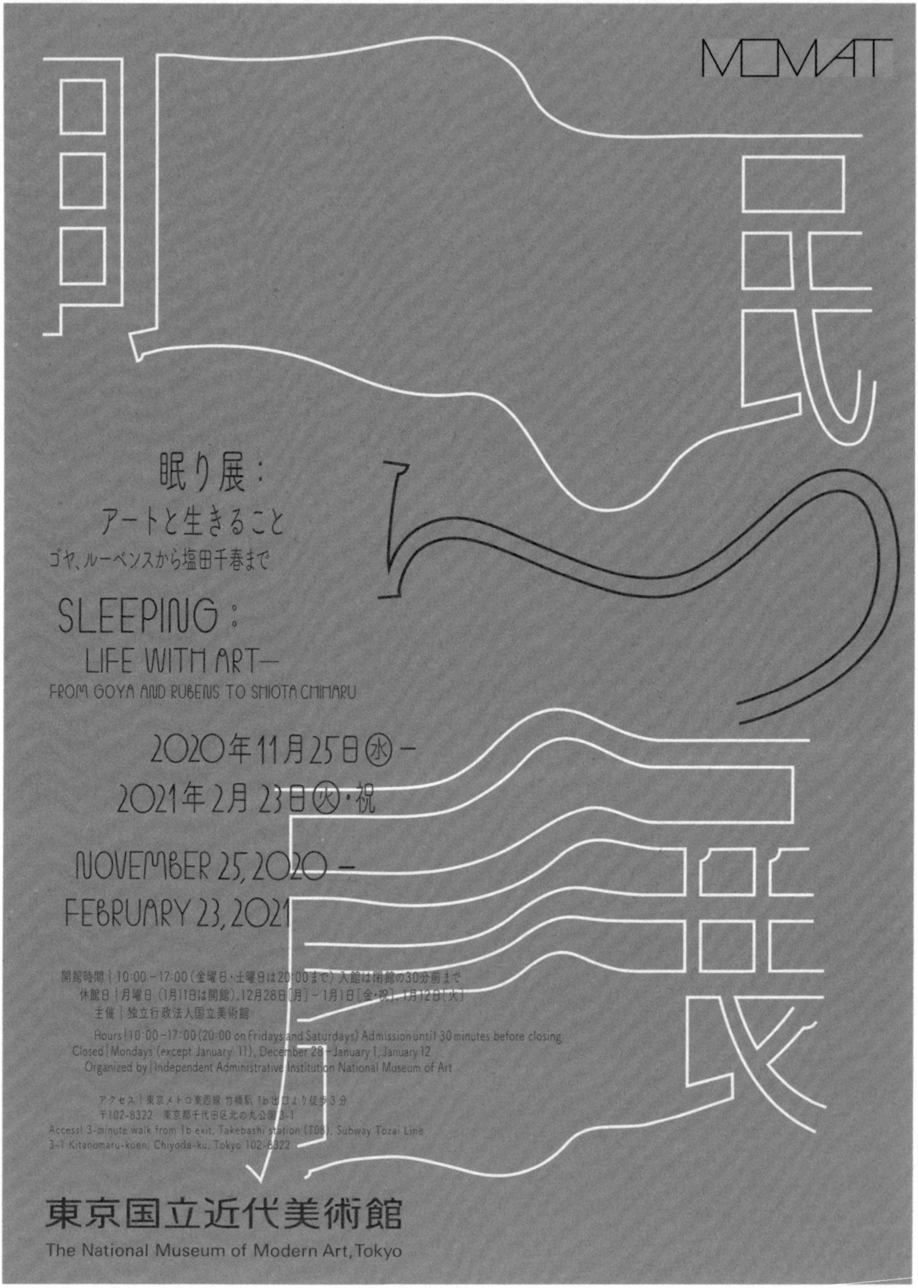
MOMAT
眠り展：
アートと生きること
ゴヤ、ルーベンスから塩田千春まで
SLEEPING:
LIFE WITH ART—
FROM GOYA AND RUBENS TO SHIOTA CHIHARU
2020年11月25日㊌－
2021年2月23日㊋・祝
NOVEMBER 25, 2020 –
FEBRUARY 23, 2021
開館時間｜10:00－17:00（金曜日・土曜日は20:00まで）入館は閉館の30分前まで
休館日｜月曜日（1月11日は開館）、12月28日［月］－1月1日［金・祝］、1月12日［火］
主催｜独立行政法人国立美術館
Hours｜10:00–17:00 (20:00 on Fridays and Saturdays) Admission until 30 minutes before closing
Closed｜Mondays (except January 11), December 28 – January 1, January 12
Organized by｜Independent Administrative Institution National Museum of Art
アクセス｜東京メトロ東西線 竹橋駅 1b出口より徒歩3分
〒102-8322　東京都千代田区北の丸公園3-1
Access｜3-minute walk from 1b exit, Takebashi station (T08), Subway Tozai Line
3-1 Kitanomaru-koen, Chiyoda-ku, Tokyo 102-8322
東京国立近代美術館
The National Museum of Modern Art, Tokyo

発行	2022.09.01
編集・発行	多摩美術大学 美術学部 グラフィックデザイン学科 https://graphic.tamabi.ac.jp/
担当教員	澤田 泰廣 堀内 恭司 平野 篤史 長澤 昌彦
デザイン	平野 篤史 萱沼 大喜
印刷	八紘美術
用紙	コート46 73kg（ポスター） コート46 110kg（スリーブ）

matohu
日　本　の　眼
日常にひそむ美を見つける
matohu
2012　7/21(SAT)～11/25(SUN)
金沢21世紀美術館デザインギャラリー
21

死なない命
Undying Life
コレクション展 2
やくしまるえつこ
エドワード・スタイケン
BCL
デミアン・ハースト
ヴィック・ムニーズ
日比野克彦
八谷和彦
ヤノベケンジ
粟津潔
川井昭夫
イ・ブル
椿昇
Chim↑Pom
Collection 2
YAKUSHIMARU Etsuko
Edward STEICHEN
BCL
Damien HIRST
Vik MUNIZ
HIBINO Katsuhiko
HACHIYA Kazuhiko
YANOBE Kenji
AWAZU Kiyoshi
KAWAI Akio
LEE Bul
TSUBAKI Noboru
Chim↑Pom
2017.7.22 sat.-
2018.1.8 mon.
主　催　金沢21世紀美術館［公益財団法人金沢芸術創造財団］
協　力　金沢工業大学、首都大学東京
休場日　毎週月曜日（ただし8/14、9/18、10/9、10/30、1/8は開場）、9/19、10/10、12/29-1/1
会　場　金沢21世紀美術館 展示室1～6、光庭（展示室5の粟津潔、光庭の川井昭夫は11月11日（土）から）
料　金　一般＝360円（280円）大学生＝280円（220円）小中高生＝無料 65歳以上の方＝280円
※（　）内は団体料金（20名以上）
21

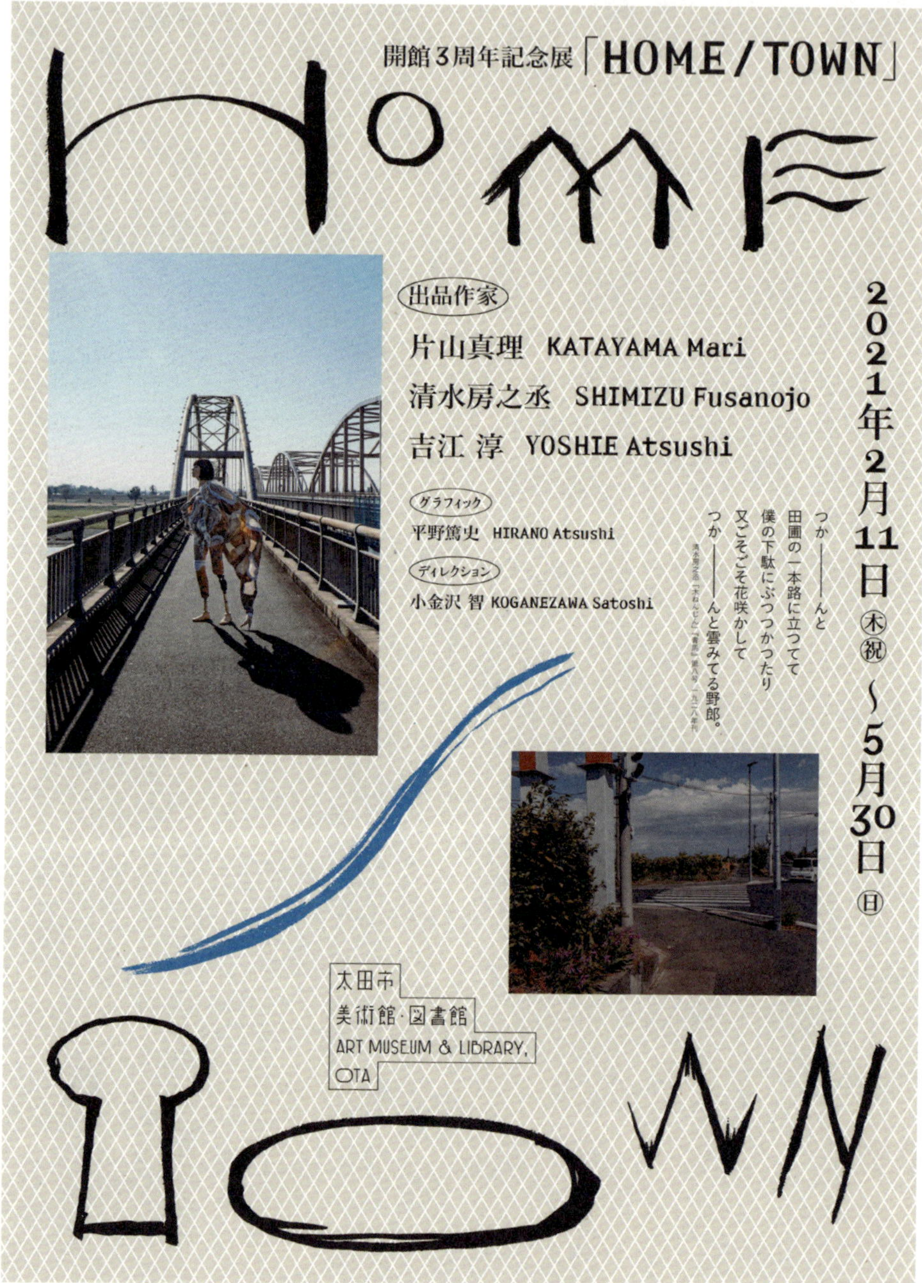
開館3周年記念展「HOME/TOWN」
HOME
出品作家
片山真理 KATAYAMA Mari
清水房之丞 SHIMIZU Fusanojo
吉江 淳 YOSHIE Atsushi
グラフィック
平野篤史 HIRANO Atsushi
ディレクション
小金沢 智 KOGANEZAWA Satoshi
2021年2月11日㊍㊗～5月30日㊐
つか——んと
田圃の一本路に立つてて
僕の下駄にぶつつかつたり
又ごそごそ花咲かして
つか——んと雲みてる野郎。
太田市
美術館・図書館
ART MUSEUM & LIBRARY, OTA
TOWN

2022年4月9日㊏
|
2022年7月3日㊐
出展作家
秋田公立美術大学 粘菌研究クラブ
鵜飼 結一朗
THE COPY TRAVELERS
ぬか つくるとこ
久村 卓
増子 博子
開館時間
10:00 ～ 18:00 ※火曜休館、5月3日（火）は開館
会場
はじまりの美術館（福島県耶麻郡猪苗代町新町 4873）
料金
障がい者手帳をお持ちの方および
付添いの方（1名まで）無料
主催
社会福祉法人安積愛育園 はじまりの美術館
協力
株式会社ぬか、kinologue、小出由紀子事務所、
公立大学法人秋田公立美術大学、
社会福祉法人やまなみ会 やまなみ工房、
MINAYOYA SAUNA、有限会社アップリンク
後援
福島県、福島県教育委員会、猪苗代町、
猪苗代町教育委員会、あさかホスピタルグループ（申請中含む）
はじまりの美術館
日常をととのえる展

おと
ミュージカル
脚本・演出：岩井
音楽：前野健太
出演：ユースケ・
藤井隆
吉原光夫
大原櫻子
川上友里
橋本さとし
演奏：佐山こうた
人生とは幼い神様が書いた落書きなのかも知れ

PARCO劇場 50th Anniversary シリーズ
2023年3月12日(日)～4月2日(日)
PARCO劇場
(渋谷PARCO 8F)

Aiko Koike

Aiko Koike is an art director and graphic designer from Tokyo who graduated from Central Saint Martins with a degree in graphic design. A freelancer since 2016, her work can be seen on collaterals for the KYOTO EXPERIMENT Kyoto International Performing Arts Festival, the Contact Gonzo+YCAM Bio Research Exhibition, PARCO's "Ai to Aimai", and KAAT Kanagawa Arts Theatre's "The Vacuum Cleaner".

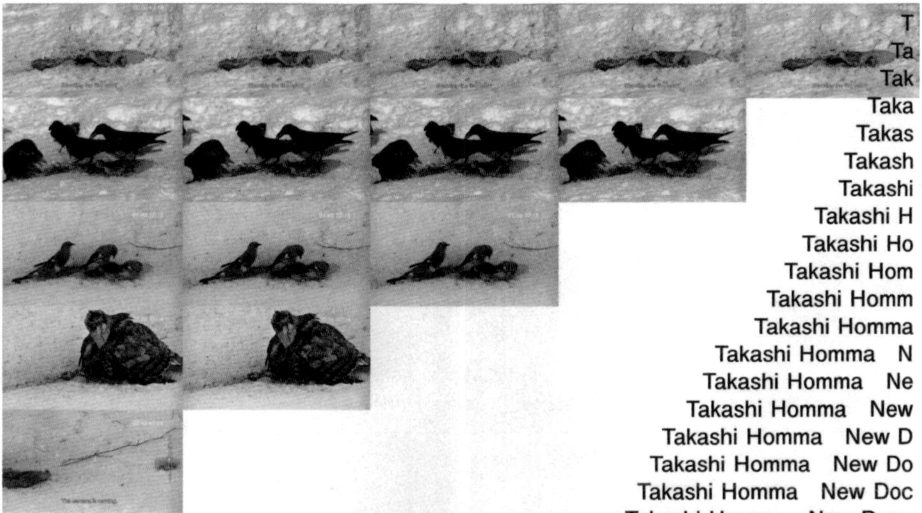

T
Ta
Tak
Taka
Takas
Takash
Takashi
Takashi H
Takashi Ho
Takashi Hom
Takashi Homm
Takashi Homma
Takashi Homma N
Takashi Homma Ne
Takashi Homma New
Takashi Homma New D
Takashi Homma New Do
Takashi Homma New Doc
Takashi Homma New Docu
Takashi Homma New Docum
Takashi Homma New Docume
Takashi Homma New Documen
Takashi Homma New Document
Takashi Homma New Documenta
Takashi Homma New Documentar
Takashi Homma New Documentary
Takashi Homma New Documentary M
Takashi Homma New Documentary Mo
Takashi Homma New Documentary Mov
Takashi Homma New Documentary Movi
Takashi Homma New Documentary Movie
Takashi Homma New Documentary Movie F
Takashi Homma New Documentary Movie Fi
Takashi Homma New Documentary Movie Fir
Takashi Homma New Documentary Movie Firs
Takashi Homma New Documentary Movie First
Takashi Homma New Documentary Movie First,
Takashi Homma New Documentary Movie First, j
Takashi Homma New Documentary Movie First, ja
Takashi Homma New Documentary Movie First, jay
Takashi Homma New Documentary Movie First, jay c
Takashi Homma New Documentary Movie First, jay co
Takashi Homma New Documentary Movie First, jay com
Takashi Homma New Documentary Movie First, jay come
Takashi Homma New Documentary Movie First, jay comes
Takashi Homma New Documentary Movie First, jay comes.

Sat, March 24, 2018
The National Museum of Modern Art, Tokyo
Artist talk (15 min.) & Film screening (25 min.)

Doors open 14:45
Talk 15:15-15:30
Screening 15:30-19:15 (Museum is open until 20:00 on the day.)
At Lecture hall
Free admission, no reservation required, 160 seats.
Organized by The National Museum of Modern Art, Tokyo
Access : A 3 minutes walk from 1b exit, Takebashi station, Subway Tozai Line (T-08)

The National Museum of Modern Art, Tokyo

I♡ München
PEACE
KISS
I ♥ MOM
PRIDE WEEK
PARCO
2022.4.15-5.9

ART LEAP 2020
特別にできない、ファンタジー
蓮沼昌宏
2021年2月20日(土)ー3月14日(日) 12時ー19時 神戸アートビレッジセンター
レッサー
Art

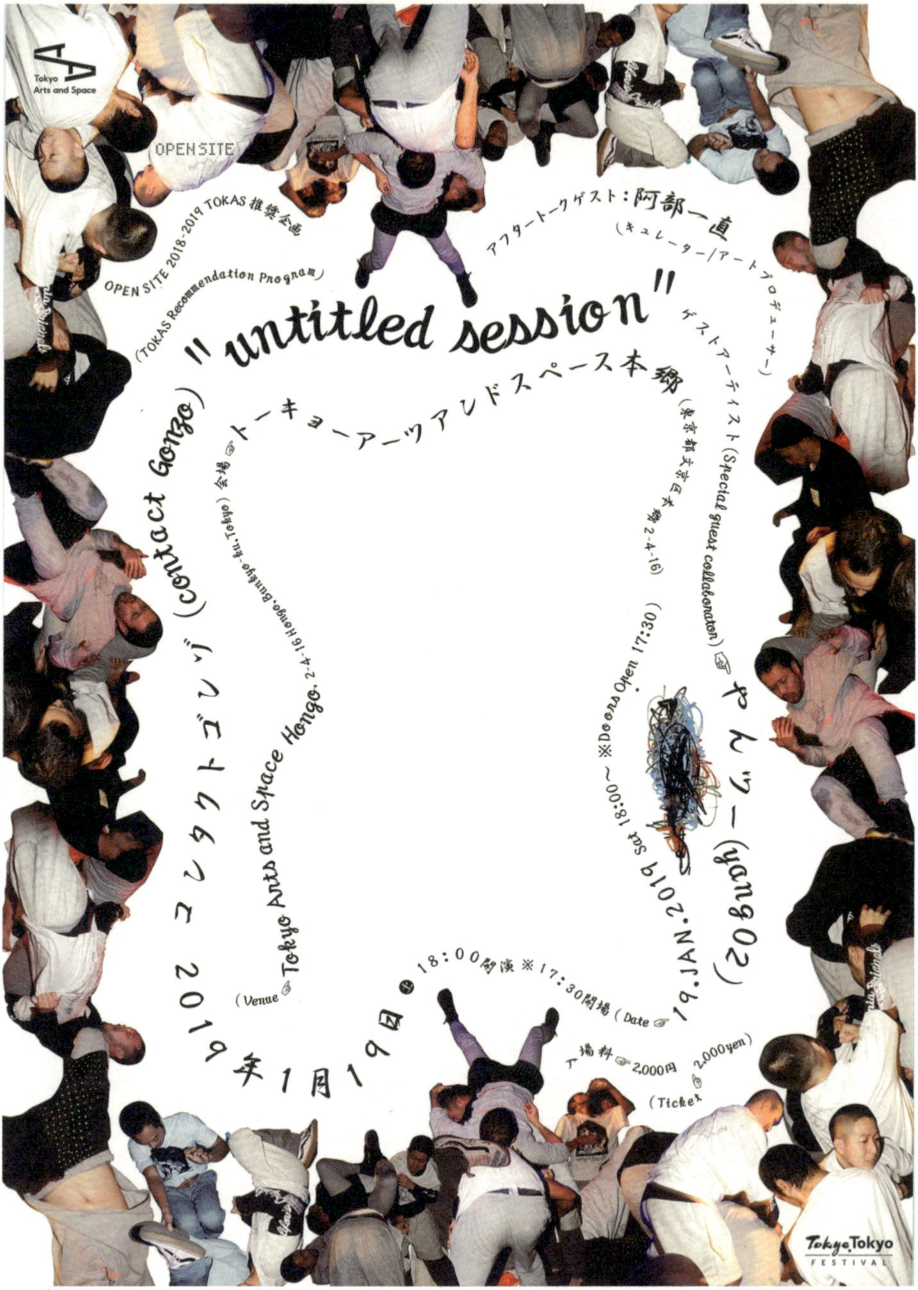
Tokyo Arts and Space
OPEN SITE
OPEN SITE 2018-2019 TOKAS 推奨企画
(TOKAS Recommendation Program)
コンタクトゴンゾ(contact Gonzo)"untitled session"
アフタートークゲスト：阿部一直
(キュレーター/アートプロデューサー)
ゲストアーティスト(Special guest collaborator)☞やんツー(yang02)
会場☞トーキョーアーツアンドスペース本郷
(東京都文京区本郷2-4-16)
(Venue☞ Tokyo Arts and Space Hongo. 2-4-16 Hongo, Bunkyo-ku, Tokyo)
2019年1月19日㊏ 18:00開演 ※17:30開場
(Date☞ 19.JAN.2019 Sat 18:00~ ※Doors Open 17:30)
入場料☞2,000円
(Ticket☞ 2,000yen)
Tokyo Tokyo FESTIVAL

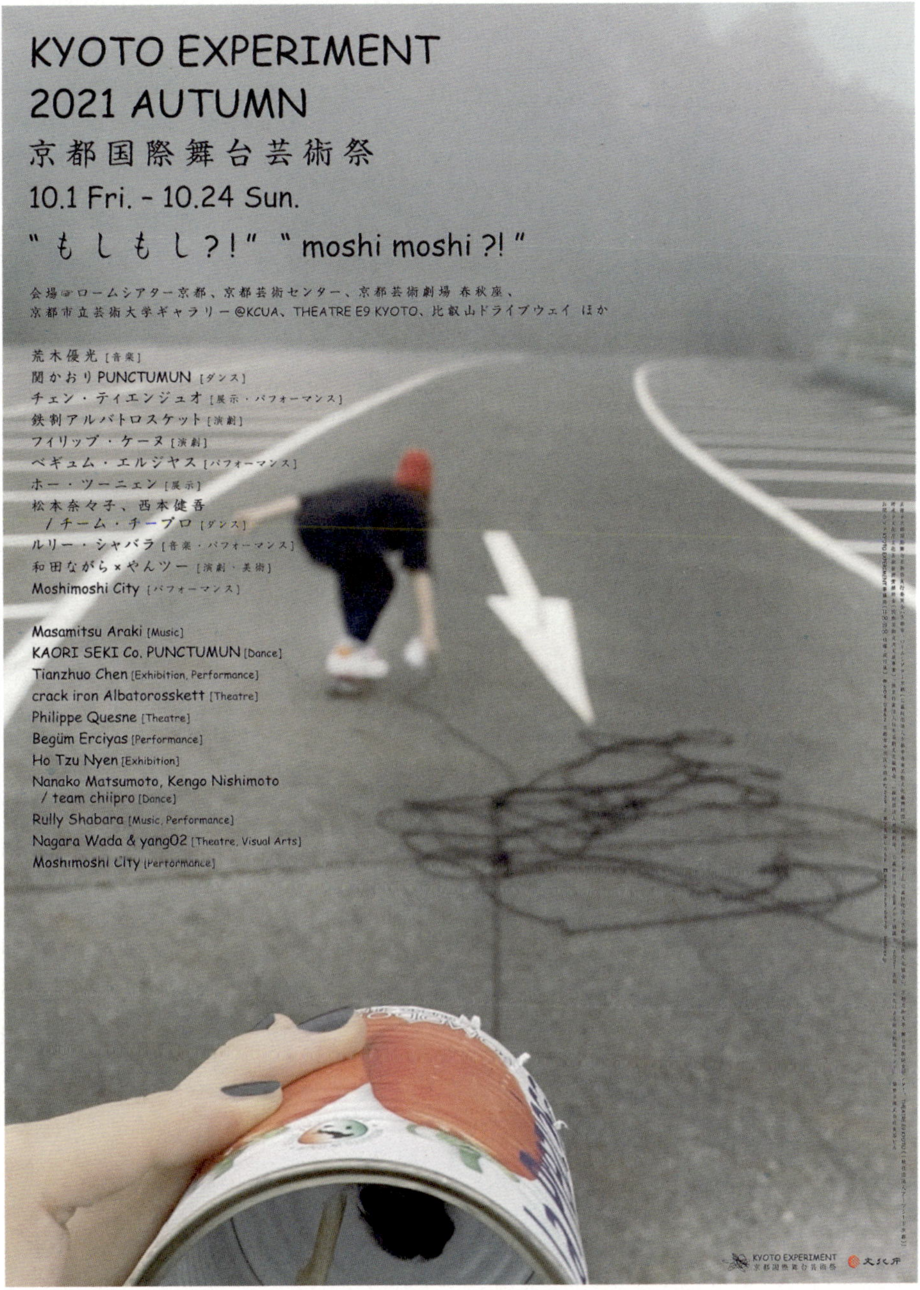

KYOTO EXPERIMENT
2021 AUTUMN
京都国際舞台芸術祭
10.1 Fri. - 10.24 Sun.
"もしもし?!" " moshi moshi ?! "
会場◎ロームシアター京都、京都芸術センター、京都芸術劇場 春秋座、
京都市立芸術大学ギャラリー@KCUA、THEATRE E9 KYOTO、比叡山ドライブウェイ ほか
荒木優光［音楽］
関かおり PUNCTUMUN［ダンス］
チェン・ティエンジュオ［展示・パフォーマンス］
鉄割アルバトロスケット［演劇］
フィリップ・ケーヌ［演劇］
ベギュム・エルジヤス［パフォーマンス］
ホー・ツーニェン［展示］
松本奈々子、西本健吾
／チーム・チープロ［ダンス］
ルリー・シャバラ［音楽・パフォーマンス］
和田ながら×やんツー［演劇・美術］
Moshimoshi City［パフォーマンス］
Masamitsu Araki [Music]
KAORI SEKI Co. PUNCTUMUN [Dance]
Tianzhuo Chen [Exhibition, Performance]
crack iron Albatorosskett [Theatre]
Philippe Quesne [Theatre]
Begüm Erciyas [Performance]
Ho Tzu Nyen [Exhibition]
Nanako Matsumoto, Kengo Nishimoto
/ team chiipro [Dance]
Rully Shabara [Music, Performance]
Nagara Wada & yang02 [Theatre, Visual Arts]
Moshimoshi City [Performance]
KYOTO EXPERIMENT
京都国際舞台芸術祭
文化庁

KYOTO EXPERIMENT
2021 SPRING
京都国際舞台芸術祭
2.6 Sat. - 3.28 Sun.
世界各地の実験的な舞台芸術が集まるフェスティバル
会場☞ロームシアター京都、京都芸術センター、京都芸術劇場 春秋座、京都伝統産業ミュージアム、
京都府立府民ホール"アルティ"、mumokutekiホール ほか
ROHM Theatre Kyoto, Kyoto Art Center, Kyoto Art Theater Shunjuza, Kyoto Museum of Crafts and Design,
Kyoto Prefectural Citizens' Hall ALTI, mumokuteki hall and other locations
小原真史 [展示]
デイナ・ミシェル [ダンス]
垣尾優 [ダンス]
フロレンティナ・ホルツィンガー [パフォーマンス]
山本精一 [音楽]
ナターシャ・トンテイ [パフォーマンス]
音遊びの会×いとうせいこう [音楽・パフォーマンス]
中間アヤカ&コレオグラフィ [ダンス]
ウィチャヤ・アータマート / For What Theatre [演劇]
ママリアン・ダイビング・リフレックス / ダレン・オドネル [演劇]
Kansai Studies (dot architects、和田ながら) [リサーチプログラム]
Masashi Kohara [Exhibition]
Dana Michel [Dance]
Masaru Kakio [Dance]
Florentina Holzinger [Performance]
Seiichi Yamamoto [Music]
Natasha Tontey [Performance]
The Otoasobi Project & Seiko Ito [Music, Performance]
Ayaka Nakama & Choreography [Dance]
Wichaya Artamat / For What Theatre [Theatre]
Mammalian Diving Reflex / Darren O'Donnell [Theatre]
Kansai Studies (dot architects, Nagara Wada) [Research program]
1.8 Fri. チケット発売スタート!
Ticket sales start 1.8 Fri.!
KYOTO EXPERIMENT
KYOTO EXPERIMENT

KYOTO EXPERIMENT
2022
京都国際舞台芸術祭
10.1 Sat. - 10.23 Sun.
世界各地の実験的な舞台芸術が集まるフェスティバル
今年のキーワードは
"ニューてくてく" "New teku teku"
会場☞ロームシアター京都、京都芸術センター、京都芸術劇場 春秋座、
THEATRE E9 KYOTO、京都市京セラ美術館、京都中央信用金庫 旧厚生センター ほか
アーザーデ・シャーミーリー [演劇]
梅田哲也 [パフォーマンス]
小野彩加、中澤陽 / スペースノットブランク [演劇]
サマラ・ハーシュ [演劇]
ジャールナン・パンタチャート [演劇]
ティノ・セーガル [ライブアート]
フォースド・エンタテインメント [演劇]
フロレンティナ・ホルツィンガー [パフォーマンス]
松本奈々子、西本健吾 / チーム・チーブロ [ダンス]
ミーシャ・ラインカウフ [展示]
メルツバウ、バラージ・パンディ、リシャール・ピナス
with 志賀理江子 [ビジュアルコンサート]
dot architects & 和田ながら [リサーチプログラム Kansai Studies]
CMTK (森千裕×金氏徹平) [ミーティングポイント]
Azade Shahmiri [Theatre]
Tetsuya Umeda [Performance]
Ayaka Ono & Akira Nakazawa / Spacenotblank [Theatre]
Samara Hersch [Theatre]
Jarunun Phantachat [Theatre]
Tino Sehgal [Live Art]
Forced Entertainment [Theatre]
Florentina Holzinger [Performance]
Nanako Matsumoto & Kengo Nishimoto / team chiipro [Dance]
Mischa Leinkauf [Exhibition]
Merzbow, Balázs Pándi & Richard Pinhas
with Lieko Shiga [Visual concert]
dot architects & Nagara Wada [Research program: Kansai Studies]
CMTK (Chihiro Mori & Teppei Kaneuji) [Meeting Point]
KYOTO EXPERIMENT
京都国際舞台芸術祭

Arata Kubota

Born in Yamanashi Prefecture in 1981, Arata Kubota graduated from Tama Art University majoring in graphic design. He has received many awards for his work — a New York ADC Gold Prize, D&AD Yellow Pencil, and Gold Cannes Lion to name a few.

SEKI
2-55-12 SANGENJAYA
SETAGAYA-KU
TOKYO 154-0024
SLICE OF HEARTLAND
sliceof.heartland.jp
HEARTLAND
BEER

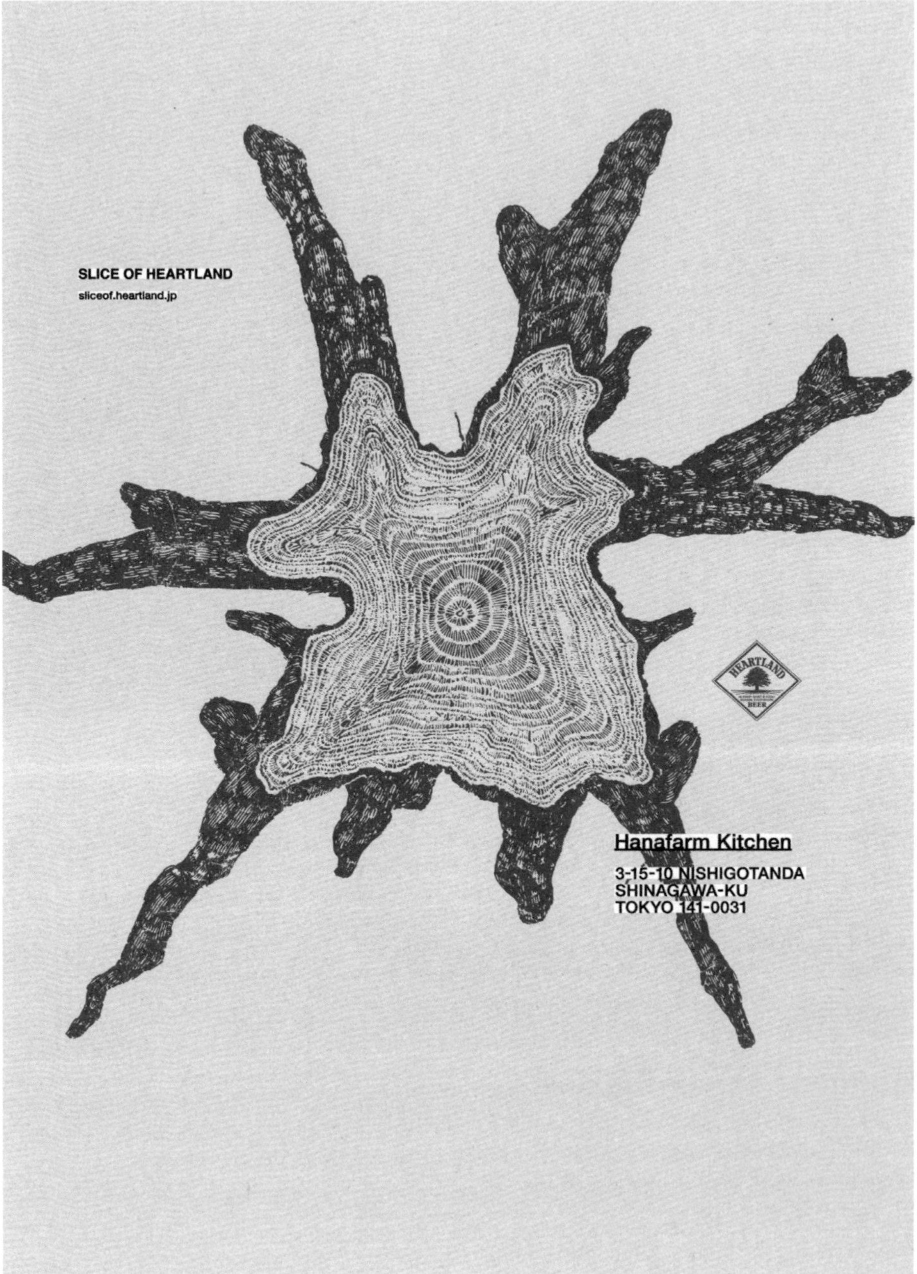
SLICE OF HEARTLAND
sliceof.heartland.jp
HEARTLAND
BEER
Hanafarm Kitchen
3-15-10 NISHIGOTANDA
SHINAGAWA-KU
TOKYO 141-0031

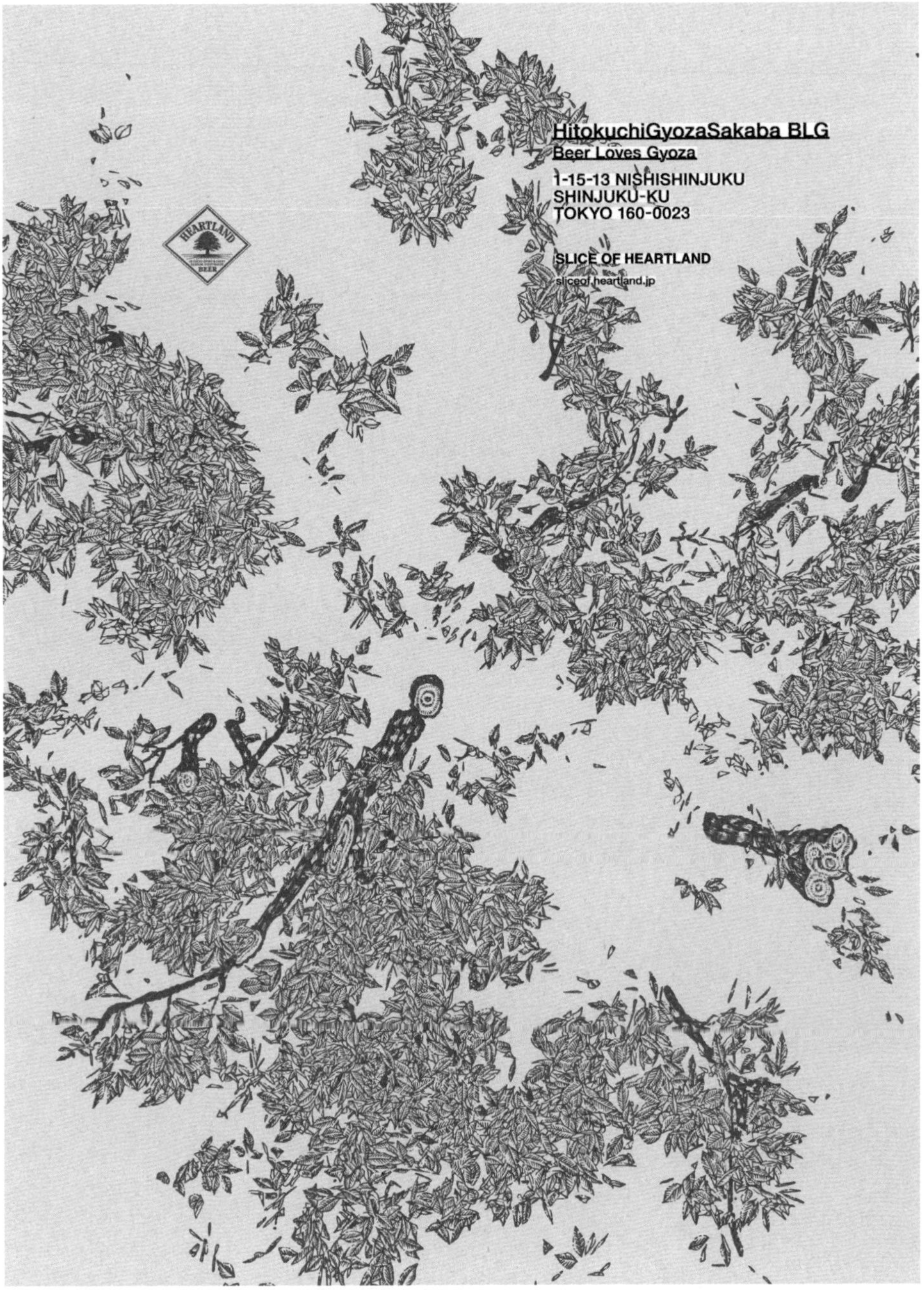
HitokuchiGyozaSakaba BLG
Beer Loves Gyoza
1-15-13 NISHISHINJUKU
SHINJUKU-KU
TOKYO 160-0023
SLICE OF HEARTLAND
sliceof.heartland.jp

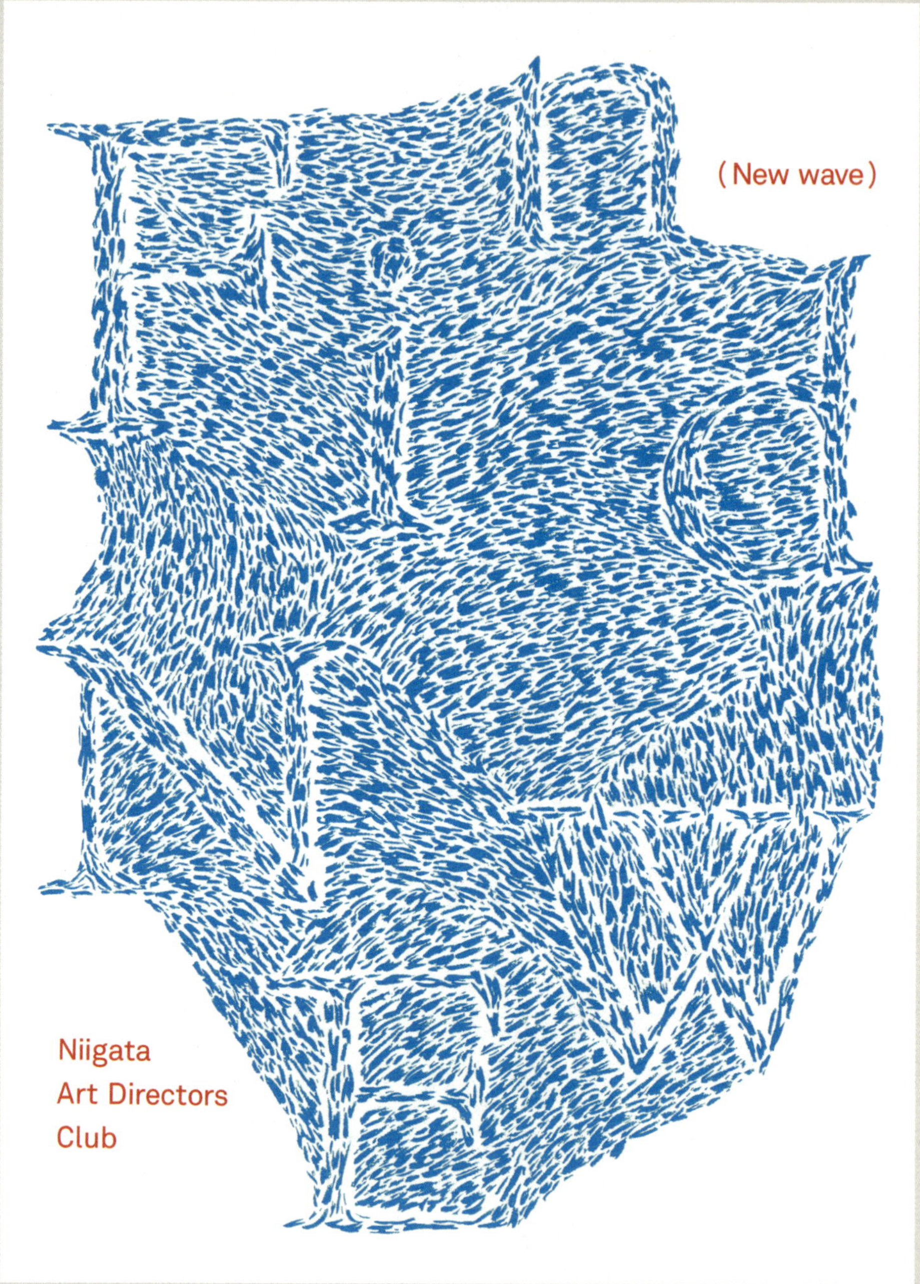
(New wave)
Niigata
Art Directors
Club

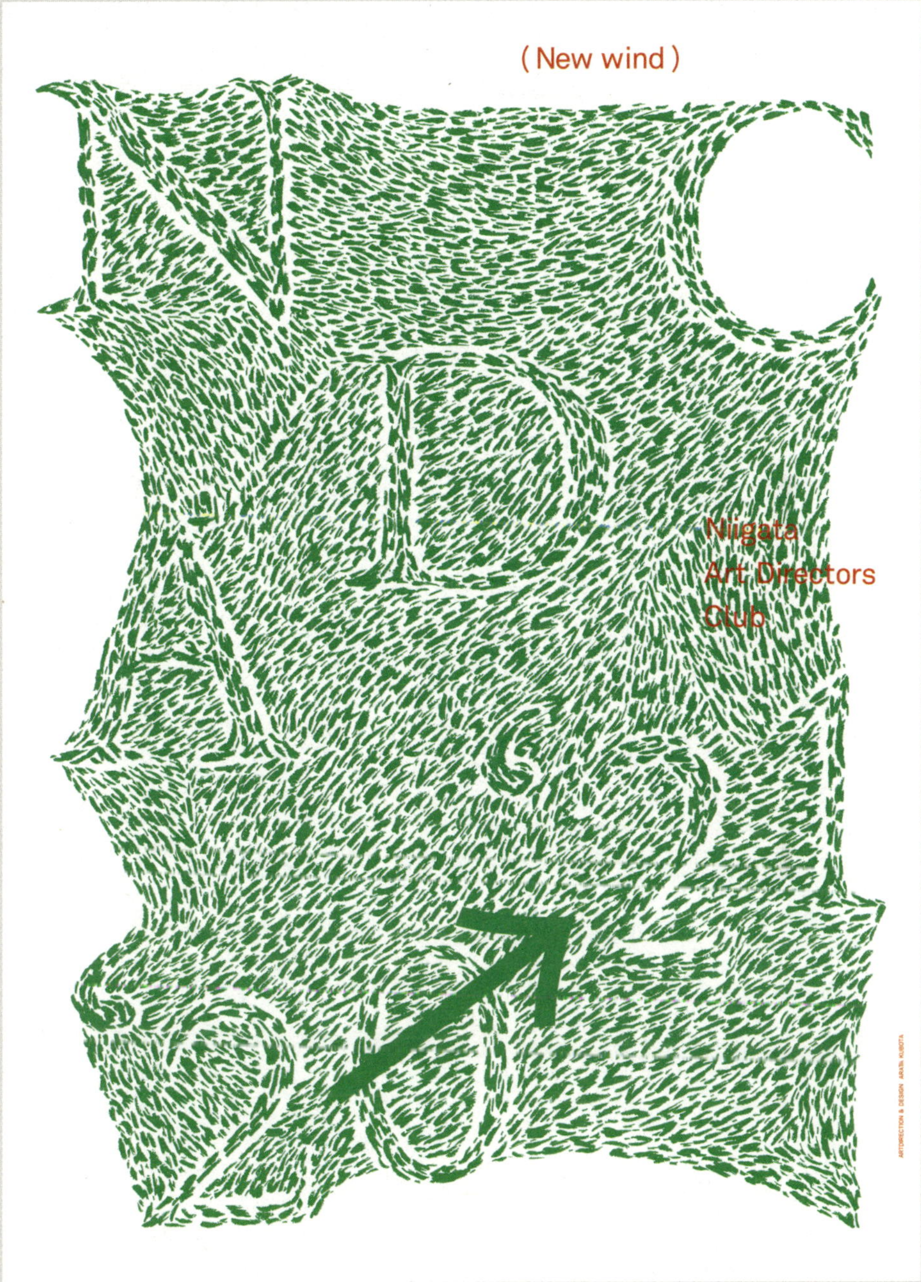
(New wind)
Niigata
Art Directors
Club

静岡新聞
静岡おでん

常識に、非をつけろ。
今年、SBSは65周年を迎えます。超FSも2年目。ともに、これまでを超えていきましょう。
平成29年(2017年)1月4日(水曜日)

（1）　平成２９年(2017年) 1月４日（水曜日）　静岡新聞　(第三種郵便物認可)

静岡新聞 第二部

昨年のアメリカ大統領選挙の投票日、静岡が話題になったことをご存知だろうか。とある解説者がテレビで、オハイオ州を獲った方が勝つとし、オハイオ州はアメリカの平均的な州で日本の静岡みたいなものだから、と言ったところ、その発言がすぐに「オハイオと静岡は似ている」という一文になってSNS上に拡散したのだ。悲しかったのは、「その例え、分かりやすい」という反応があったことで、はからずも静岡が「日本の平均」として捉えられていることを再認識させられることになった。標準、普通、一般的、日本の縮図、日本の平均県。だから静岡では、メーカーの発売前の新商品のサンプリングがよく行われるそうだ。引き続きサンプル商品は欲しいが、普通だと思われ続けるのはよくない。特徴がないと言われているみたいで気分がよくない。現状からの脱却を急がねばならない。2020年、次のアメリカ大統領選挙のときは、オハイオ州の引き合いに出されるのを防がなくてはいけない。全米は変わることを選んだ。全茶はどうする？ 今年65周年を迎えるSBSは、静岡の変わりゆく姿を報道したい。FMデビューを果たしたSBSラジオは、静岡の前に進もうとする声をクリアな音で流したい。新しい静岡、オハヨー州といきませんか的なそんな2017年の正月。

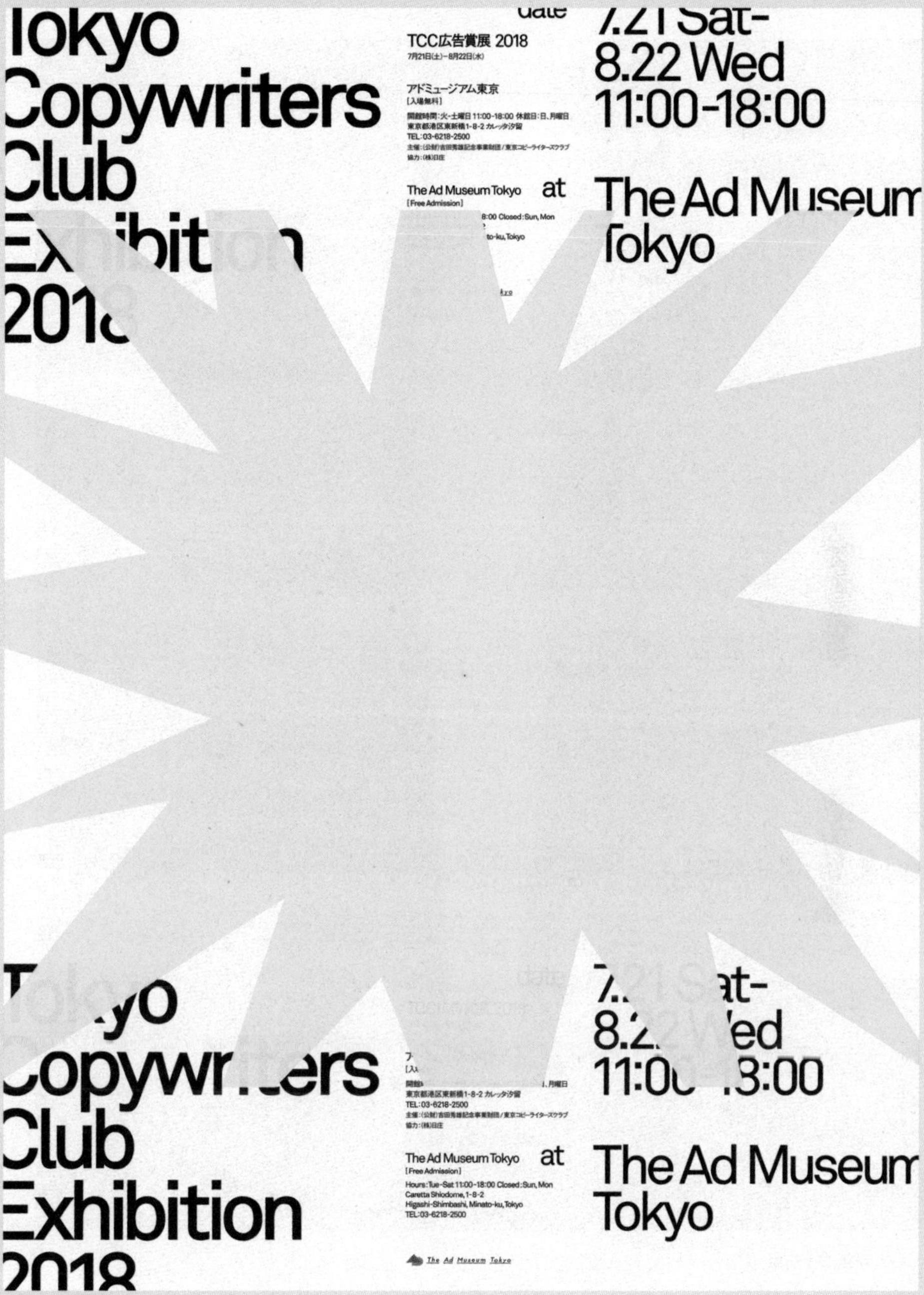
Tokyo Copywriters Club Exhibition 2018
date
TCC広告賞展 2018
7月21日(土)–8月22日(水)
アドミュージアム東京
[入場無料]
開館時間:火-土曜日 11:00-18:00 休館日:日、月曜日
東京都港区東新橋1-8-2 カレッタ汐留
TEL:03-6218-2500
主催:(公財)吉田秀雄記念事業財団/東京コピーライターズクラブ
協力:(株)日庄
The Ad Museum Tokyo
[Free Admission]
Hours: Tue-Sat 11:00-18:00 Closed: Sun, Mon
Caretta Shiodome, 1-8-2
Higashi-Shimbashi, Minato-ku, Tokyo
TEL:03-6218-2500
at
7.21 Sat-
8.22 Wed
11:00-18:00
The Ad Museum Tokyo

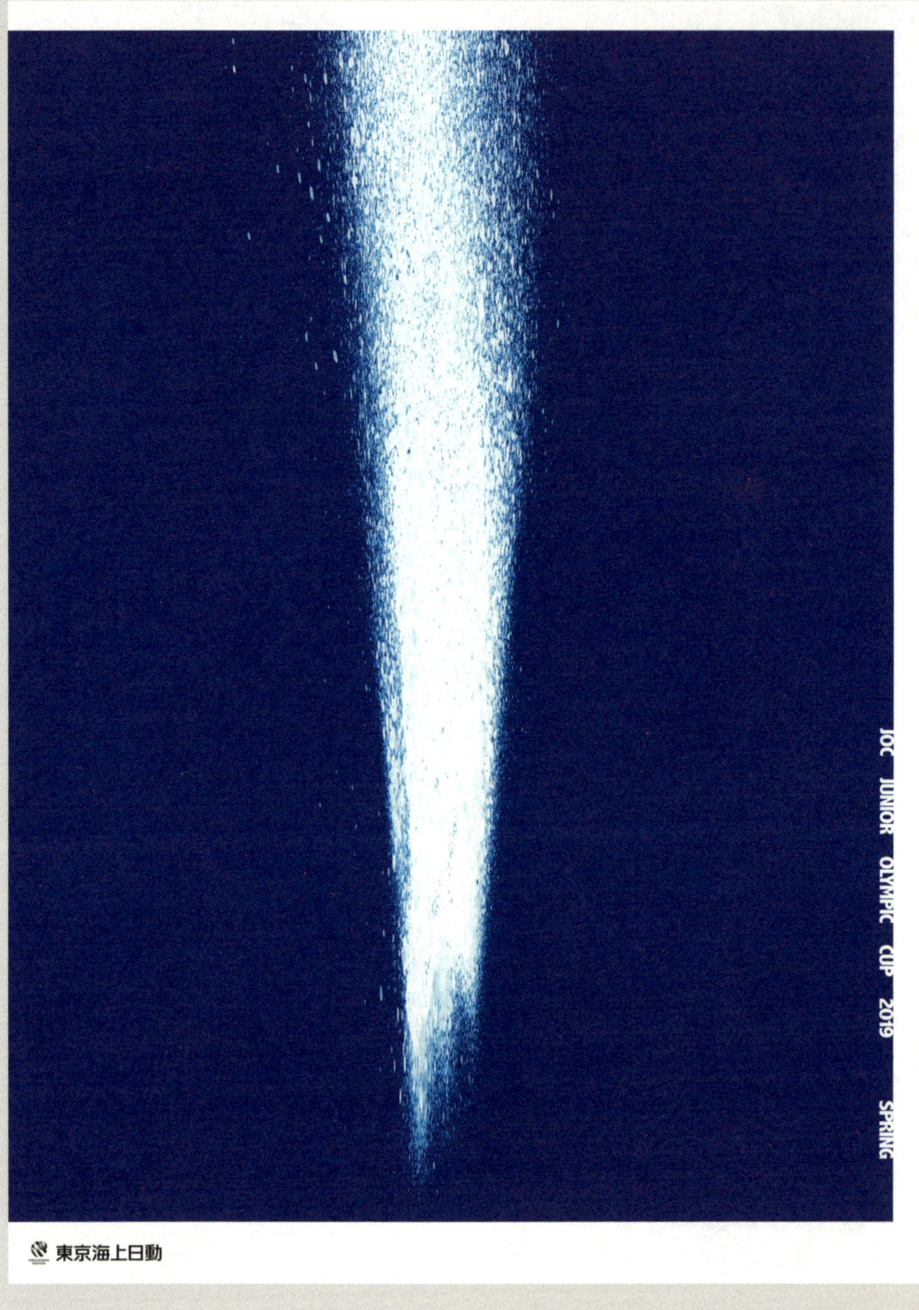
JOC JUNIOR OLYMPIC CUP 2019 SPRING
東京海上日動

Otsuka 大塚製薬
LIVE
LOVE
LOVE
LOVE
熱中したら
対策ポカリ
POCARI SWEAT

秩父山系
松岡 純米吟釀
醸造 生原酒
硬度 127mg/l
埼玉県 小川町
Saitama Ogawa

松
岡
醸
造
純米吟醸
生原酒
硬度　127mg/l　埼玉県　小川町
Saitama Ogawa

asianvoice

asianvoice is a branding and graphic design studio dedicated to making the world a little more fun. Its founder and representative, Rico Honda, is a member of the Japan Graphic Designers Association and Japan Typography Association, as well as a board member of the DAS Designers Association.

ZERO is empty.
ZERO EXHIBITION 2020

o
o
DAS
ZERO POSTERS
EXHIBITION
2022
Rico Honda

NUIT BLANCHE KYOTO 2022
Nuit Blanche Kyoto
ニュイ・ブランシュ KYOTO 2022
パリ白夜祭への架け橋 - 現代アートと過ごす夜
10.01.sat
※一部のプログラムは前後数週間実施
京都市内各所で実施　入場無料
Opening 10.01.sat 16:00 | 会場：京都駅ビル駅前広場（ホテルグランヴィア京都前特設会場） ※雨天時は7階東広場北ピロティ
京都市とアンスティチュ・フランセ関西が毎秋開催するニュイ・ブランシュKYOTOは、
京都市の姉妹都市であるパリ市発祥のニュイ・ブランシュ（白夜祭）に着想を得た現代アートの祭典です。
12年目を迎える今年は「遊び場（Aires de jeux）」をテーマに、日仏アーティストによるビジュアルアートや
パフォーマンス、展覧会など、バラエティ豊かなプログラムをお届けします。
フランスの4つの文化機関、そして開館30周年を迎えるヴィラ九条山とのコラボレーションにもぜひご注目ください。
OFFICIAL WEB SITE

FURO ふ SHIKI
EXHI BITION
2021

The 68th
New York
Type Directors Club
Exhibition
June 6th–
July 1st, 2022
The World's
Best
Typography
THE
ONE CLUB
FOR
CREATIVITY
THE ONE SHOW

あじあん
うおいす

ZERO
POSTER
DESIGN
EXHIBITION
2019
ZERO
FACTORY
MADE IN
RICO HONDA

画面越しの君は、時々遠くて、時々近い。

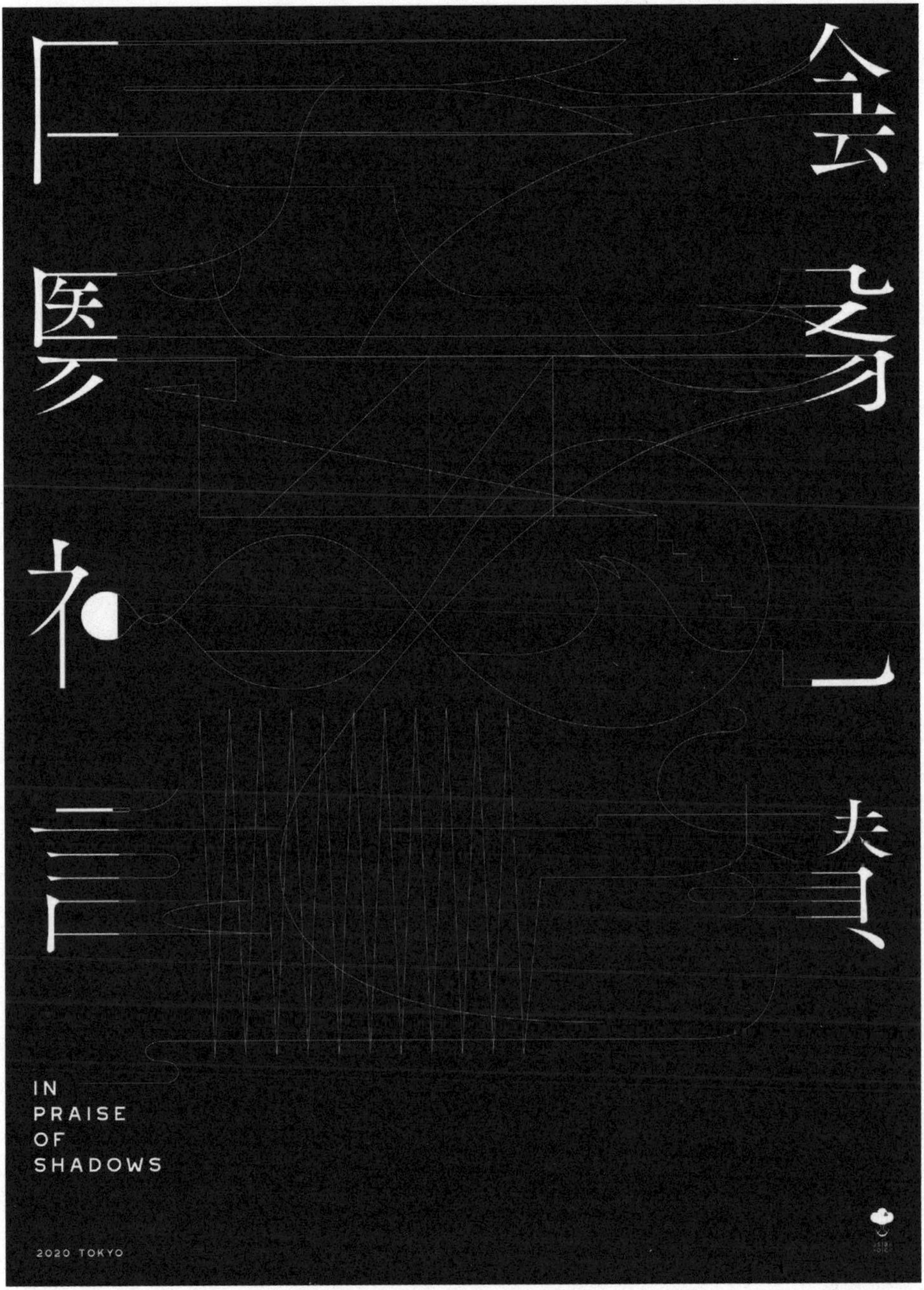
IN
PRAISE
OF
SHADOWS
2020 TOKYO

Asuka Watanabe

Asuka Watanabe is a graphic designer and illustrator based in Tokyo.

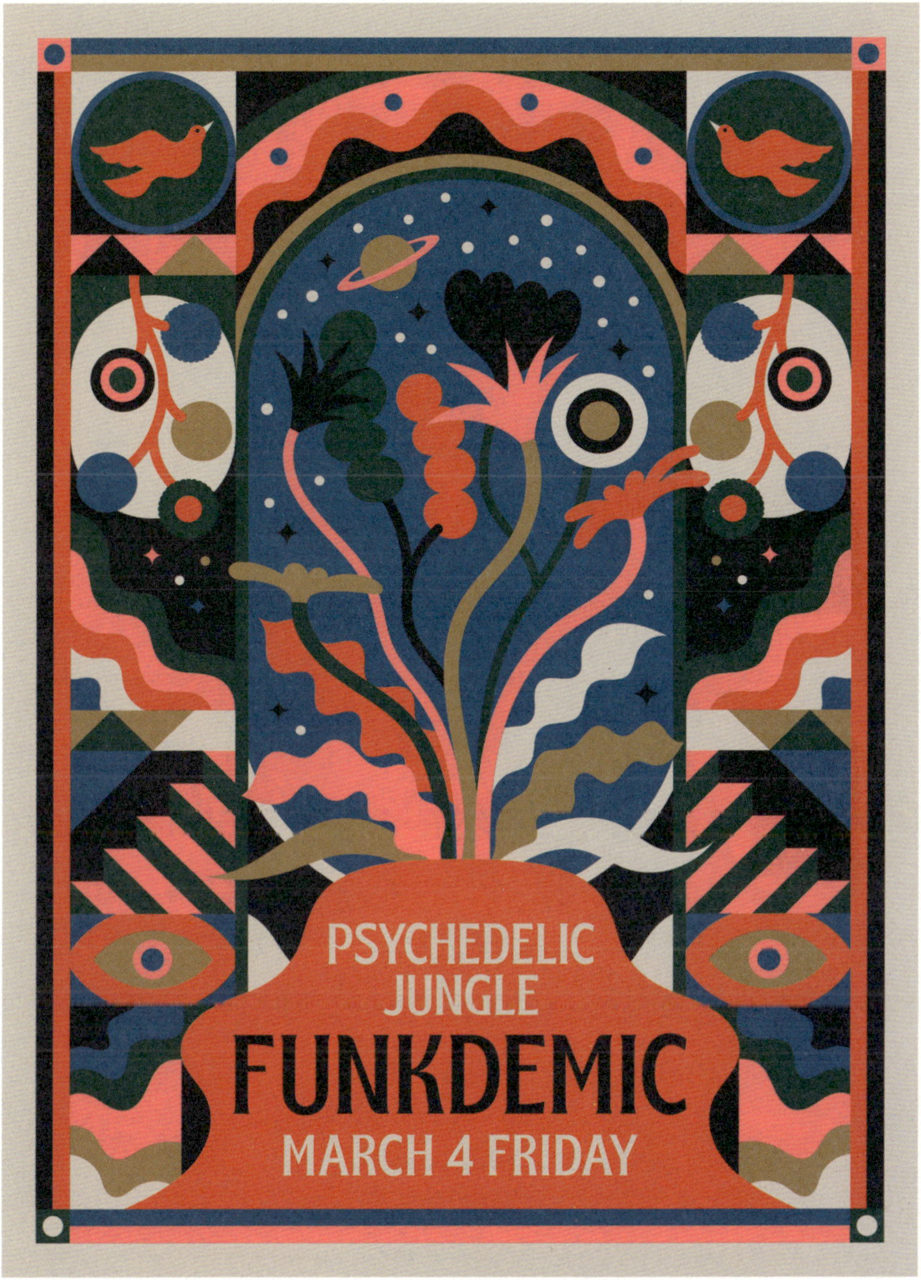
PSYCHEDELIC
JUNGLE
FUNKDEMIC
MARCH 4 FRIDAY

Open Air
FUNKDEMIC
OCTOBER 14-16
Autocamp Mogura

Solar Pot
NUSIC & HIRANYA ACCESS present
@Secret semi-outdoor location in the center of Tokyo
Mori Ra
Akie
Akiram En
7e
MARCH 14 SUN, 2021
13:00 - 20:00
Info: solarpotmusic@gmail.com

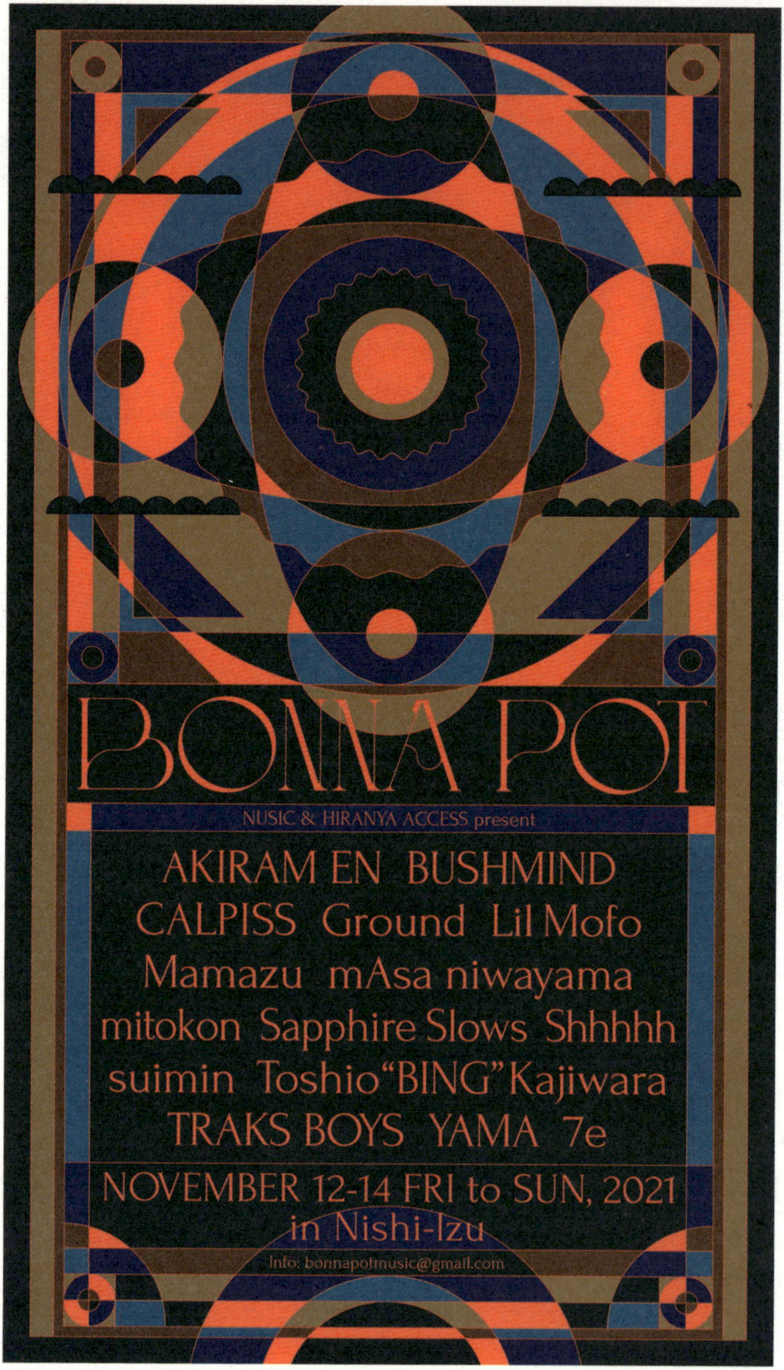
BONNA POT
NUSIC & HIRANYA ACCESS present
AKIRAM EN BUSHMIND
CALPISS Ground Lil Mofo
Mamazu mAsa niwayama
mitokon Sapphire Slows Shhhhh
suimin Toshio "BING" Kajiwara
TRAKS BOYS YAMA 7e
NOVEMBER 12-14 FRI to SUN, 2021
in Nishi-Izu
Info: bonnapotmusic@gmail.com

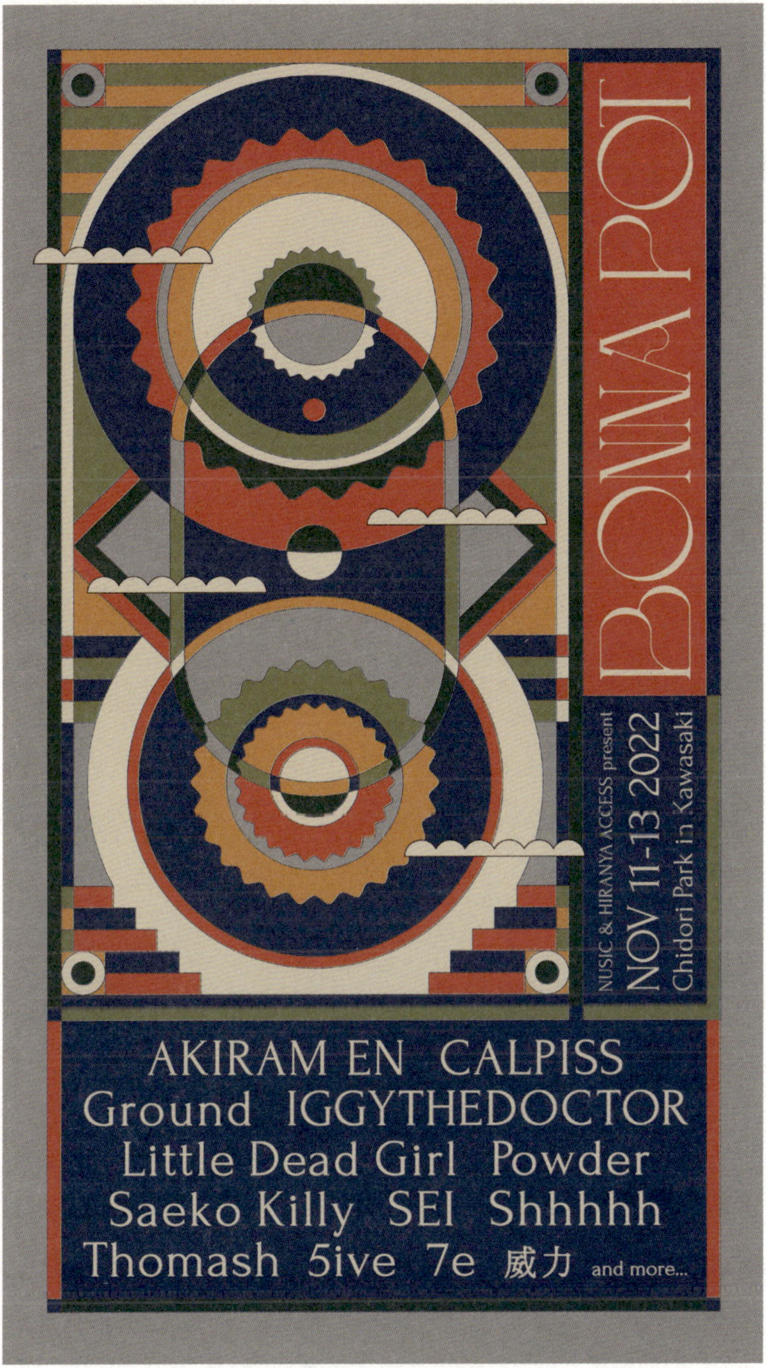
BONNA POI
NUSIC & HIRANYA ACCESS present
NOV 11-13 2022
Chidori Park in Kawasaki
AKIRAM EN CALPISS
Ground IGGYTHEDOCTOR
Little Dead Girl Powder
Saeko Killy SEI Shhhhh
Thomash 5ive 7e 威力 and more...

Atsushi Ishiguro

Atsushi Ishiguro is an art director and graphic designer who runs the award-winning creative studio OUWN in Tokyo. Known for its impressive, dynamic, and multifaceted approach, OUWN pursues the essence of design through “People and Thought” (p-a-t.jp), an artistic practice that centres on achieving a sustainable society.

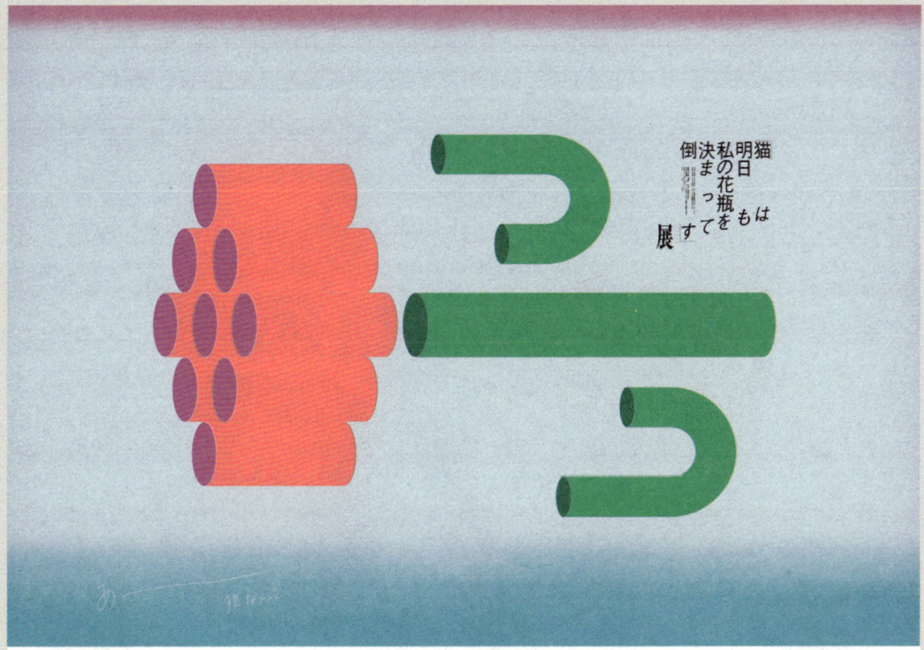
猫は
明日も
私の花瓶を
決まって
倒す
展

The cat will do it again.

猫は
明日も
私の花瓶を
決まって
倒す

The cat will do
again.

猫は
明日も
私の花瓶を
決まって
倒

蘆雪化猫
蘆雪化猫
The cat will do it again.

DELUSION TO
HEDI SLIMANE

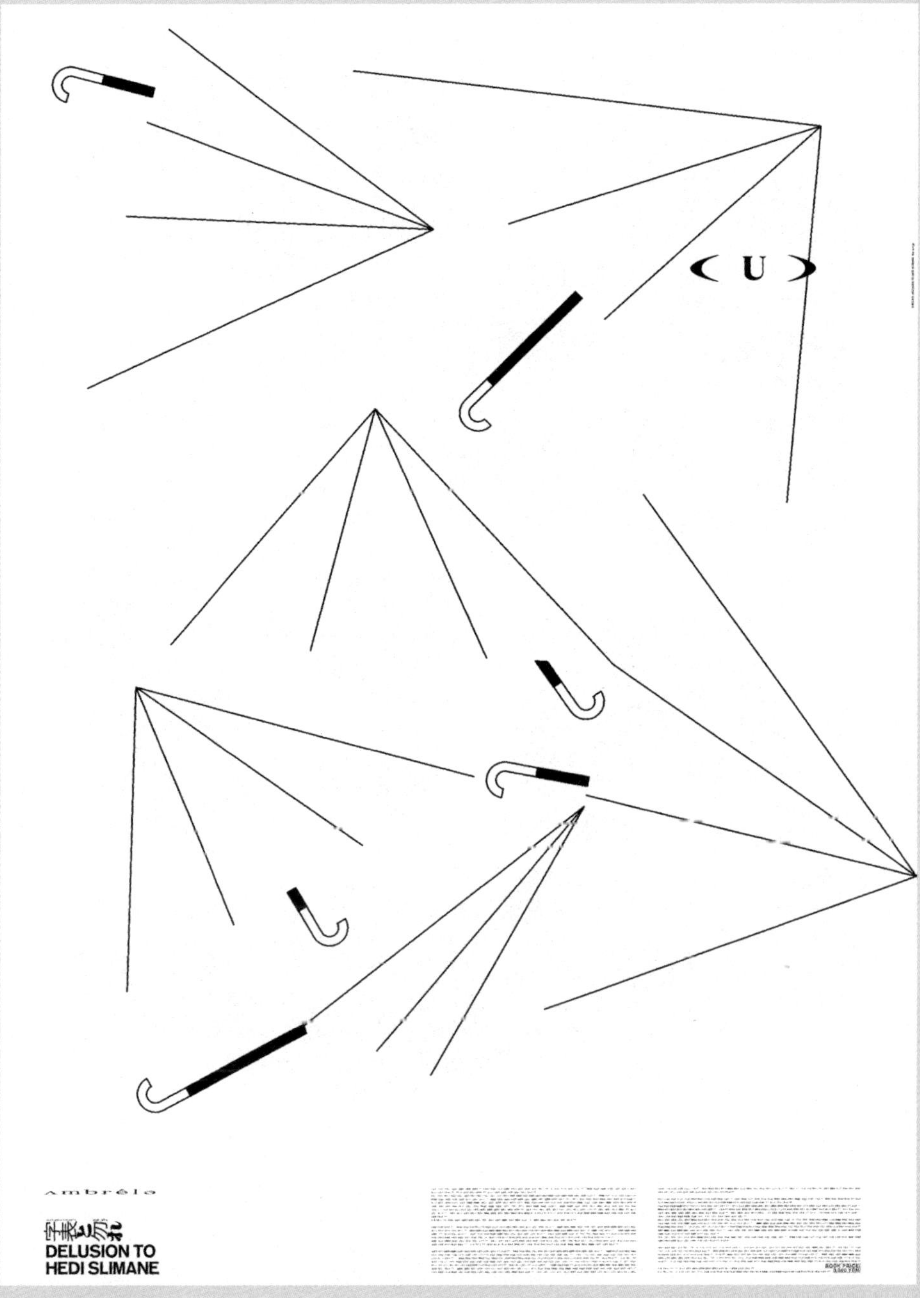

U
ambrélo
DELUSION TO
HEDI SLIMANE
BOOK PRICE

(K)
DELUSION TO
HEDI SLIMANE

DELUSION TO
HEDI SLIMANE

露
誰にもいわずにおきましょう
朝のお庭のすみっこで
花がほろりと泣いたこと
もしも噂がひろがって
蜂のお耳へはいったら
わるいことでもしたように
蜜をかえしに行くでしょう
金子
みすゞ
BUNKITSU

海の向う
北原白秋
BUNKITSU

みんないつか死ぬんだ
プラトーン
オリバー・ストーン
ウィレム・デフォー
トム・ベレンジャー
チャーリー・シーン
ジョニー・デップ
stall

金は必要だが、重要ではない
ナイト・オン・ザ・プラネット
ジム・ジャームッシュ
ウィノナ・ライダー
ロベルト・ベニーニ
ジーナ・ローランズ

stall

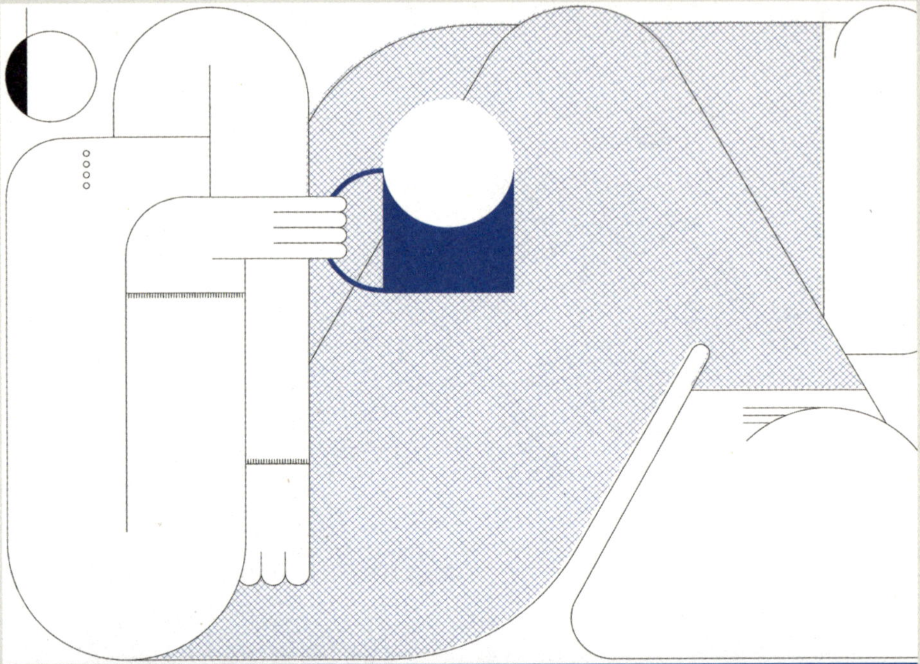

collé

Born in Tokyo and raised in Fukuoka, Tokyo University of the Arts alumnus Agata Yamaguchi founded the collé design studio in 2021. In 2022, he launched "omise" — a brand and web store for which he develops original products. He is also a member of the Japan Graphic Designers Association.

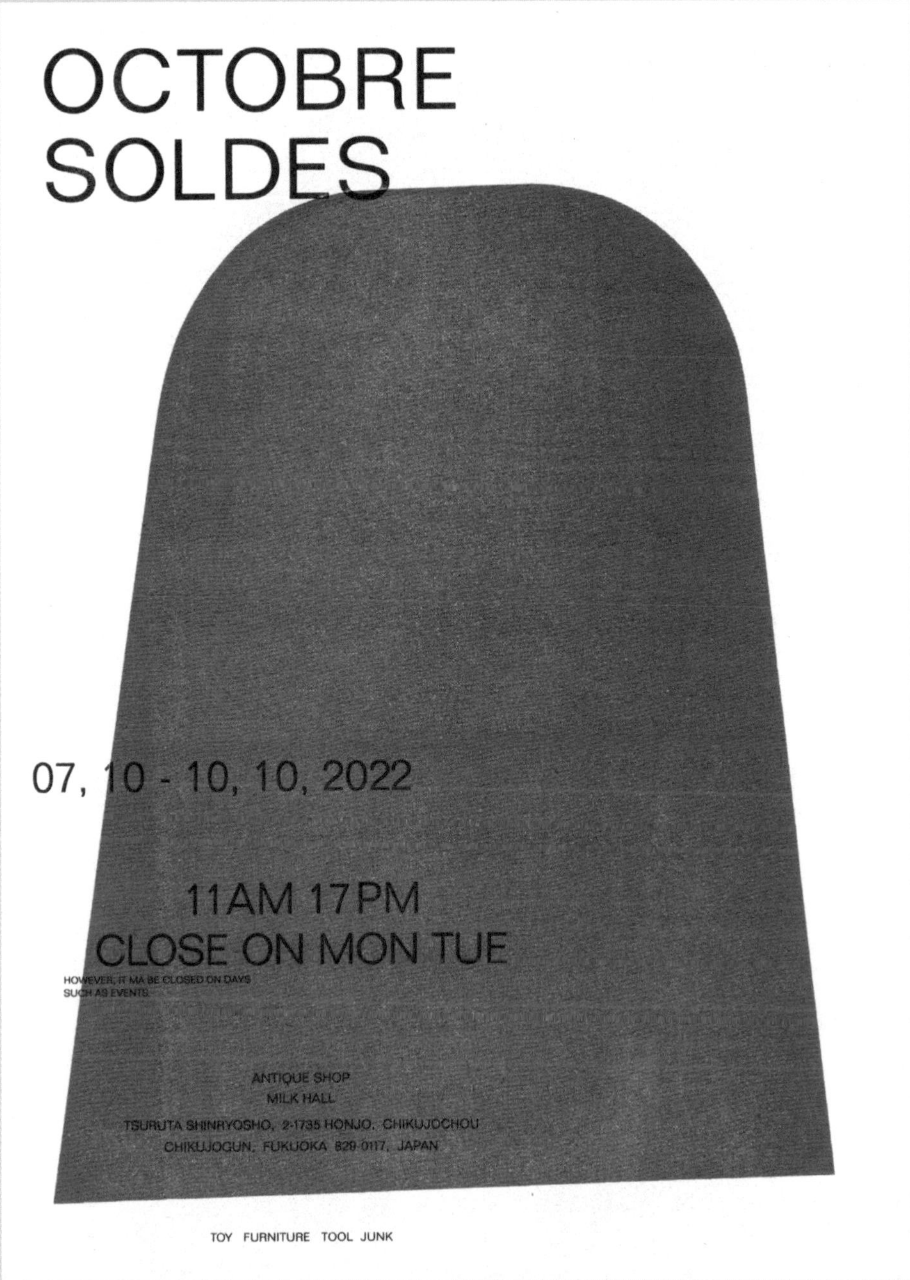
OCTOBRE
SOLDES
07, 10 - 10, 10, 2022
11AM 17PM
CLOSE ON MON TUE
HOWEVER, IT MA BE CLOSED ON DAYS
SUCH AS EVENTS.
ANTIQUE SHOP
MILK HALL
TSURUTA SHINRYOSHO, 2-1735 HONJO, CHIKUJOCHOU
CHIKUJOGUN, FUKUOKA 829-0117, JAPAN
TOY FURNITURE TOOL JUNK

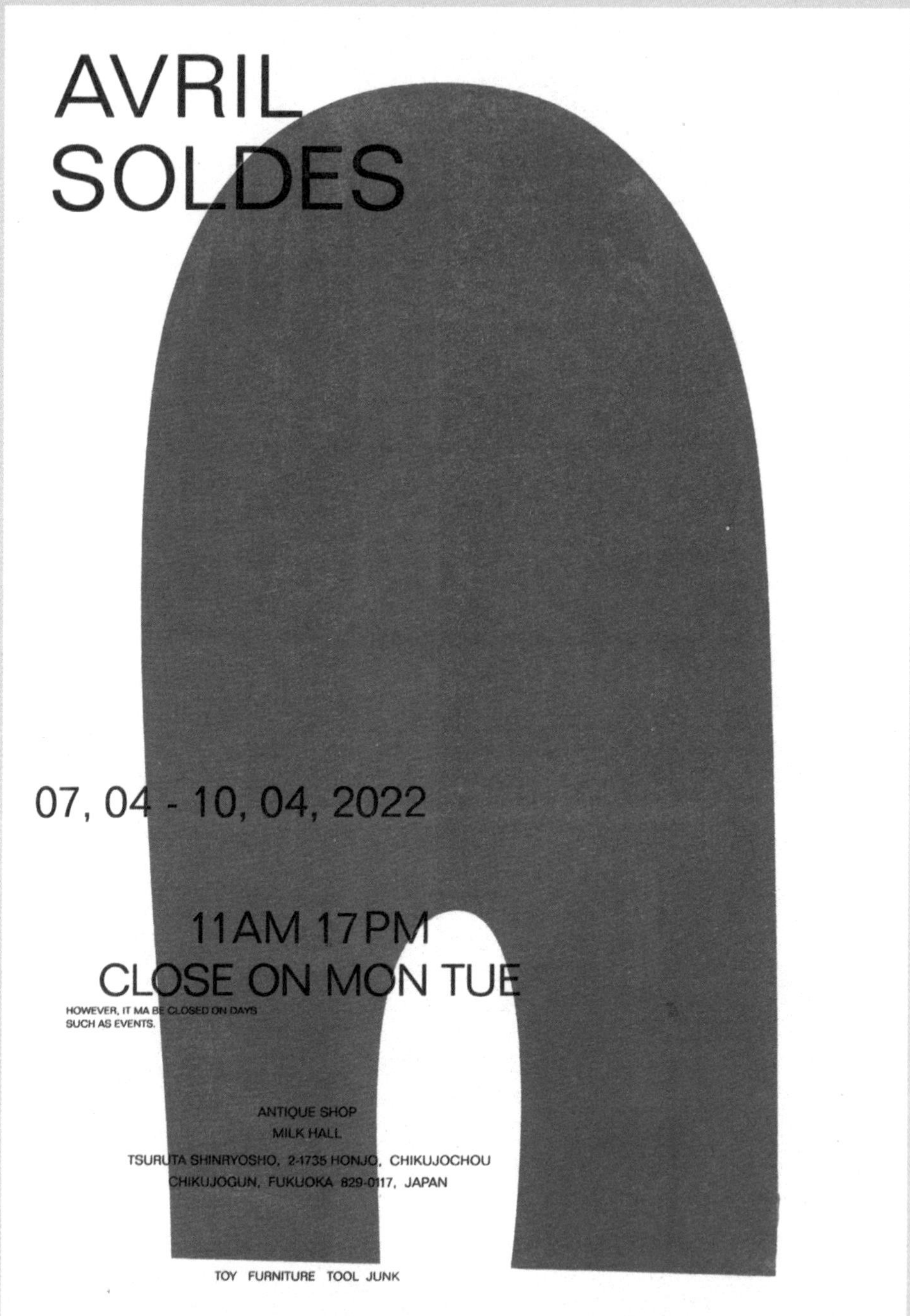
AVRIL
SOLDES
07, 04 - 10, 04, 2022
11AM 17PM
CLOSE ON MON TUE
HOWEVER, IT MA BE CLOSED ON DAYS
SUCH AS EVENTS.
ANTIQUE SHOP
MILK HALL
TSURUTA SHINRYOSHO, 2-1735 HONJO, CHIKUJOCHOU
CHIKUJOGUN, FUKUOKA 829-0117, JAPAN
TOY FURNITURE TOOL JUNK

JANVIER
SOLDES
05, 01 - 08, 01, 2022
11AM 17PM
CLOSE ON MON TUE
HOWEVER, IT MA BE CLOSED ON DAYS
SUCH AS EVENTS.
ANTIQUE SHOP
MILK HALL
TSURUTA SHINRYOSHO, 2-1735 HONJO, CHIKUJOCHOU
CHIKUJOGUN, FUKUOKA 829-0117, JAPAN
TOY FURNITURE TOOL JUNK

shopping
AGATA YAMAGUCHI EXHIBITION
at Alt_Medium
2-6-3-102 SHIMOOCHIAI,
SHINJUKU-KU,
TOKYO 161-0033
DATE: 10/15THU-
10/20TUE/2020
TIME: 12:00-20:00
*LAST DAY 17:00
Fun shape vol.1 X 5 ¥0,00
Fun shape vol.2 X 7 ¥0,00
Fun shape vol.3 X 6 ¥0,00
Cucumber ¥78
Tooth paste ¥270
Softener ¥899
Conpact car ¥1,903,000
22 Items
Tax 10% ¥190,424
Total ¥2,094,671
Alt_Medium

shopping
AGATA YAMAGUCHI EXHIBITION
at Alt_Medium
2-6-3-102 SHIMOOCHIAI,
SHINJUKU KU,
TOKYO 161-0033
DATE: 10/15 THU-
10/20 TUE / 2020
TIME: 12:00-20:00
• LAST DAY 17:00
Fun shape vol.1 X 4 ¥0,00
Fun shape vol.2 X 2 ¥0,00
Fun shape vol.3 X 1 ¥0,00
Fan
8 Items
Tax 10% ¥5,113,240
Total ¥56,245,640
Alt_Medium

sho
AGATA YAMAGUCHI EXHIBITION
at Alt_Medium
DATE:
10/20TUE/2020
TIME:
12:00-20:00
• LAST DAY 17:00
Softener ¥899
Water ¥103
Sedan ¥5,283,000
Toothbrush ¥245
Shampoo ¥699
Pear ¥230
Banana ¥89
Apple ¥130
Fun shape vol.2 X 9 ¥0,00
Tax 10%
Total ¥56,245,640
Alt_Medium

shopping
AGATA YAMAGUCHI EXHIBITION
at Alt_Medium
2-6-3-102 SHIMOOCHIAI,
SHINJUKU-KU,
TOKYO 161-0033
DATE: 10/15THU-
10/20TUE/2020
TIME: 12:00-20:00
*LAST DAY 17:00
Fun shape vol.1 X 5 ¥0,00
Fun shape vol.2 X 6 ¥0,00
Fun shape vol.3 X 7 ¥0,00
Blance Ball ¥1,500
Plastic Bottle ¥78
Tomate ¥100
17 Items
Tax 10% ¥164
Total ¥1,806
Alt_Medium

(Grandpa self-checkout)
1B 9516 P

FAMILY

(Mr. flower garden)
7U 9721 A
FAMILY

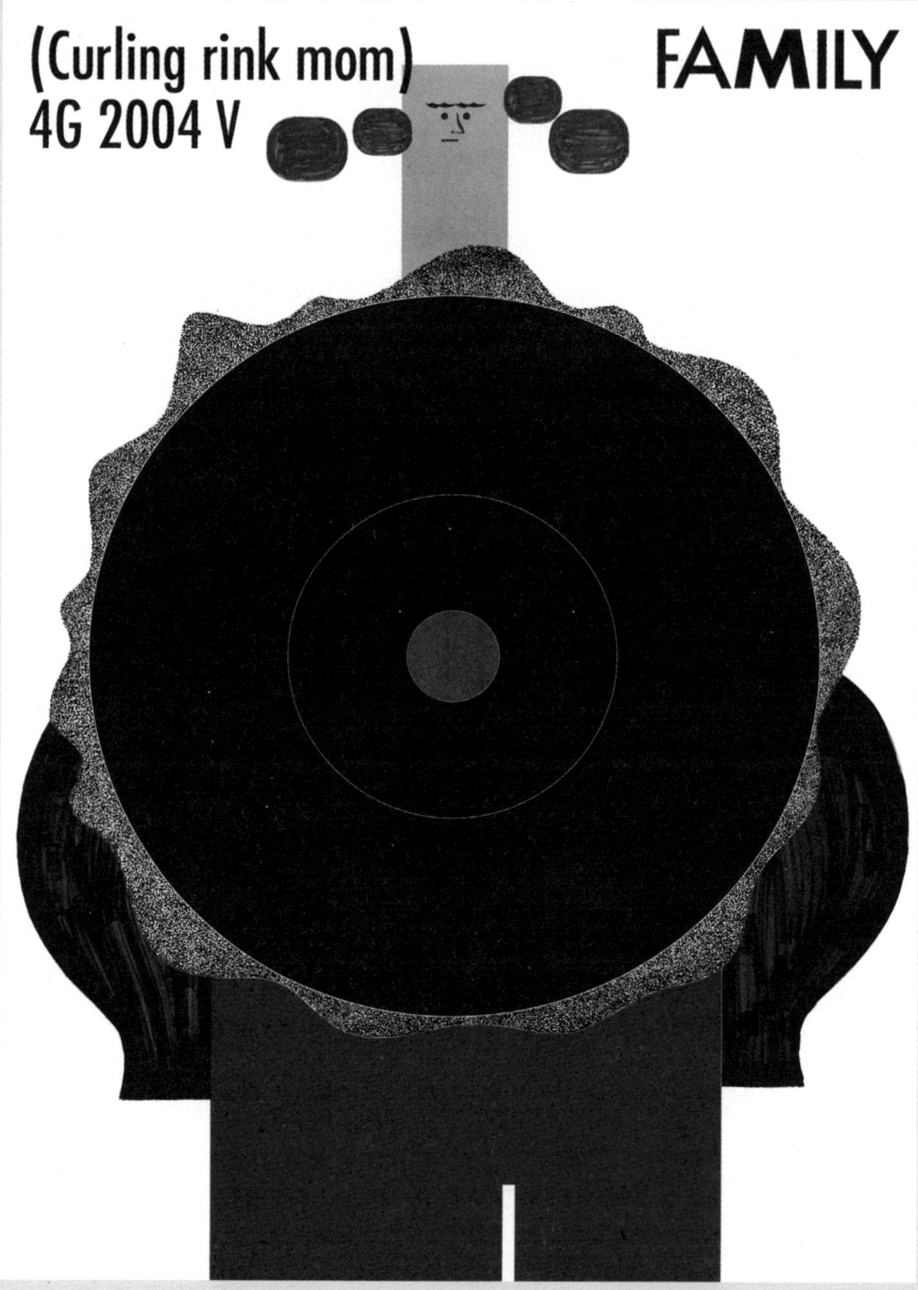
(Curling rink mom)
4G 2004 V
FAMILY

(Datemaki gal)
#B 4728 T
FAMILY

face myself

face myself

coton design

Hiroko Sakai pivoted to graphic design after studying psychology in university. Since founding coton design in 2011, she has received various awards, including the Bronze Award and Judges Award at the 2010 Hong Kong International Poster Triennial, as well as a Certificate of Honour at the Lahti XVIII Poster Biennial. Born in 1981, she currently lives and works in Tokyo.

Natural beauty and one's feelings are expressed by using scissors to adjust the length of the stems and to modify the shape of the leaves and by using the hands to add curvature. Today, avant-garde ikebana that doesn't even use plants is one genre of the art.
TRADITIONAL WAY
& FRESH IDEA

コンとロール
control
下北沢 OFF・OFFシアター
2021年1月19日㊋～1月25日㊊
作・演出　細川洋平
出演　鈴政ゲン　藤井千帆　細井じゅん　松浦祐也　三浦俊輔　宮城茉帆
ほろびて
https://horobite.com

ポロポロ、に
作・演出 細川洋平
浅井浩介
齊藤由衣
高野ゆらこ
はぎわら水雨子
藤代太一
和田華子（青年団）
ほろびて
BUoY
2021年10月27日 wed ―― 11月1日 mon

hair
cut
for
yourself
CREEK

Please arrange
fresh and tasty vegetables
on your table.
harimazaka
marche

LIVING WITH FARMING

local farmers' market

第32回下北沢演劇祭参加作品
Plant the seedlings
苗をうえる
作・演出 細川洋平
下北沢OFF・OFFシアター
'22年2月16日(水)ー23日(水・祝)
ほろびて

いけばな龍生展
植物の貌
二〇二〇
'20年11月22日［日］・23日［月・祝］
渋谷ストリーム ホール
時間　10：00－18：00
※入場は閉場の30分前まで　※本展は日時指定制です
会場　渋谷ストリーム ホール　東京都渋谷区渋谷 3-21-3
入場料　1,500円　高校生以下無料
主催　龍生派家元吉村華洲＋龍生派本部
龍生派

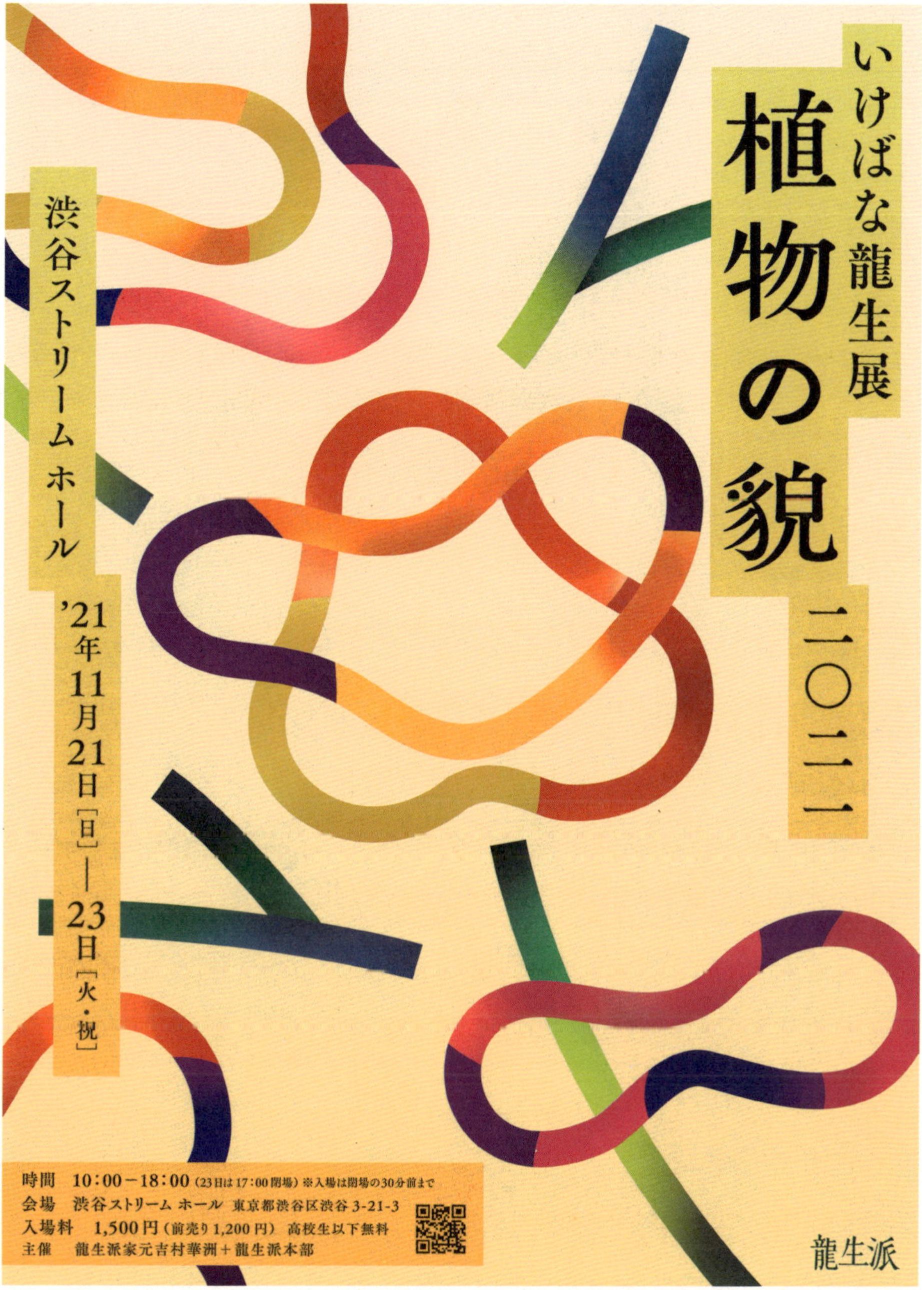
いけばな龍生展
植物の貌
二〇二一
渋谷ストリーム ホール
'21年11月21日〔日〕— 23日〔火・祝〕
時間 10:00—18:00（23日は17:00閉場）※入場は閉場の30分前まで
会場 渋谷ストリーム ホール 東京都渋谷区渋谷3-21-3
入場料 1,500円（前売り1,200円） 高校生以下無料
主催 龍生派家元吉村華洲＋龍生派本部
龍生派

些細な差異が、とめどなくなっていくさ。
こころはしろいままで世界に、あるのさ。
kohaku
加瀬澤 拓未（劇団献身）
葛堂 里奈（ブルドッキングヘッドロック）
佐藤 滋（青年団／滋企画）
鈴政 ゲン
藤代 太一
作・演出 細川洋平
調布市せんがわ劇場
2022. 6. 1 wed — 6. 5 sun
ほろびて
第11回せんがわ劇場演劇コンクール「グランプリ」受賞公演

border
border
ほろびて
ぼうだあ
'20 2月27日(木) – 3月2日(月)
下北沢 OFF・OFFシアター
作・演出 細川洋平
出演 三浦俊輔 藤代太一 三森麻美 大場みなみ 久具巨林 平井友稀奈

DENTSU

From corporate identity branding and design communications to product conceptualisation and development, DENTSU offers a streamlined suite of services with design at its core. It has been recognised by the New York ADC, ADFEST, and TOPAWARDS ASIA to name a few.

PHOTO BY
SHOHEI TAKENAKA

ICRP KYOK UKAI

2020.5.25.Mon
14:00-15:30

#01

2020.5.25.Mon
14:00-15:30

#02

ICRP KYOKUKAI

PHOTO BY
MARIKO OHYA

PHOTO BY
KATSUTOSHI SAWACHIKA

ICRP
KYOK
UKAI

2020.5.25.Mon
14:00-15:30

#03

2020.5.25.Mon
14:00-15:30

#04

ICRP KYOKUKAI

PHOTO BY
YOICHI ONODA

PHOTO BY
KEITA GOTO

ICRP KYOKUKAI

2020.5.25.Mon
14:00-15:30

#05

ようこそ糸魚川へ。
国石"ヒスイ"の産地でもあるこの地の石には、
さまざまな物語が潜んでいます。
色、形、模様、手ざわり。
個性あるそのひとつひとつから、
糸魚川の壮大な自然を感じてみてください。

01

石を知る

石のまち糸魚川
ISHI NO MACHI ITOIGAWA

新旧の地質が隣り合う糸魚川の石たちは、
ブルー、グリーン、淡いピンクなど
ひとつひとつが個性的。
運が良ければヒスイを発見できるかも!?
ぜひ、あなただけの石をみつけてくださいね。

02

石を拾う

石のまち糸魚川
ISHI NO MACHI ITOIGAWA

03

石に祈る

はるか昔のこと。

糸魚川の地を治める奴奈川姫のもとへ、

出雲国からはるばる大国主命がやってきました。

その時、彼女が身につけていたのが"ヒスイ"。

以来、糸魚川の石には

不思議な力があると信じられています。

石のまち糸魚川

ISHI NO MACHI ITOIGAWA

東西の地層の境目に位置する
糸魚川は、まさに自然の恵みの集合地点。
名物の紅ズワイガニや地酒、
そして泉質の異なる数々の温泉。
糸魚川の幸を、
どうぞ味わい尽くしてください。

04

石を味わう

石のまち糸魚川
ISHI NO MACHI ITOIGAWA

ジオ・パーク教授
地球の研究をしている。
特に興味があるのが地層について。
こだわりはちょびヒゲ。
毎日こまめに形を整えている。
石のまち糸魚川
ISHI NO MACHI ITOIGAWA
https://ishinomachi.com

ARTWORK BY tupera tupera

アライナミ

よく笑ってよく食べて、
いつも元気いっぱい波とおどる。
その笑い声につられて魚たちもおどりだす。
泣くと嵐がくるから気をつけて。

石のまち糸魚川
ISHI NO MACHI ITOIGAWA

https://ishinomachi.com

emuni Inc.

Founded in 2012 by Takashi Murakami and Masashi Murakami, emuni Inc. is an award-winning art direction and design practice based in Tokyo. Its packaging, way-finding, and editorial design work spans across multiple mediums and platforms.

東京芸術祭2022
2022.
9.1㊍-
12.11㊐
ひらく きわめる つながる
Open Refining Connecting
東京芸術祭
Tokyo Festival
東京芸術劇場、GLOBAL RING THEATRE〈池袋西口公園野外劇場〉、
豊島区立芸術文化劇場〈東京建物 Brillia HALL〉ほか東京・豊島区池袋エリア

ミントデザインズ大百科
2022年6月8日水〜6月19日日 11時〜20時
会場 スパイラルガーデン 入場無料
“Mintpedia”
主催：有限会社ミントデザインズ
協賛：株式会社山田写真製版所、株式会社グランマーブル、
株式会社セブンユニフォーム
協力：株式会社竹尾、株式会社かまわぬ、大阪成蹊大学
会場協力：株式会社ワコールアートセンター

金沢21世紀美術館 デザインギャラリー
2020.7.18土 – 2021.3.21日
開場時間：10時〜18時（金曜日・土曜日は20時まで） 料金：入場無料
Museum of The People,
by The People, for The People
Period: 18 July 2020 (Sat) – 21 March 2021 (Sun)
Open: 10:00 – 18:00 (Until 20:00 on Fridays and Saturdays)
Admission: Free
21

VENT
NOUVEAU
DIGITAL

NO
U
DIGITAL

VENT
ITAL

VENT
NOUVEAU
DIGITAL

VENT
NOUVEAU
DIGITAL

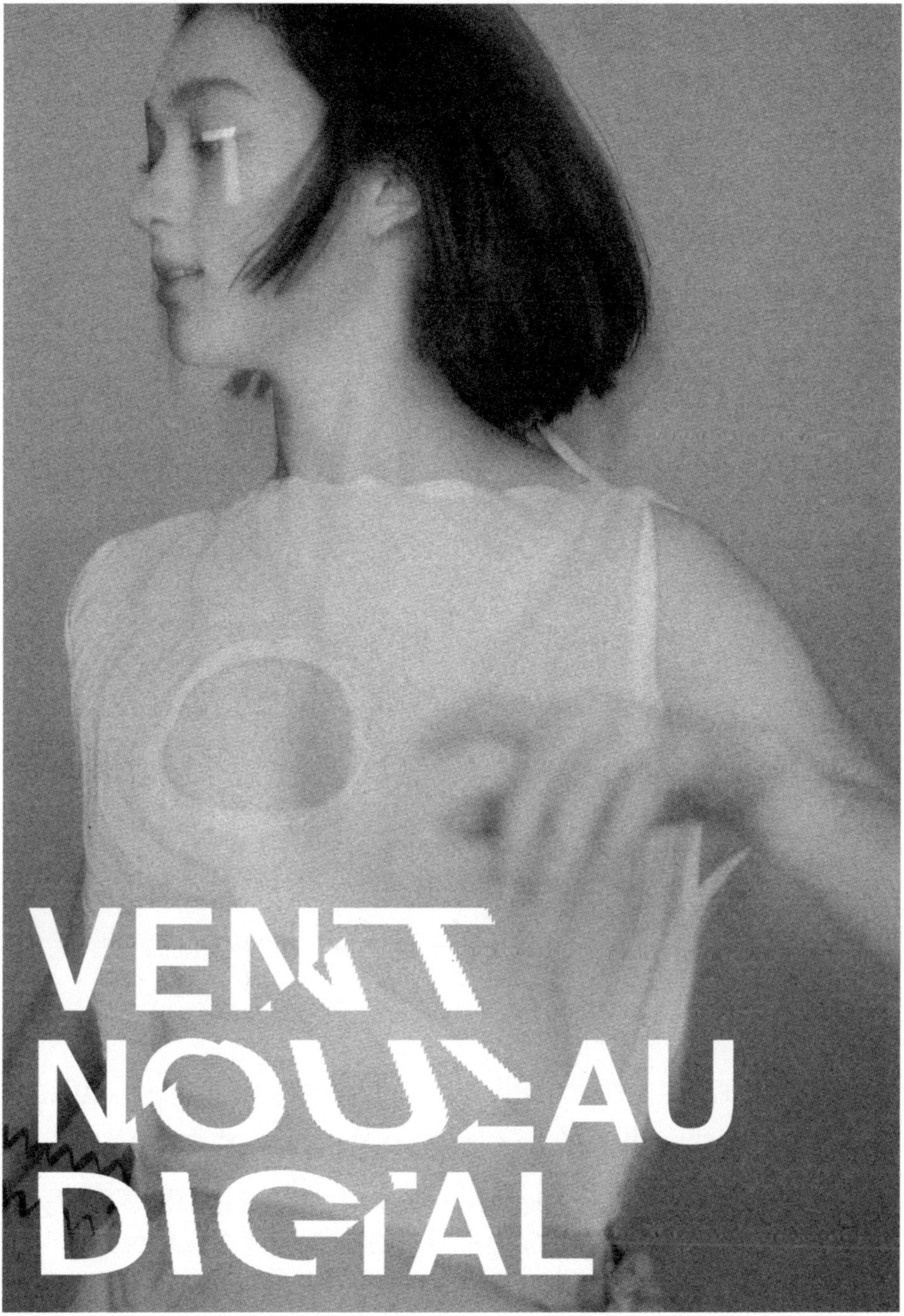
VENT
NOUVEAU
DIGITAL

Eri Ishihara

Eri Ishihara is an art director and designer who has been involved in a wide range of projects with a focus on graphics and packaging. She is also an author whose most recent release is the picture book, “Mochibake Omochi Dakedo Obake Desu” — published by Iwasaki Publishing Co.,Ltd.

SPRING HAS COME.
fiore soffitta

SPRING HAS COME.
fiore soffitta
Custom Made Flower Shop

PAK-IT
All Purpose Cleaner
SPRING HAS COME.
fiore soffitta
Custom Made Flower Shop

SPRING HAS COME.
Photographing & Graphic design : Eri Ishihara
fiore soffitta
Custom Made flower Shop

SPRING HAS COME.
fiore soffitta
Custom Made flower Shop

Landscape
砂と水玉 第2回公演『ランドスケープ』
日時：2017年 4月
14日（金）19:30
15日（土）14:00、19:00
16日（日）14:00 ※開場は開演30分前
会場：シャトー2F
東京都小金井市本町6-5-3 シャトー小金井 2F
http://www.chateau21.com
前売：2,500円／当日：2,800円 ※全席自由席
構成・演出・振付
市松
出演・振付
甲斐美奈寿
渡川いくみ
野瀬山瑞希
http://sand-and-polkadots.blogspot.jp/

Landscape
砂と水玉 第2回公演『ランドスケープ』
日時：2017年 4月
14日(金) 19:30
15日(土) 14:00、19:00
16日(日) 14:00
会場：シャトー2F
前売：2,500円／当日：2,800円
構成・演出・振付
市松
出演・振付
甲斐美奈寿
渡川いくみ
野瀬山瑞希
http://sand-and-polkadots.blogspot.jp/

B
B
日時/二〇二〇年
二月六日(木)十九時半
二月七日(金)十四時・十九時半
二月八日(土)十四時・十九時半
二月九日(日)十四時
場所/北千住BUoY
blue
bird,
black
hole
出演・振付/
甲斐美奈寿
河原舞
新宅一平
出﨑洋樹
永山香月
根本和歌菜
米澤一平
BLUE BIRD, BLACK HOLE. BLUE BIRD, BLACK HOLE.
作・演出・振付/市松
B
H
https://sunatomizutama.com/

B
B
blue bird, black hole
日時／二〇二〇年
二月六日(木)十九時半
二月七日(金)十四時・十九時半
二月八日(土)十四時・十九時半
二月九日(日)十四時
場所／北千住BUoY
出演・振付／
甲斐美奈寿
河原舞
新宅一平
出﨑洋樹
永山香月
根本和歌菜
米澤一平
BLUE BIRD BLACK HOLE, BLUE BIRD, BLACK HOLE
作 演出・振付／市松
B
H
https://sunatomizutama.com/

たとえばの風景
出演と振付：根本和歌菜、宮本悠加、柒谷樹
演出と振付：市松　主催：砂と水玉
公演日：2022年8月19日(金)、20日(土)、21日(日)
会場：カフェムリウイ
IF SO, WHAT WOULD WE SEE?

たとえばの風景
出演と振付：根本和歌菜、宮本悠加、梁谷樹
演出と振付：市松 主催：砂と水玉
公演日：2022年8月19日(金)、20日(土)、21日(日)
会場：カフェムリウイ
IF SO, WHAT WOULD WE SEE?
https://sunatomizutama.com/

Harajuku DESIGN Inc.

Harajuku DESIGN Inc. is a branding agency based in its namesake Tokyo location. Its wide range of services involve brand consultations, marketing strategies, creative and art direction, as well as design solutions for companies looking to expand globally.

Musubi, Inc.
18-2 Naka-cho,Shinjuku-ku,
Tokyo, Japan
www.musubi.tokyo.jp
musubi

Musubi, Inc.
18-2 Naka-cho,Shinjuku-ku,
Tokyo, Japan
www.musubi.tokyo.jp
musubi

Musubi, Inc.
18-2 Naka-cho,Shinjuku-ku,
Tokyo, Japan
www.musubi.tokyo.jp
musubi

Musubi, Inc.
18-2 Naka-cho,Shinjuku-ku,
Tokyo, Japan
www.musubi.tokyo.jp
musubi

Musubi, Inc.
18-2 Naka-cho,Shinjuku-ku,
Tokyo, Japan
www.musubi.tokyo.jp
musubi

おはぎさん
6 13 20 27
7 14 21 28
1 8 15 22 29
2 9 16 23 30
3 10 17 24 31
4 11 18 25
5 12 19 26
1 2 3 4 5 6 7 8 9 10 11 12

おはぎさん

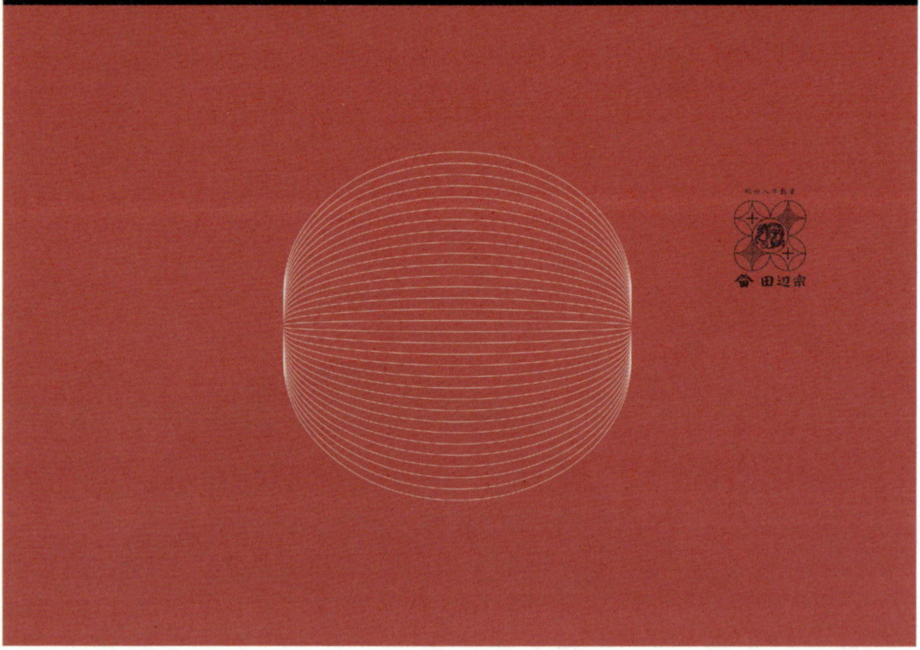
田辺宗

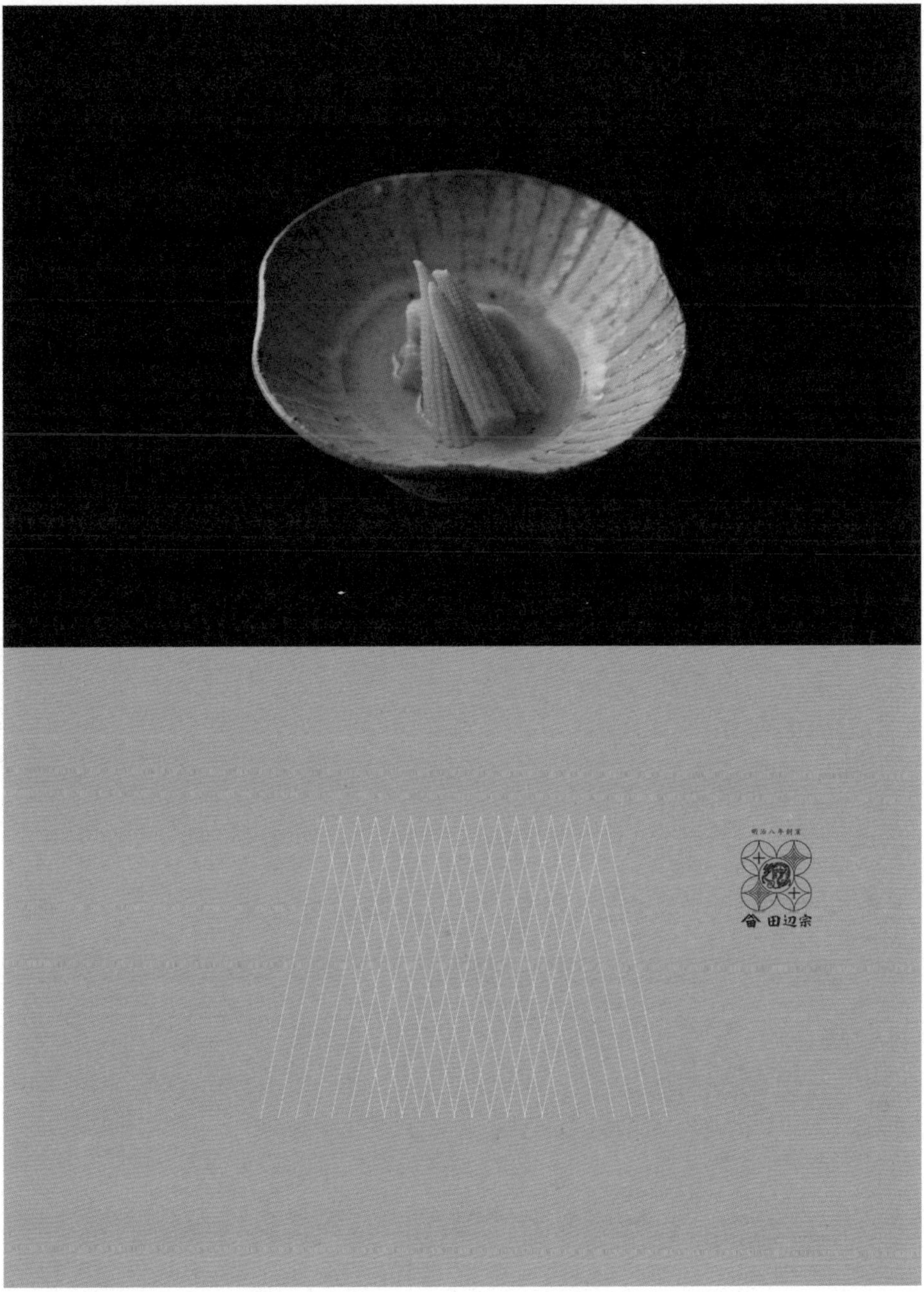

明治八年創業

田辺宗

春、草は芽吹き、島は歌い、
鬼が踊る季節です。
海を渡ると、急がなかった日本がある。
佐渡島
Sado shima
鬼太鼓

海を渡ると、急がなかった日本がある。

佐渡島

Sado shima

Sado Tourism Association

Haro, Inc.

Haro, Inc. is run by Shinpei Nakaya, a Tokyo native who graduated from Musashino Art University and worked with the Handsome Design Office before becoming a freelance graphic designer and art director. He is also one of the faces behind the "ZA" web store, which he set up in collaboration with fellow graphic designer GUCCIMAZE in 2019.

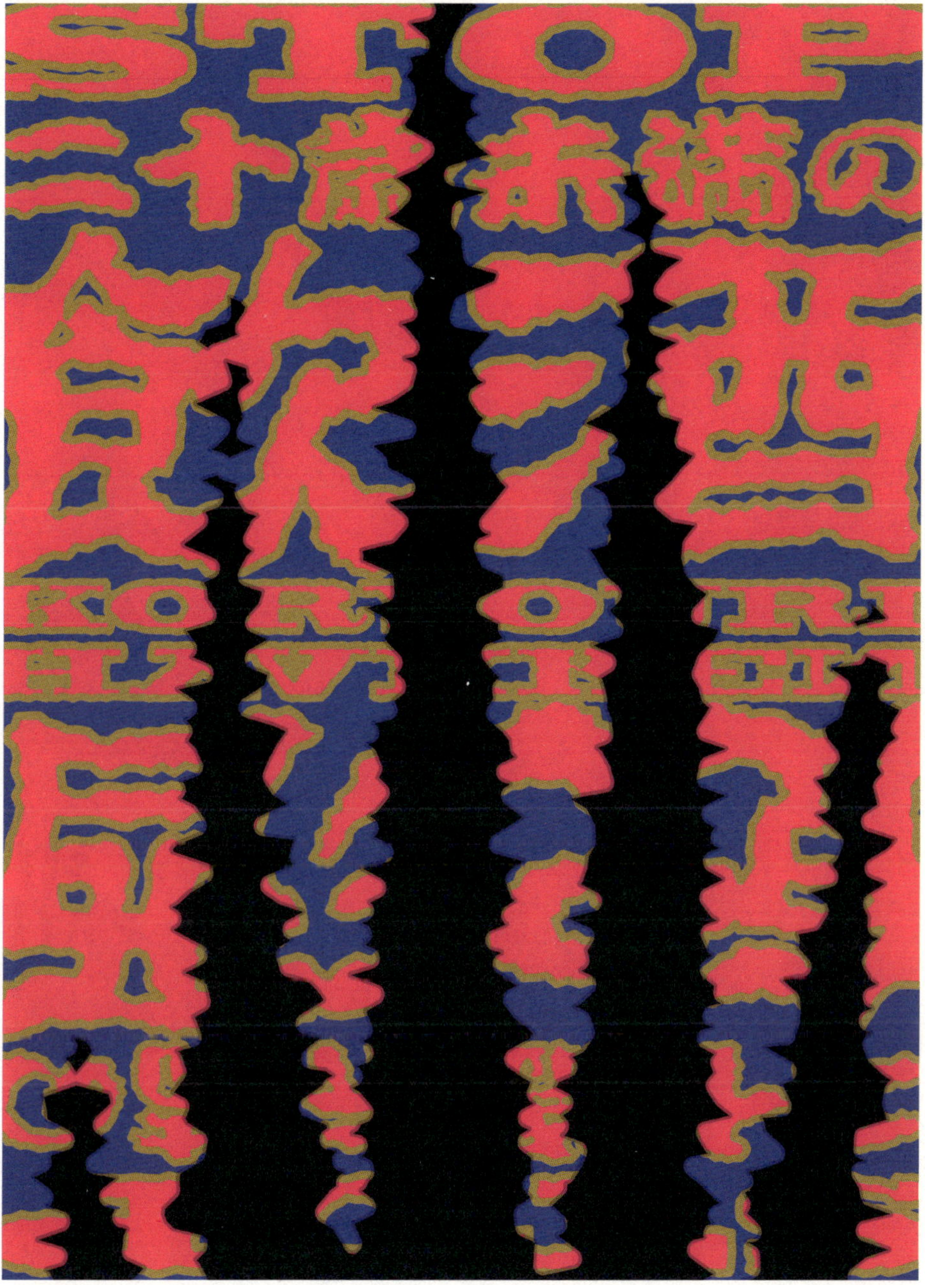
STOP
二十歳未満の

LIGHT
SHADOW

HATE
LOVE
KANJICAMO

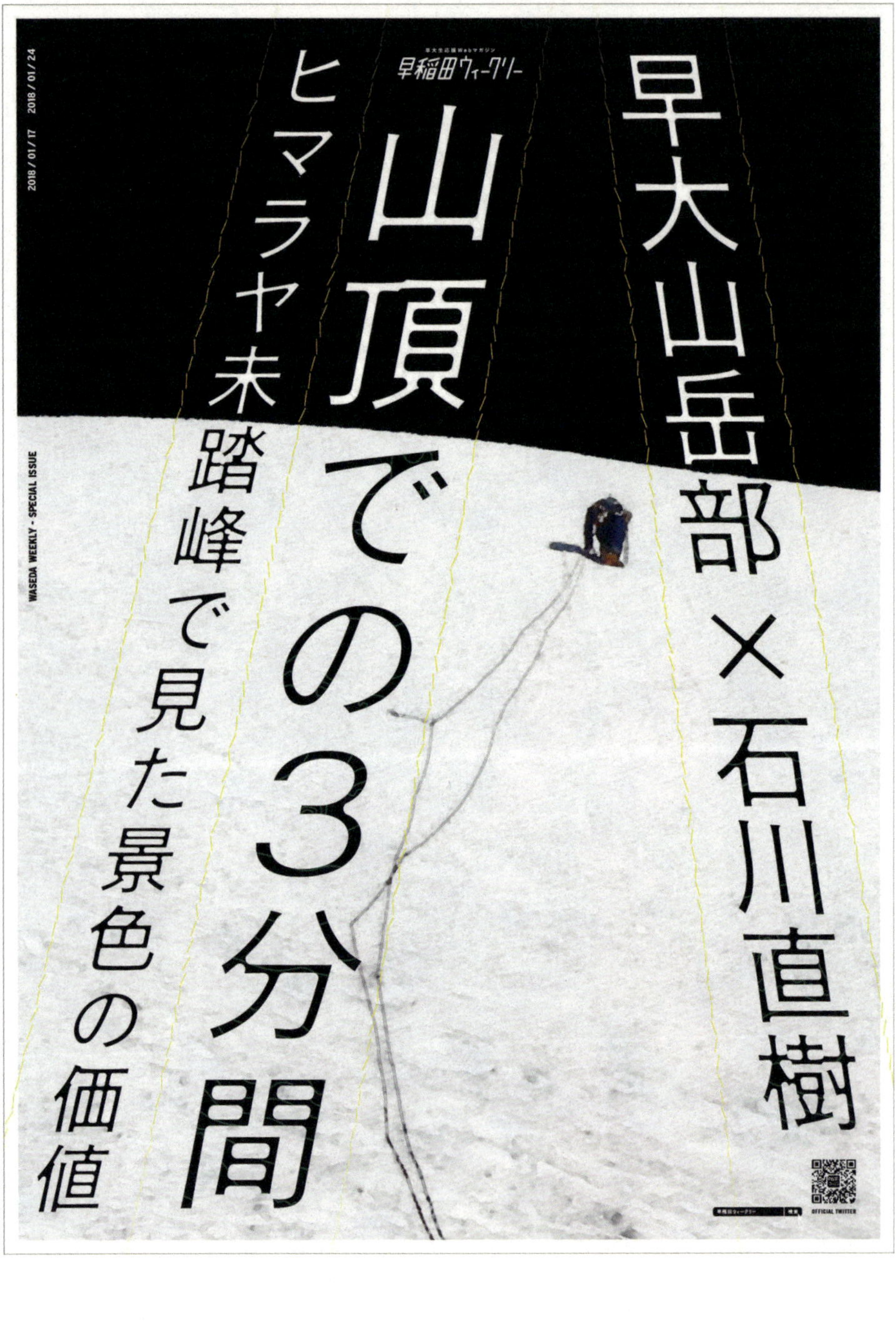
2018 / 01 / 17　2018 / 01 / 24
早大生応援Webマガジン
早稲田ウィークリー
早大山岳部×石川直樹
山頂での3分間
ヒマラヤ未踏峰で見た景色の価値
WASEDA WEEKLY - SPECIAL ISSUE
OFFICIAL TWITTER

WASEDA WEEKLY SPECIAL
普通の大学生ってなんだ
カミナリまなぶ
×
ジョイマン高木
×
サンキュータツオ
早稲田ウィークリー
5.23
5.30

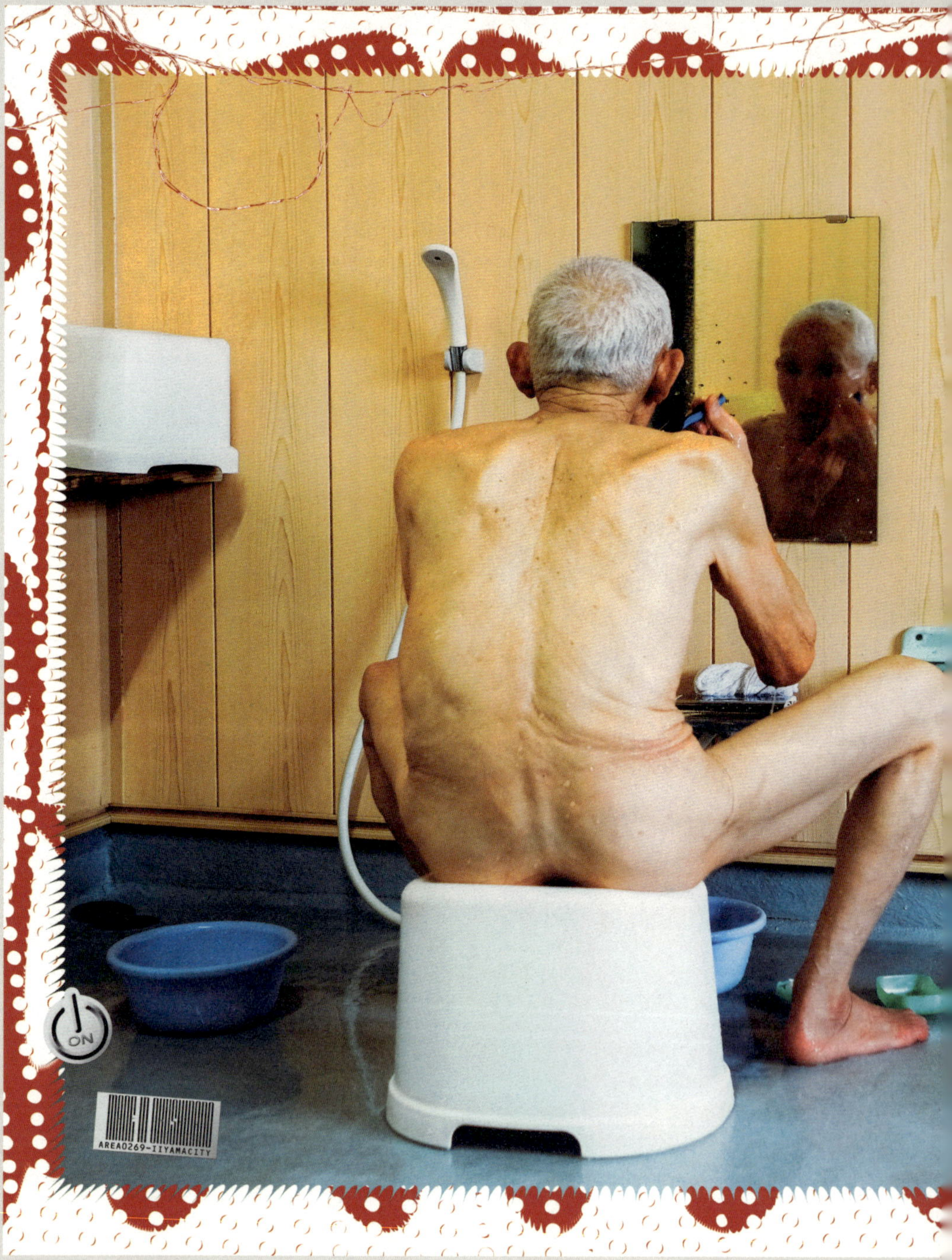
ON
AREA0269-IIYAMACITY

鶴と亀

AREA0269-IIYAMACITY
ON

奥飛騨
鶴と亀
TSURU TO KAME

PASOCOM MUSIC CLUB
COMPLEX
Super Pasocom Party
SHIBUYA WWW X
ACT パソコン音楽クラブ / dj newtown / RYOKO2000
OPENING DJ tomad
VJ Kazuki Homma
TICKET 前売 3200yen（1DRINK 別途）

LIVE パソコン音楽クラブ
GUEST VOCAL 川辺素（ミツメ） / 猪爪東風（ayU tokiO） / Tomoyuki Sagesaka（ isagen）
VJ Kazuki Homma
TICKET 前売 3900yen（1DRINK 別途）
Release One-man Live
OPEN 14:00 / START 15:
CLOSE 16:30

Hiroki Fujimaki

Hiroki Fujimaki was born in 1988 and is currently based in Tokyo.

Design:Hiroki Fujimaki Photo:Shuhei Yoshida
Print:Yamada Photo Process Co., Ltd

Design:Hiroki Fujimaki Photo:Shuhei Yoshida
Print:Yamada Photo Process Co., Ltd

Design:Hiroki Fujimaki Photo:Shuhei Yoshida
Print:Yamada Photo Process Co., Ltd

生活
せいかつ

生活

せいかつ

ON
Body
A fusion of
yoga ×
beauty ×
chiropractic

ON Body

A fusion of yoga × beauty × chiropractic

Photo: Jiang Xulei on Unsplash

ZYLA is a design studio creating meaningful impact through graphic design, motion graphic design and art direction.
We partner with visionary clients to translate bold ideas into beautifully articulated identities, visual communications, and experiences.

Tokyo Studio
2-5-1 Ebisunishi, Shibuya-ku, Tokyo 150-0021 Saison Daikanyama # 202
Company Name: ZYLA Inc. / Founded: April 2019

Advertisements, Logo / Symbol Mark Design, CI Design, Package Design, Promotion Video Producing, Tittle Back Producing, Motion Graphic Design.

Poster Design: Hiroki Fujimaki

a normal situation
a normal situation

-九谷の光景-
銀座 蔦屋書店

絢
深
剛
輝
-九谷の光景-
2021年3月2日(火)－3月12日(金)
GINZA ATRIUM
11:00－20:00
銀座 蔦屋書店

Hirotoshi Shiki

Born in Fukuoka, graphic designer Hirotoshi Shiki joined good design company after working at Message Design Centre. He is also a member of the Japan Graphic Designers Association.

LOOK, LOOK! LOOKS EXHIBITION
2021.11.27 SAT.–12.5 SUN.
11:00–21:00 (LAST DAY -18:00)
@ART-IN-GALLERY

LOOK, LOOK! LOOKS EXHIBITION
2021.11.27 SAT. - 12.5 SUN.
11:00 - 21:00 (LAST DAY - 18:00)
@ART·IN·GALLERY

LOOK. LOOK! LOOKS EXHIBITION
2021.11.27 SAT. – 12.5 SUN.
11:00 – 21:00 (LAST DAY - 18:00)
@ART·IN·GALLERY

Geographical Features of Curry

CURRY IS THE BEST THING EVER INVENTED. IT'S THE HIGHEST FROM OF LIFE ON THIS EARTH. THE WORLD REVOLVES AROUND OF CURRY!

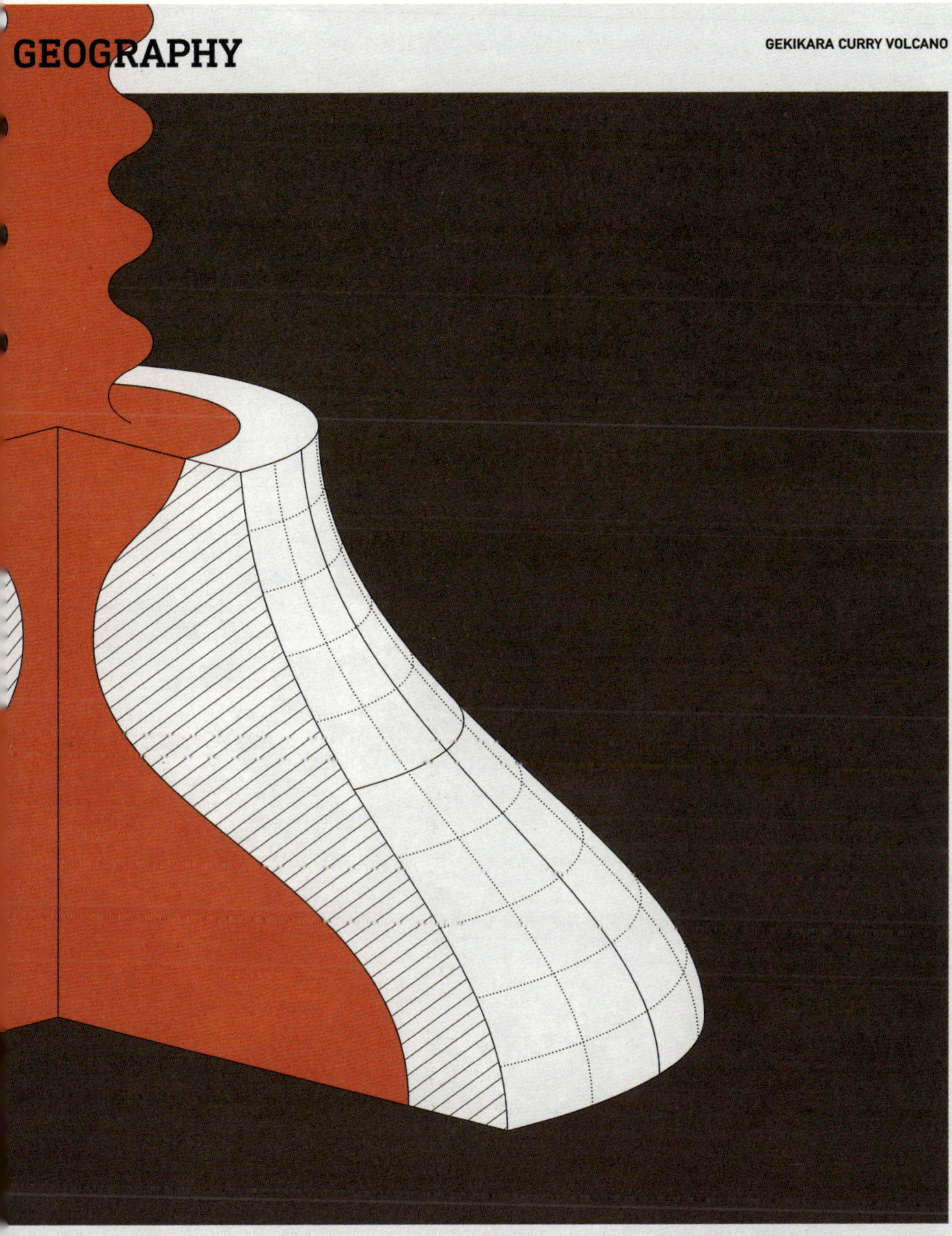

SOMEDAY, TROOPS, SOMEONE WILL ASK YOU WHY EAT CURRY, AND YOU CAN ANSWER SIMPLY, "BECAUSE IT WAS THERE!"

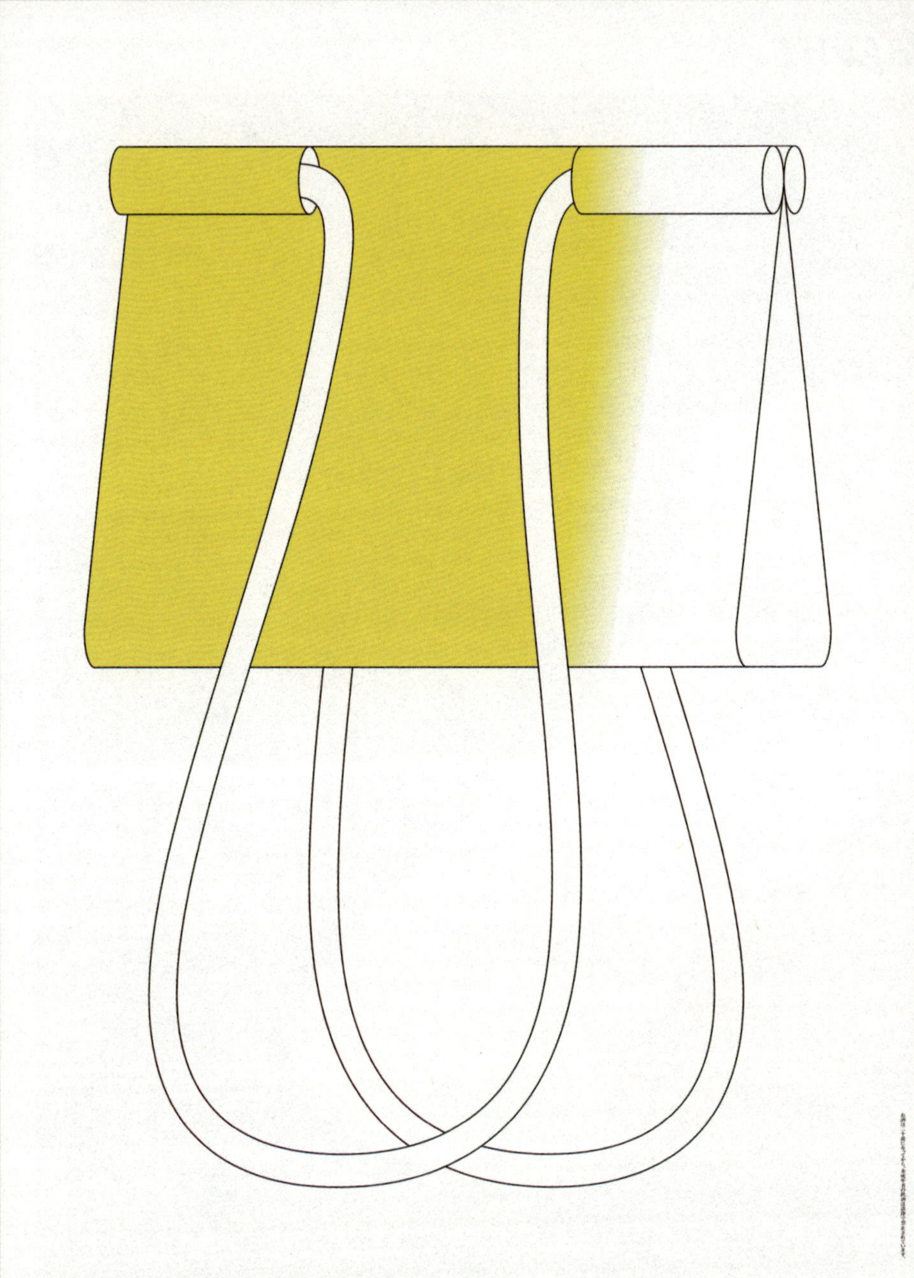

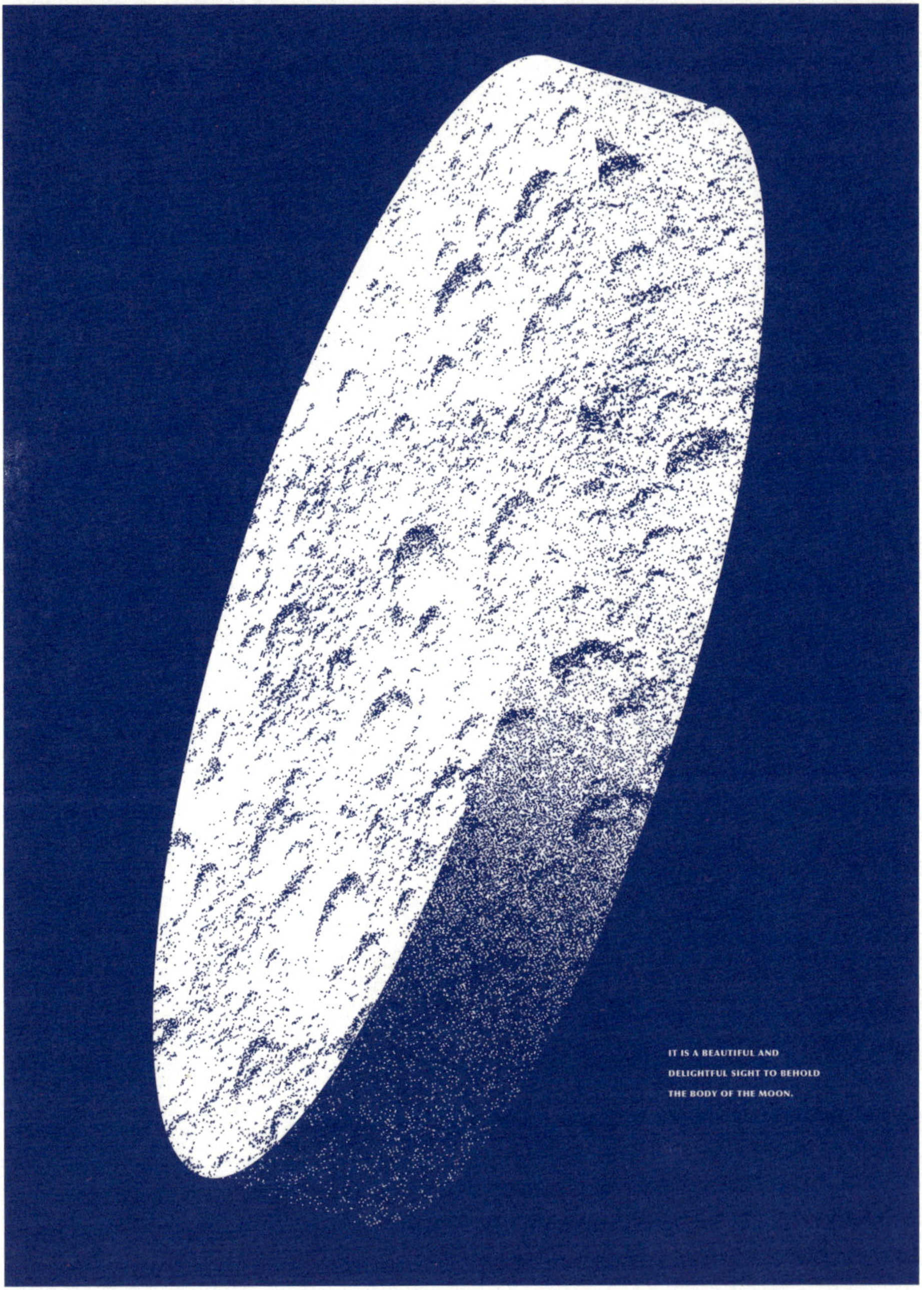
IT IS A BEAUTIFUL AND
DELIGHTFUL SIGHT TO BEHOLD
THE BODY OF THE MOON.

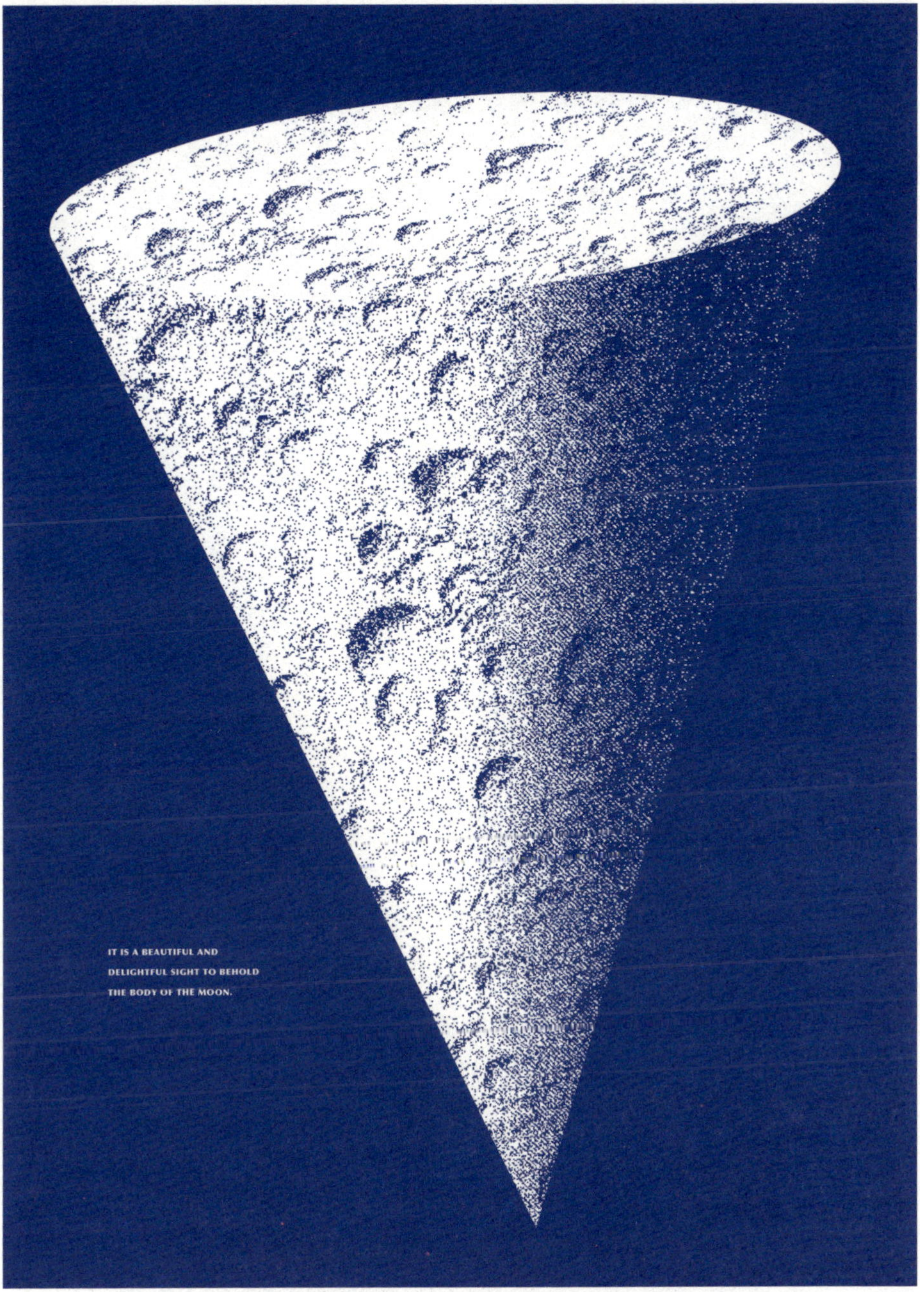
IT IS A BEAUTIFUL AND
DELIGHTFUL SIGHT TO BEHOLD
THE BODY OF THE MOON.

Print of
Pudding

Print of Pudding

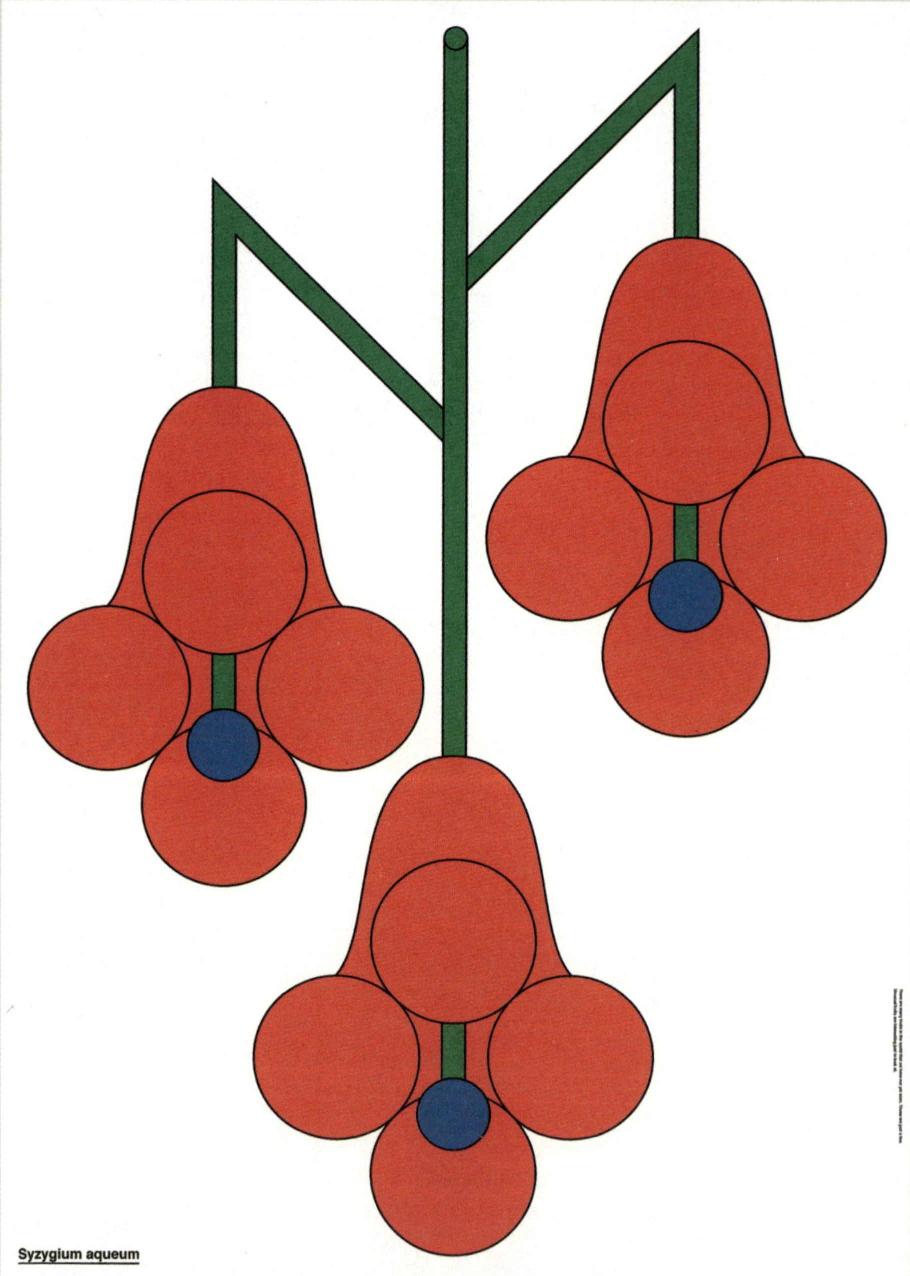
Syzygium aqueum

Jaboticaba

Star Fruit

Pitanga

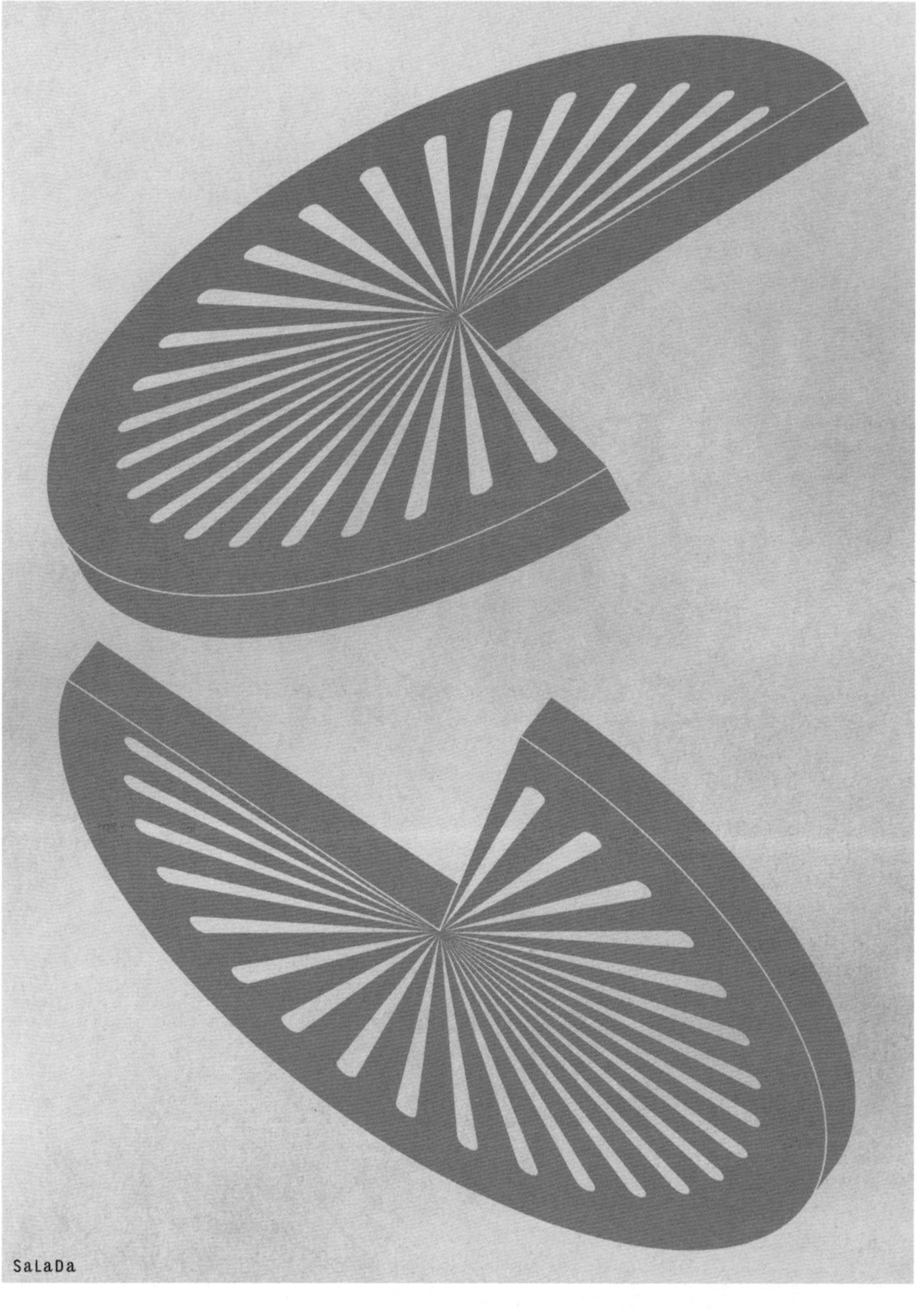
SaLaDa

SaLaDa

homesickdesign

Headquartered in Iwate, homesickdesign was founded in 2017 by Shinsuke Shimizu, who is also its creative and art director. The studio specialises in offering high-quality branding and design solutions.

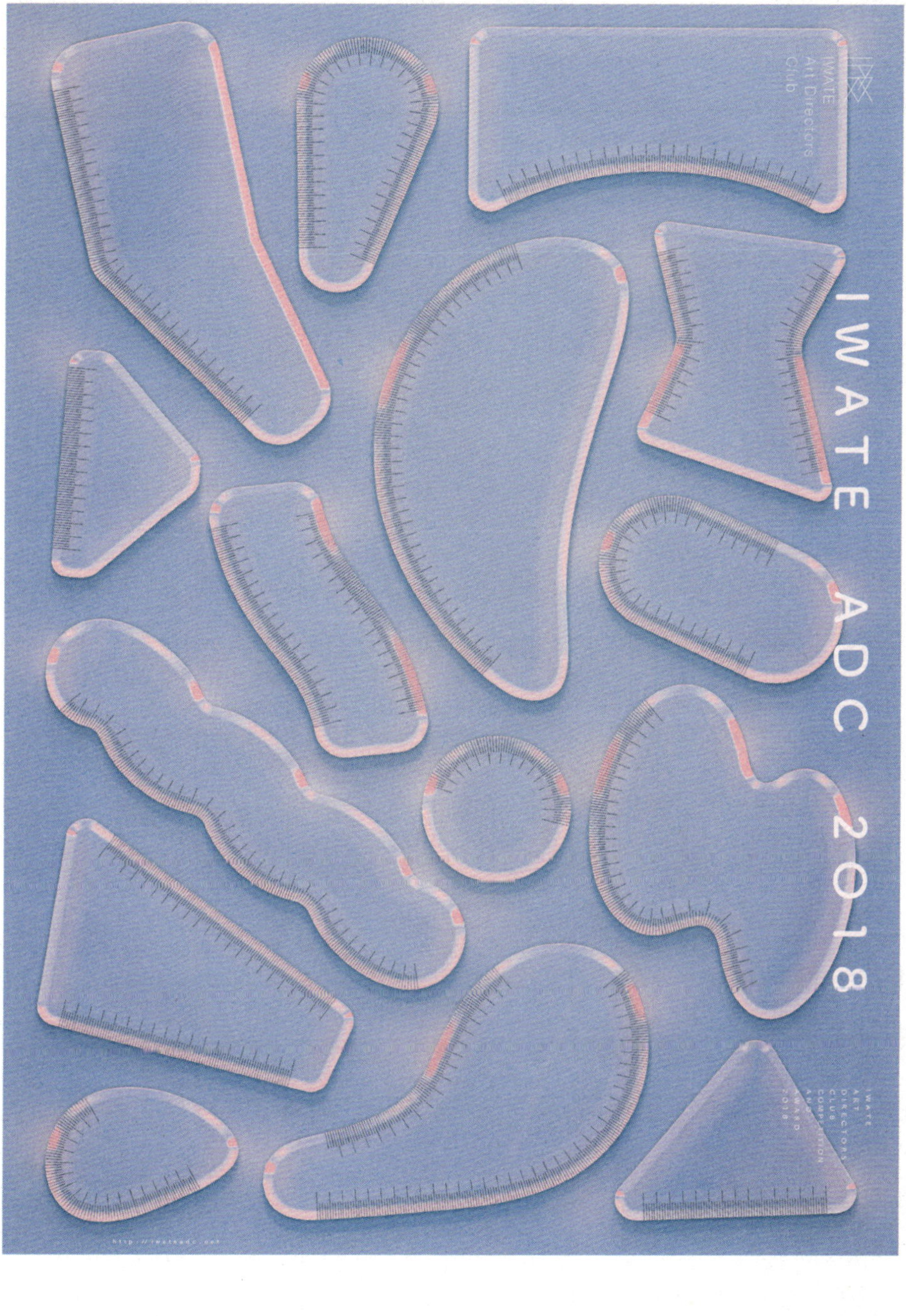
IWATE
Art Directors
Club
IWATE ADC 2018

文化庁 統括団体によるアートキャラバン事業
（コロナ禍からの文化芸術活動の再興支援事業）
「JAPAN LIVE YELL project」
アーツライブいわて
2022年8月から2023年1月迄
参加アーティスト
開催地 → 盛岡市／二戸市／野田村／宮古市／北上市

文化庁 統括団体によるアートキャラバン事業
（コロナ禍からの文化芸術活動の再興支援事業）
「JAPAN LIVE YELL project」
アーツライブいわて
2022年8月から2023年1月迄
開催地 → 盛岡市／二戸市／野田村／宮古市／北上市

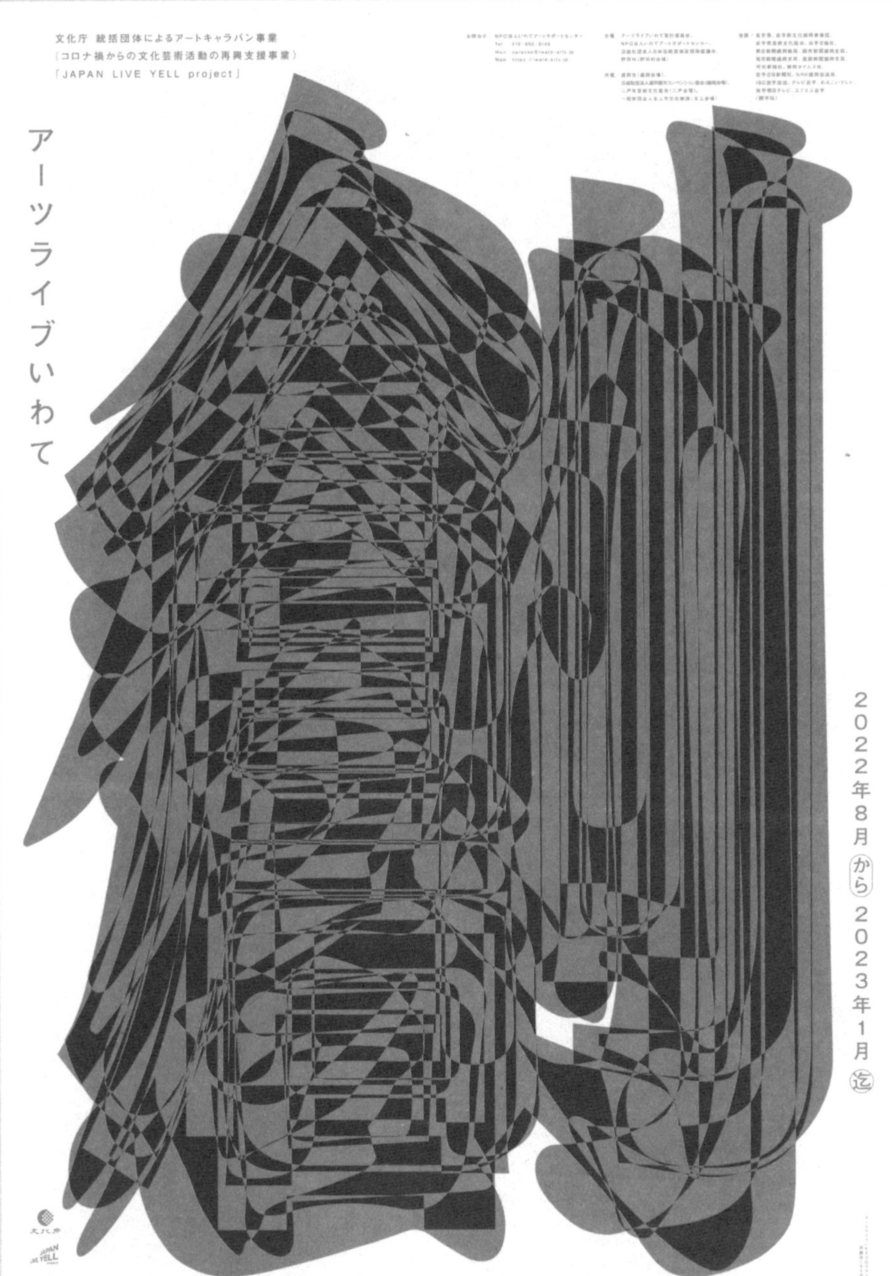
文化庁 統括団体によるアートキャラバン事業
（コロナ禍からの文化芸術活動の再興支援事業）
「JAPAN LIVE YELL project」
アーツライブいわて
2022年8月から2023年1月迄
参加アーティスト
開催地 ⟶ 盛岡市／二戸市／野田村／宮古市／北上市

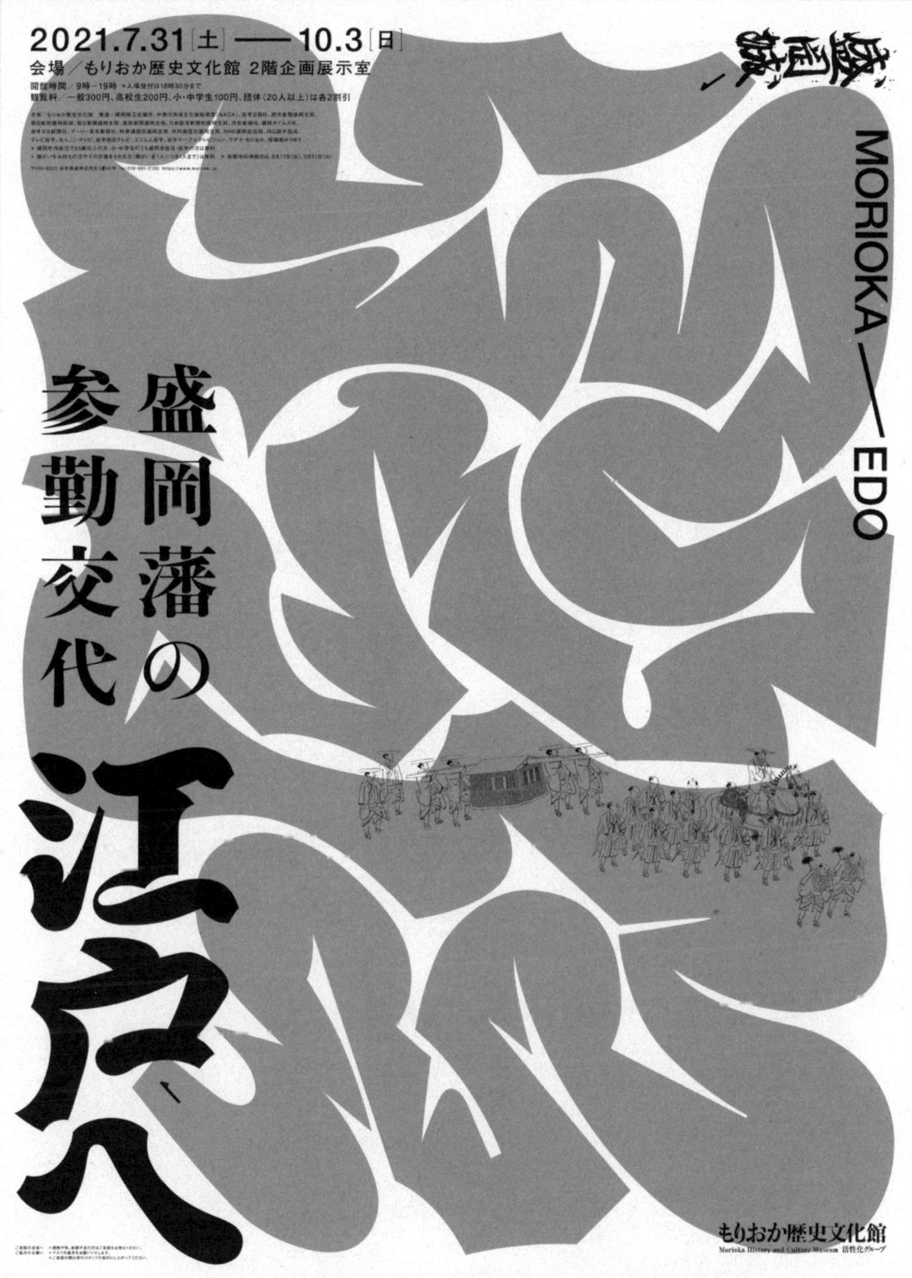

2021.7.31［土］——10.3［日］
会場／もりおか歴史文化館 2階企画展示室
開館時間／9時－19時 ＊入場受付は18時30分まで
観覧料／一般300円、高校生200円、小・中学生100円、団体（20人以上）は各2割引
MORIOKA — EDO
盛岡藩の
参勤交代
江戸へ
もりおか歴史文化館
Morioka History and Culture Museum 活性化グループ

ポートフォリオ大募集
シグでは、東北のアートシーンで活動するアーティストを探しています。
Cyg
東北ポートフォリオ(展)
Tohoku Portfolio Exhibition 2023

ポートフォリオ大募集
シグでは、東北のアートシーンで活動するアーティストを探しています。
Cyg
東北ポートフォリオ(展)
Tohoku Portfolio Exhibition 2023

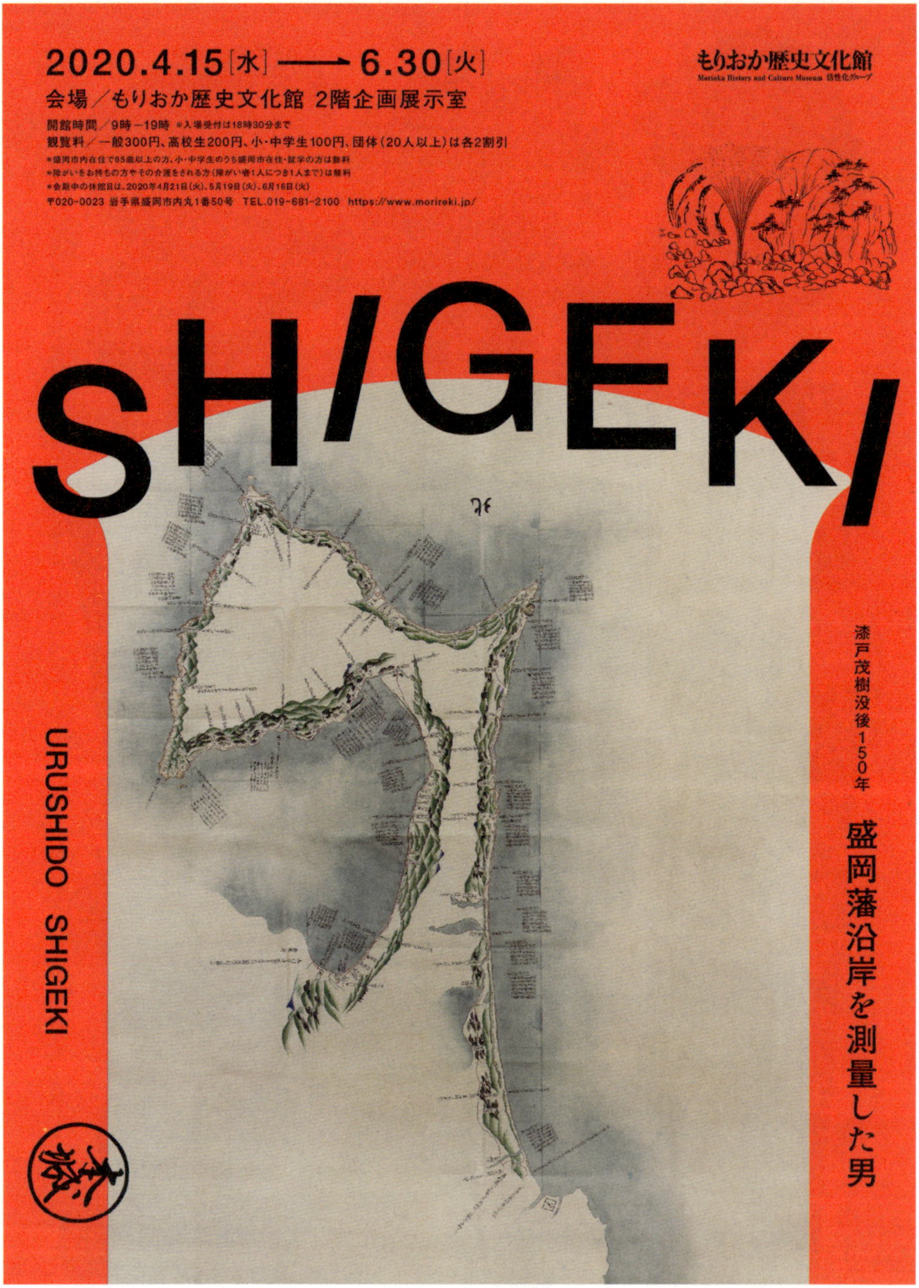
2020.4.15［水］——→6.30［火］
会場／もりおか歴史文化館 2階企画展示室
開館時間／9時－19時 ※入場受付は18時30分まで
観覧料／一般300円、高校生200円、小・中学生100円、団体（20人以上）は各2割引
※盛岡市内在住で65歳以上の方、小・中学生のうち盛岡市在住・就学の方は無料
※障がいをお持ちの方やその介護をされる方（障がい者1人につき1人まで）は無料
※会期中の休館日は、2020年4月21日（火）、5月19日（火）、6月16日（火）
〒020-0023 岩手県盛岡市内丸1番50号 TEL.019-681-2100 https://www.morireki.jp/
もりおか歴史文化館
Morioka History and Culture Museum 活性化グループ
SHIGEKI
URUSHIDO SHIGEKI
漆戸茂樹没後150年
盛岡藩沿岸を測量した男

漆戸茂樹没後150年
盛岡藩沿岸を測量した男
URUSHIDO SHIGEKI
SHIGEKI
会場／もりおか歴史文化館 2階企画展示室
開館時間／9時－19時 ＊入場受付は18時30分まで
観覧料／一般300円、高校生200円、小・中学生100円、団体（20人以上）は各2割引
＊盛岡市内在住で65歳以上の方、小・中学生のうち盛岡市在住・就学の方は無料
＊障がいをお持ちの方やその介護をされる方（障がい者1人につき1人まで）は無料
＊会期中の休館日は、2020年4月21日（火）、5月19日（火）、6月16日（火）
〒020-0023 岩手県盛岡市内丸1番50号 TEL.019-681-2100 https://www.morireki.jp/
2020.4.15［水］→6.30［火］
もりおか歴史文化館
Morioka History and Culture Museum

2022.12.3㊏から
2023.2.20㊊まで
もりおか歴史文化館／2階企画展示室
宝裕館コレクション寄贈40周年記念展
裕(ゆた)かなる宝
OUR PRECIOUS COLLECTION
三顧図〈狩野存信〉
観覧料／一般300円、高校生200円、小・中学生100円、団体（20人以上）は各2割引
開館時間／9時－18時 ＊入場受付は17時30分まで
もりおか歴史文化館
Morioka History and Culture Museum
＊盛岡市内在住で65歳以上の方、小・中学生のうち盛岡市在住・就学の方は無料 ＊障がいをお持ちの方やその介護をされる方（障がい者1人につき1人まで）は無料 ＊会期中の休館日は、12月20日(火)、31日(土)、1月1日(日)、17日(火)、2階展示室の閉室日は12月21日(水)、22日(木) ＊会期中に展示替えを実施予定／前期：12月3日(土)～1月16日(月)、後期：1月18日(水)～2月20日(月)
〒020-0023 岩手県盛岡市内丸1番50号
Tel.019-681-2100 https://www.morireki.jp/

2022.12.3㊏から
2023.2.20㊊まで
もりおか歴史文化館／2階企画展示室
宝裕館コレクション寄贈40周年記念展
裕（ゆた）かなる宝
OUR PRECIOUS COLLECTION
不動明王打出五枚胴具足
観覧料／一般300円、高校生200円
小・中学生100円、団体（20人以上）は各2割引
開館時間／9時～18時 ＊入場受付は17時30分まで
もりおか歴史文化館
Morioka History and Culture Museum
＊盛岡市内在住で65歳以上の方、小・中学生のうち盛岡市在住・就学の方は無料 ＊障がいをお持ちの方やその介護をされる方（障がい者1人につき1人まで）は無料 ＊会期中の休館日は、12月20日(火)、31日(土)、1月1日(日)、17日(火)、2階展示室の閉室日は12月21日(水)、22日(木) ＊会期中に展示替えを実施予定／前期：12月3日(土)～1月16日(月)、後期：1月18日(水)～2月20日(月)
〒020-0023 岩手県盛岡市内丸1番50号
Tel.019-681-2100 https://www.morireki.jp/

Kango Shimizu

Kango Shimizu is a Japanese graphic designer who likes to create cute designs.

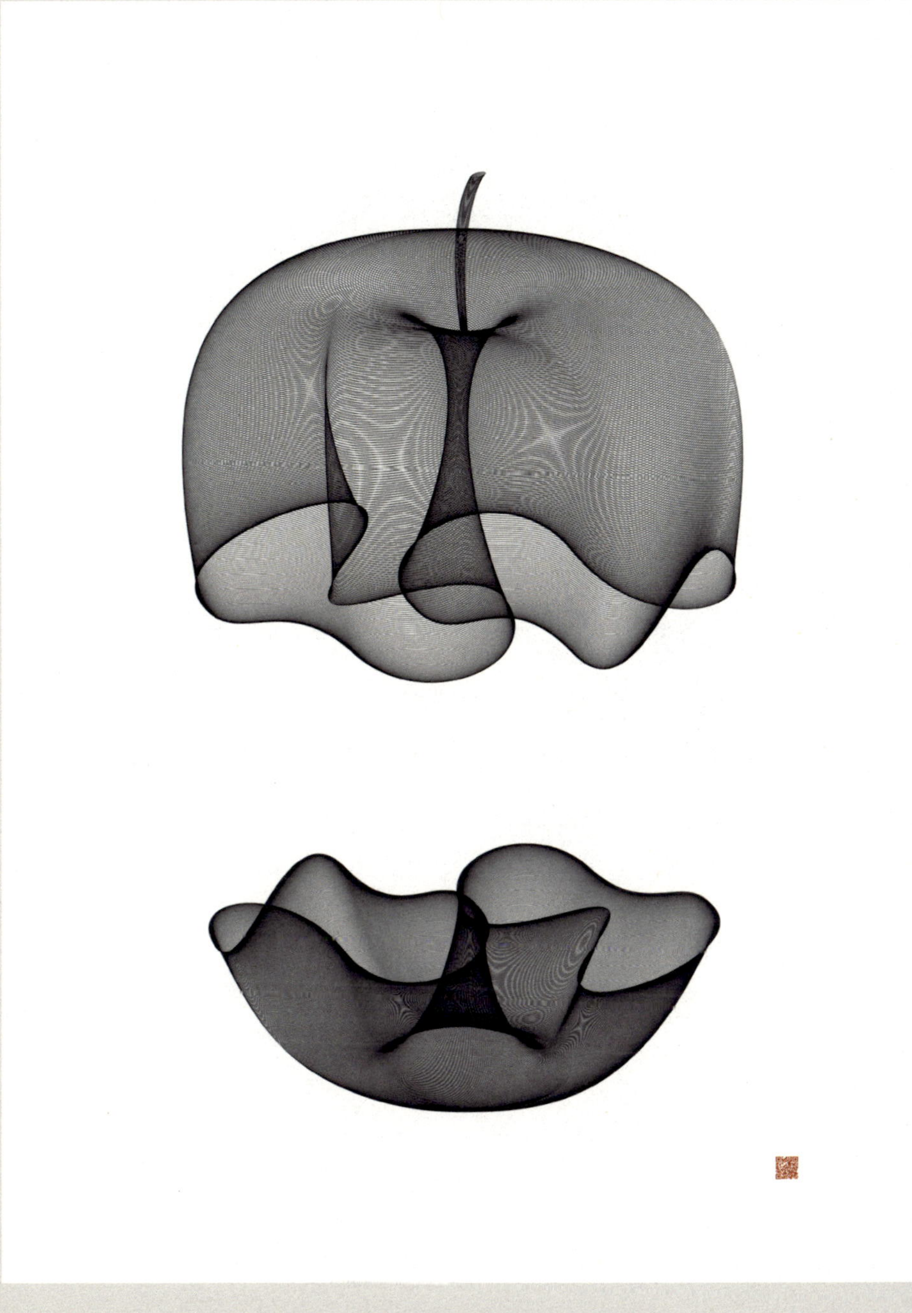

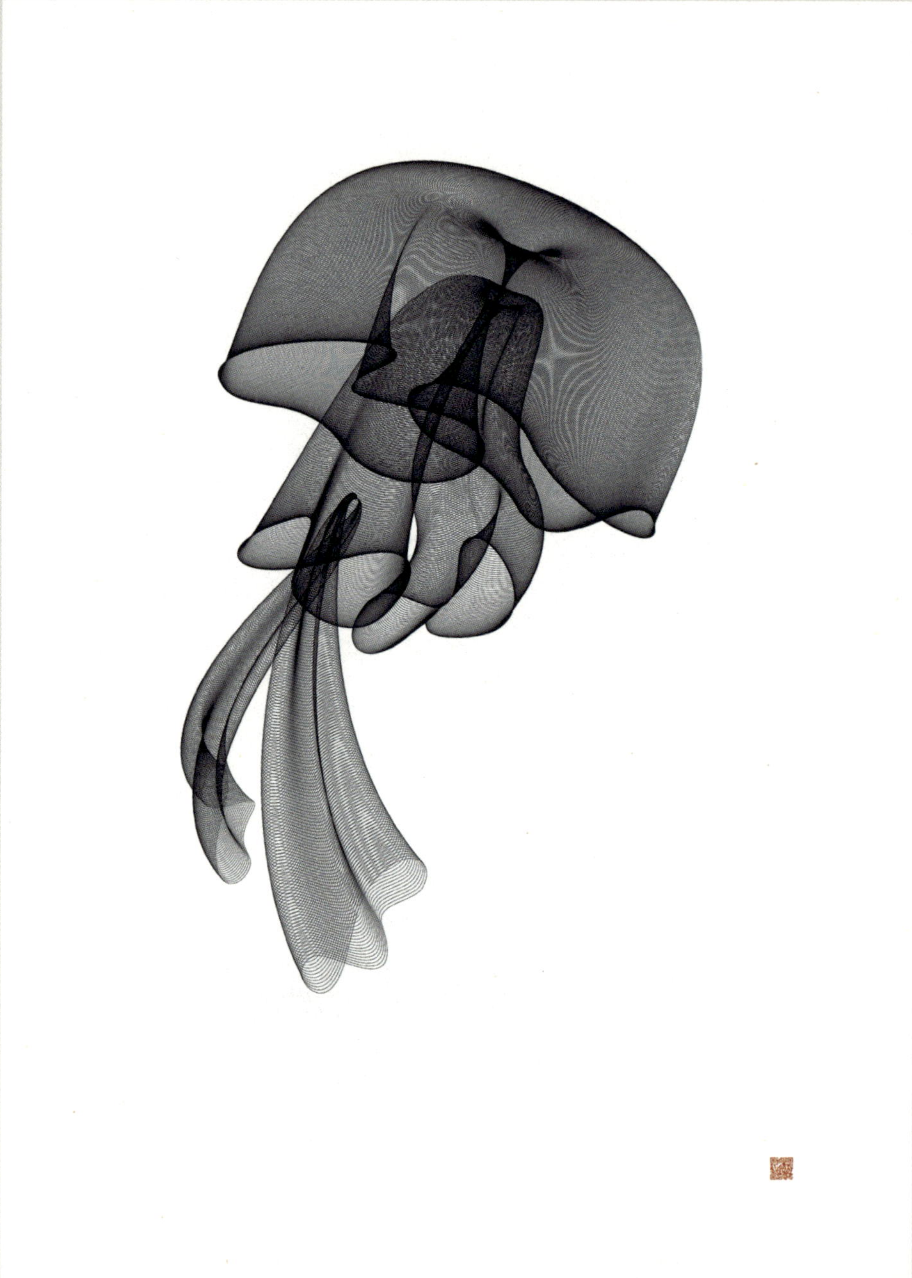

Karaoke Bar
Manhattan
in Echigo Yuzawa
Niigata Prefecture.

It all started when the first owner Takehara and his crew landed in Echigo-Yuzawa and established the first strip theater Pieroza in the hot spring resort town of Echigo-Yuzawa. The bar space on the basement floor became very popular. The Clownza was a great success but as the times have changed, the business format has also changed, and the second owner, Keijiro Hoshi, has established a karaoke bar + style that is more in line with the times. And from June 2019, the third owner, Masako Hoshi, will be creating a high-quality space where.

E BAR
TTAN
enjoy drinks in a relaxed atmosphere.
araoke.
enjoy playing musical instruments.
play darts games.
We will continue to improve our service for all of our customers.
We are now open for business as Karaoke Bar Manhattan with a new look and new atmosphere.
We are now open for business as Karaoke Bar Manhattan, with a new look and new energy.
Please come and enjoy our unique space in Echigo-Yuzawa.

Karaoke Bar
Manhattan
in Echigo Yuzawa
Niigata Prefecture.
It all started when the first owner Takehara and his crew landed in Echigo-Yuzawa and
in the hot spring resort town of Echigo-Yuzawa. The bar space on the basement floor became
but as the times have changed, the business format has also changed, and the second owner,
style that is more in line with the times. And from June 2019, the third owner, Masako Hoshi,

KE BAR
ATTAN
ter Pieroza
was a great success,
hed a karaoke bar + izakaya
ality space where.
Want to enjoy drinks in a relaxed atmosphere.
Enjoy karaoke.
Want to enjoy playing musical instruments.
Want to play darts games.
We will continue to improve our service for all of our customers.
We are now open for business as Karaoke Bar Manhattan with a new look and new atmosphere.
We are now open for business as Karaoke Bar Manhattan, with a new look and new energy.
Please come and enjoy our unique space in Echigo-Yuzawa.

PEACEFUL GOOOOD HOLIDAY
I want to spend a peaceful holiday.
Like, for example, lying down in the shade of a tree.
That would be a very nice day.

PEACEFUL GOOOOD HOLIDAY
I want to spend a peaceful holiday.
Like, for example, running around freely on a bicycle.
It would be a very nice day.

There are many different types of families.

Kozuka Gothic Family font.

There are many different types of families.

Andale Mono Regular

Family font.

Keita Asaoka

Keita Asaoka is a creative production company that goes beyond the boundaries of advertising to exceed client expectations. It assembles the right team of people to build brand strategies and carry out projects that combine high-level skill sets in production, direction, planning, copywriting, design, web development, digital experiences, and global marketing.

NOT JUST ONE,
GRAB BOTH EXTREMES.
Is avoiding the main road the only way to be unique?
Is it only sincere to follow a tradition?
Picking one is easier than trying to pick "both".
Good design, yet functional. Traditional, but free spirited.
Our choice is "both".
RUFFLOG™
WWW.RUFFLOG.JP

NOT JUST ONE,
GRAB BOTH EXTREMES.
RUFFLOG™
WWW.RUFFLOG.JP

NOT JUST ONE,
GRAB BOTH EXTREMES.
WWW.RUFFLOG.JP
RUFFLOG.

birds

birds

Overhead view of
the sea at Ako
To maintain Ako's water quality, we have decided to donate a portion of
our proceeds from the sales of goods of AKO OYSTER PRODUCTS.
We hope to provide everyone with delicious products by keeping the
Ako seas forever clean, thereby letting delicious oysters grow under its surface.
Sustainable activities to protect the ocean
AKO
OYSTER PRODUCTS

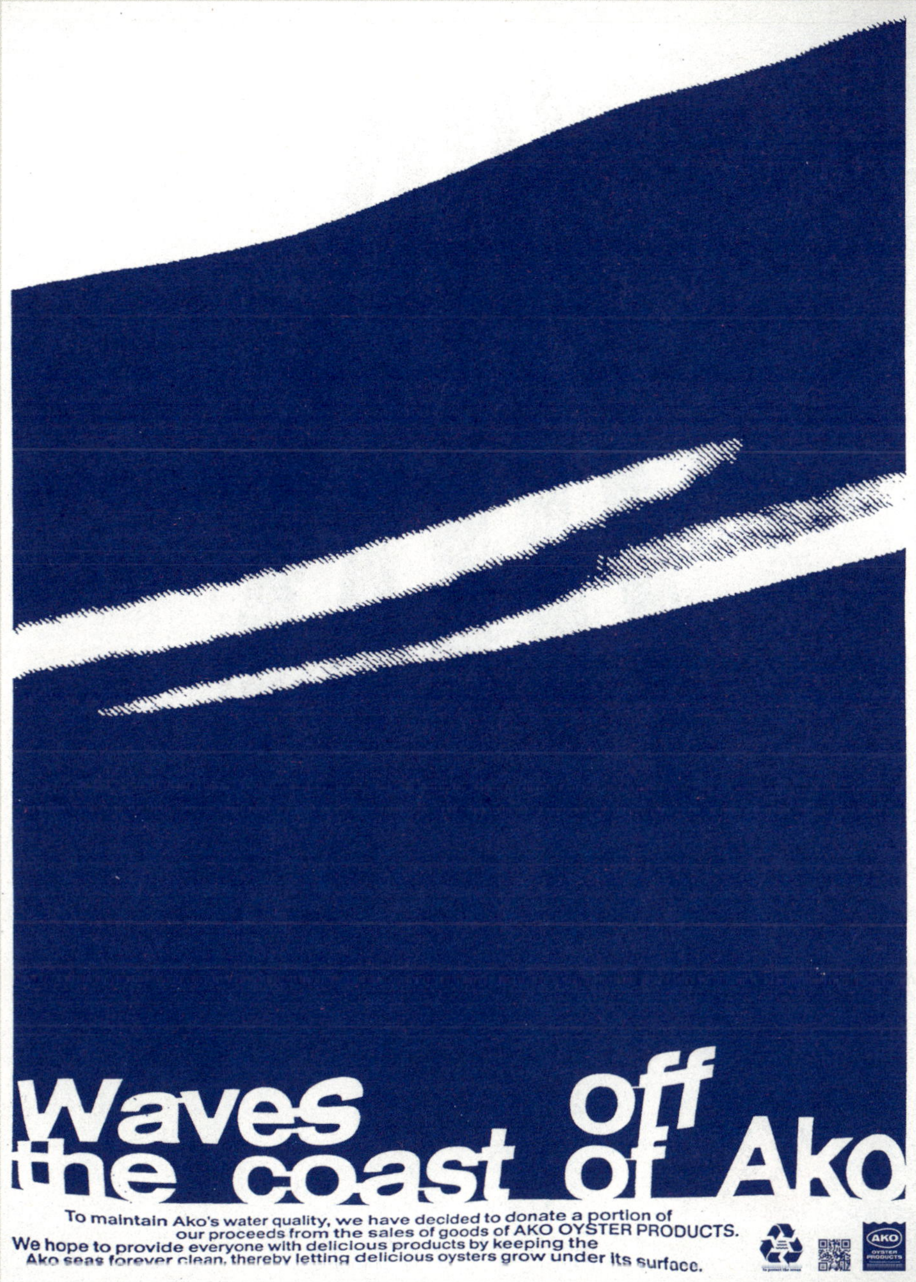
waves off
the coast of Ako
To maintain Ako's water quality, we have decided to donate a portion of
our proceeds from the sales of goods of AKO OYSTER PRODUCTS.
We hope to provide everyone with delicious products by keeping the
Ako seas forever clean, thereby letting delicious oysters grow under its surface.
AKO
OYSTER
PRODUCTS

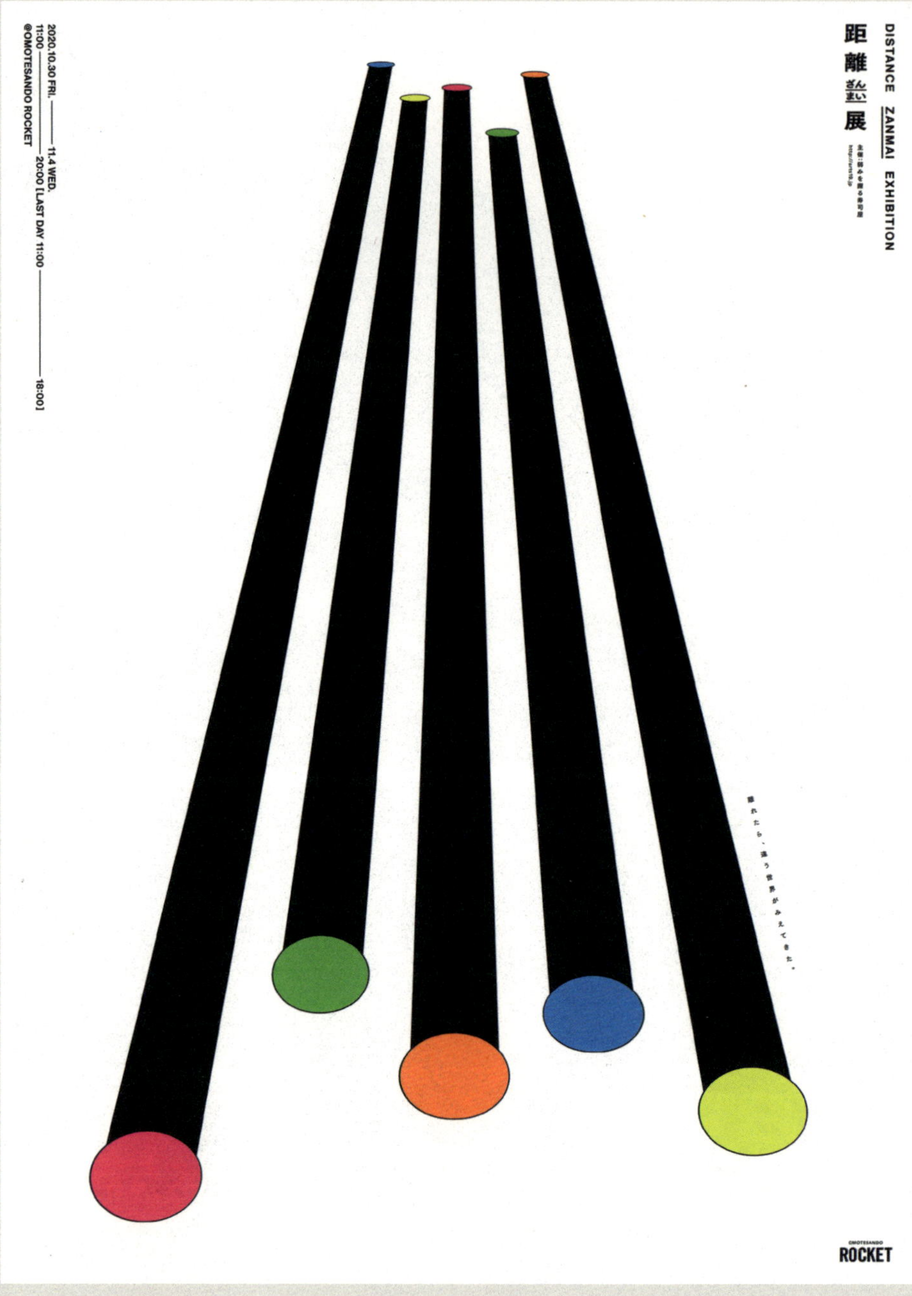
DISTANCE ZANMAI EXHIBITION
距離ざんまい展
2020.10.30 FRI. —— 11.4 WED.
11:00 —— 20:00 [LAST DAY 11:00 —— 18:00]
@OMOTESANDO ROCKET
離れたら、違う世界がみえてきた。
OMOTESANDO
ROCKET

DISTANCE ZANMAI EXHIBITION
距離ざんまい展
もっと距離を、楽しむには？
2020.10.30 FRI. — 11.4 WED.
11:00 — 20:00【LAST DAY 11:00 — 18:00】
@OMOTESANDO ROCKET
OMOTESANDO
ROCKET

Kenichi Kuromaru

A member of homesickdesign since 2018, Kenichi Kuromaru is skilled at designing with a focus on typography — in particular, by mixing Japanese letters and the Roman alphabet in his work. He also excels in geometric expressions and experiments with volumetric representations through 3D renders. He continues to seek out methods that allow for new and analogue textures to co-exist in advanced 3D forms.

Ill tration: Tomomi Kawamura
Exhibition: L Link Posters
Venue: Galler Dazzle
ate: 9.27 tue—10.2 su 2:00-19:00

Morioka Takamatsu Pond / October 15th (1956)

Morioka Takamatsu Pond / October 15th (1956)

Maiko Higuchi

Maiko Higuchi is a Tokyo-based graphic designer who specialises in print.

WARUI SHIBAI
VOL.22&23

野性の恋

悪い芝居 VOL.22

交互上演

作・演出 ― 山崎彬

音楽 ― 岡田太郎

暴動のあと、さみしい
ポップニューワールド

悪い芝居 VOL.23

14歳になった。学校に友達はいない。
家でひとり、ラジオを聞きながら、
誰にも見せない漫画を描いていた。
僕の部屋があの時のすべてだった。
それだけでよかった。

東京芸術劇場 シアターウエスト
TOKYO 2019.5.24FRI ― 6.2SUN

HEP HALL
OSAKA 2019.6.7FRI ― 6.10MON

BOKAN
MY
LOVE
2022
3.18
金
3.21
月・祝
下北沢・本多劇場

螢
27 han
×
uwanosora
“hotaru”
愛の、みちしるべだ。

WAS IN UNS IST, FLIESST IN DER WELT BEREITS ÜBER.
DAHER IST ES EINE LEHRE, DAS INNERE ZU POLIEREN, INDEM EIN ÄUSSERER REIZ EMPFANGEN WIRD.

WAS IN UNS IST, FLIESST IN DER WELT BEREITS ÜBER.

DAHER IST ES EINE LEHRE, DAS INNERE ZU POLIEREN, INDEM EIN ÄUSSERER REIZ EMPFANGEN WIRD.

体験的生態学

Experiential Ecology

Tone In Nature

落ち葉が演じる〈住居のトーン〉

トーン（Tone）とは、生物が身のまわりのモノに与える役割の事である。自然界のトーンは、生物の種類や気分によって異なる。例えば、水中に暮らすコバントビケラの幼虫は、落ち葉を切りとって身を守る布団をつくる。裸のコバントビケラに注目してみよう。葉っぱを見つけると、その裏に潜り、楕円状に切り込みを入れてゆく。付近にある枝や砂利などには何ら関心をもたない。このとき、コバントビケラから見た世界では、目の前に現れた落ち葉だけが〈住居のトーン〉を演じるのである。

The "tone of the dwelling" acted out by fallen leaves

Tone refers to the role that living things play in the world around them. Tone in nature depends on the type of organism and its mood. For example, larvae of Anisocentropus kawamurai, which live in the water, cut off fallen leaves to make bedding to protect themselves. We would like to focus on the larvae of Anisocentropus kawamurai, which has lost its bedding. When they find a leaf, they burrow behind it and make an oval cut. They pay no attention to branches or gravel. At this time, only the fallen leaves that appear in front of them can act as the "tone of the dwelling".

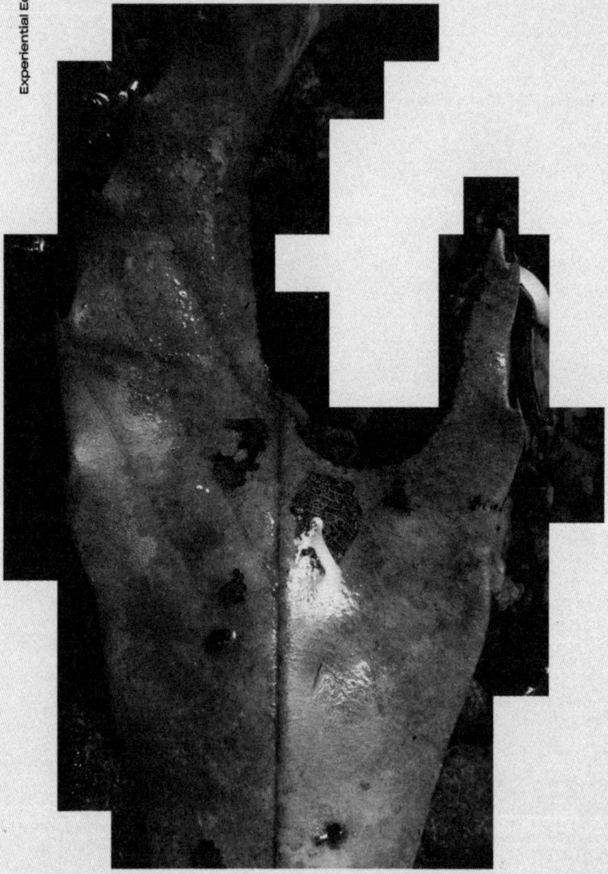

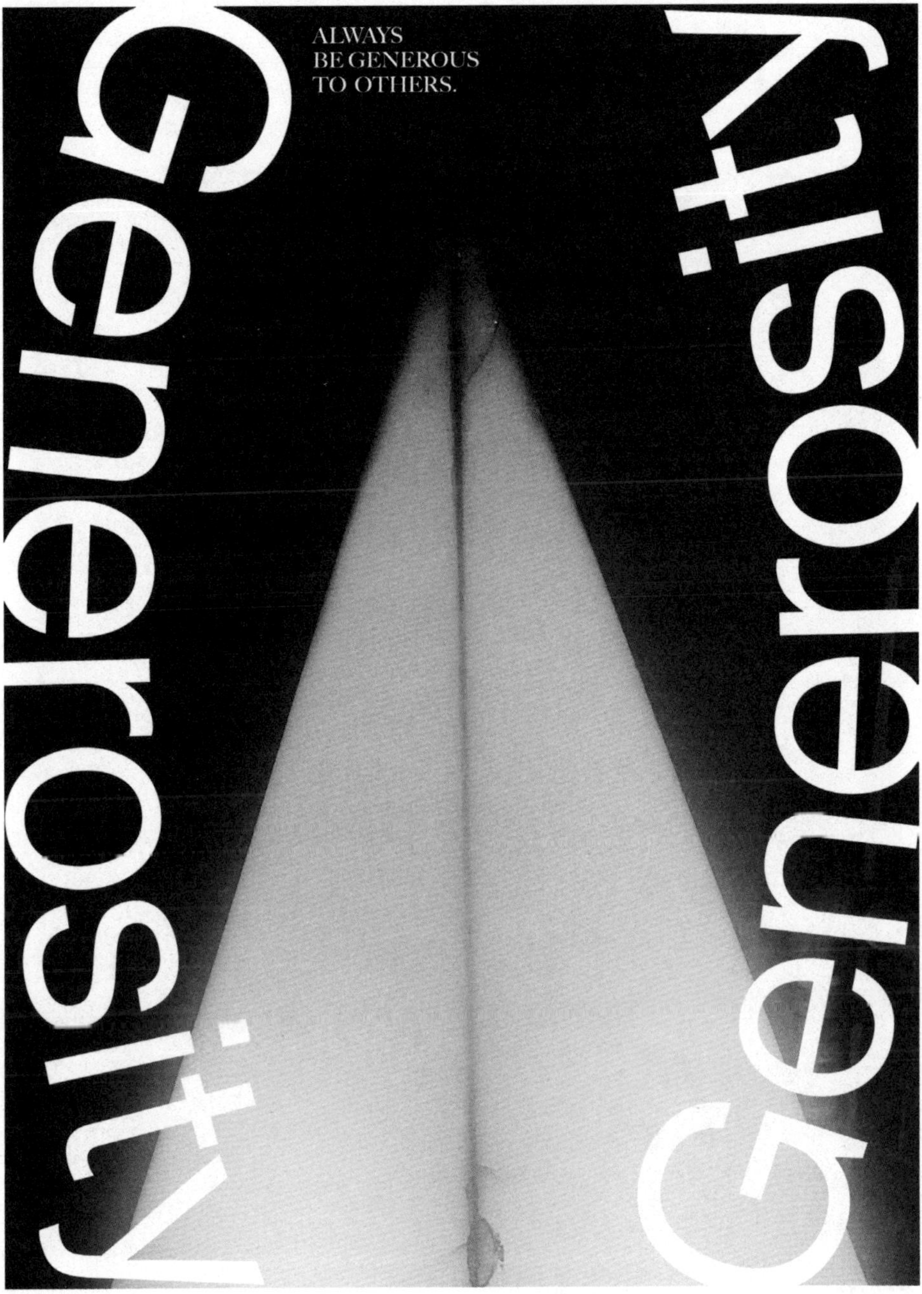
Generosity
ALWAYS
BE GENEROUS
TO OTHERS.
Generosity

KEI TO MAI

KEI KOBAYASHI
AND
MAIKO HIGUCHI
SUPER MARKET.

1151 450039/03
16.8.2016 13:07
OBD RRR RPM
K: 9/4 M: 7/12

Verified by PIN

KEI TO MAI

KEI KOBAYASHI
AND
MAIKO HIGUCHI
SUPER MARKET.

1151 450039/03
16.8.2016 13:07
OBD RRR RPM
K: 9/4 M: 7/12

Verified by PIN

KEI TO MAI

KEI KOBAYASHI
AND
MAIKO HIGUCHI
SUPER MARKET.

1151 450039/03
16.8.2016 13:07

OBD RRR RPM
K: 9/4 M: 7/12

Verified by PIN

KEI TO MAI

KEI KOBAYASHI
AND
MAIKO HIGUCHI
SUPER MARKET.

1151 450039/03
16.8.2016 13:07

OBD RRR RPM
K: 9/4 M: 7/12

Verified by PIN

UA 25th→30
"UA" 25th to 30th Anniversary Calendar
We wish to be with you every day.
May many happiness come to you.
2022 Calendar
UA 25th→→→30th??
25
30

UA 25th→30
"UA" 25th to 30th Anniversary Calendar
We wish to be with you every day.
May many happiness come to you.
2022 Calendar
UA 25th→→→30th??
25
30

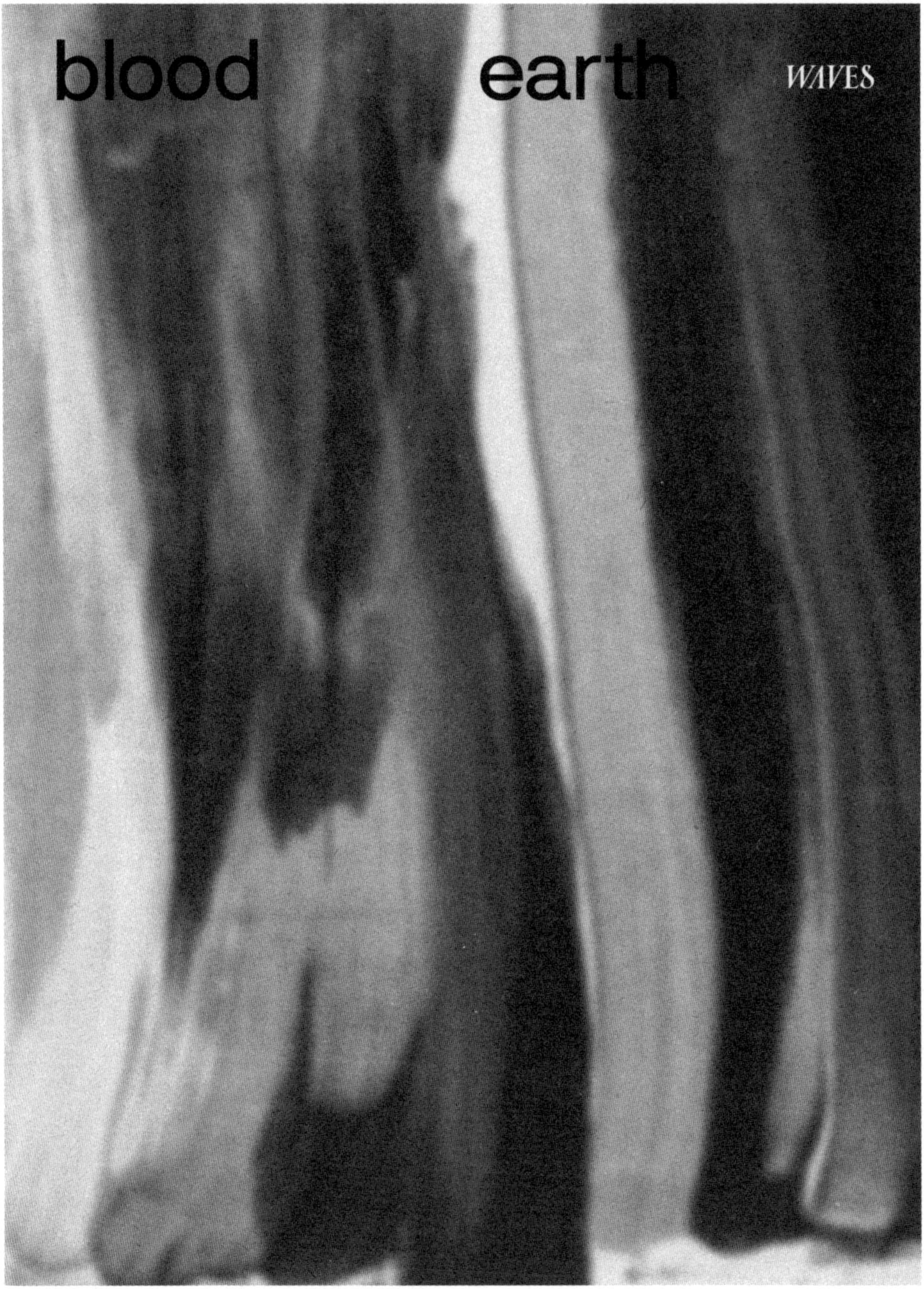
blood
earth
WAVES

blood
WAVES

Mayuka Nanbu

Born in Osaka, Mayuka Nanbu graduated from the Kyoto City University of Arts Visual Design Department and currently works at Taste Inc. with a focus on branding and graphic design. She also researches and produces work centred on typography.

花
AUTUMN
鳥

Overcome
Together
×
Design
Power
I Believe.
2020 The International Exhibition of Professional Artists

Overcome
Together
×
Design
Power
I Believe.
2020 The International Exhibition of Professional Artists

Strange Feeling
Strange feeling that shakes our daily lives.

Strange feeling that shakes our daily lives.
Strange Feeling

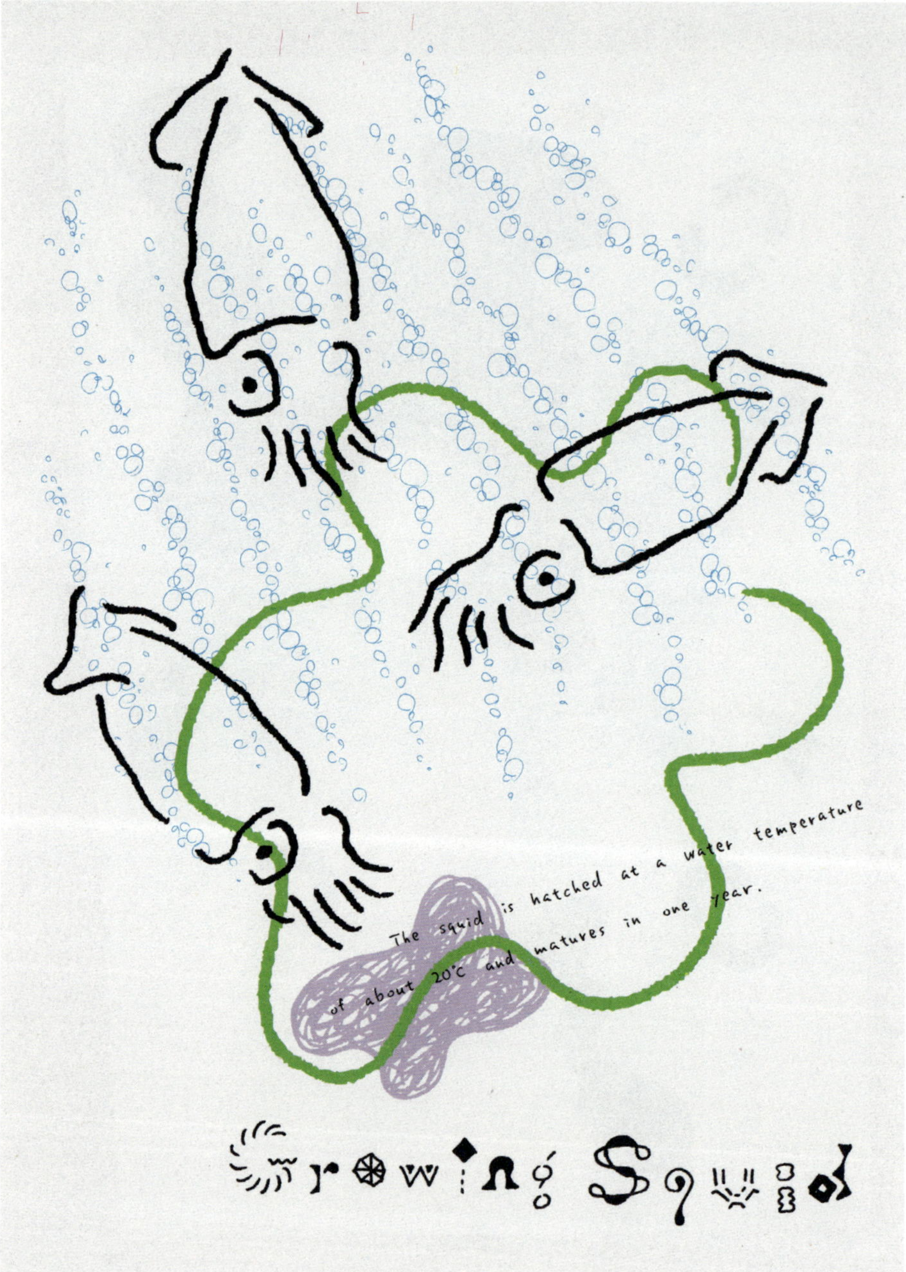
The squid is hatched at a water temperature of about 20°C and matures in one year.
Growing Squid

Male fawns begin to grow their horns at
the age of one and then grow to about 60 cm.
Growing
Fawn

The ladybug larva molts 3 times and takes about 20 days to become an adult.
Growing Ladybug

Growing Chick
The chick becomes a chicken and
lays eggs in about 150 days.

Moeta Wakamatsu

Born in Tokyo, Musashino Art University alumnus Moeta Wakamatsu is a graphic designer with a focus on typography. His work has been awarded and recognised by various organisations, including the International Poster Triennial in Toyama and the Japan Typography Yearbook.

『混乱と結束』

これはなんだ。これはわからぬ何かだ。
わからぬから怖い。皆が怖がっている。世界が混乱している。
私もどうなのかわからないが、とりあえず混乱しているのかもしれない。
対処法もわからない。本当に恐ろしいものなのか、或いはこれほど騒ぎたてるものではないのか。いつの日か、あれは愚かだったと笑える日が来るのか。
わからない。確かなことがわからない。だから怖い。皆、混乱している。
ならば今こそ結束するときか。皆の結束を願う。
再び日常が戻れば簡単に結束は解けるだろう。
たとえ束の間でも、皆が結束することを願う。

東京芸術劇場
Tokyo
Metropolitan
Theatre
2021
生前遺作展

東京芸術劇場
Tokyo Metropolitan Theatre
2021
7.2 金 – 7.10 土
開場時間 11時–18時（最終日のみ16時まで）
入場料 無料
会場 東京芸術劇場 アトリエイースト Atelier East(B1F)
〒171-0021 東京都豊島区西池袋1-8-1
JR・東京メトロ・東武東上線・西武池袋線 池袋駅西口より徒歩2分

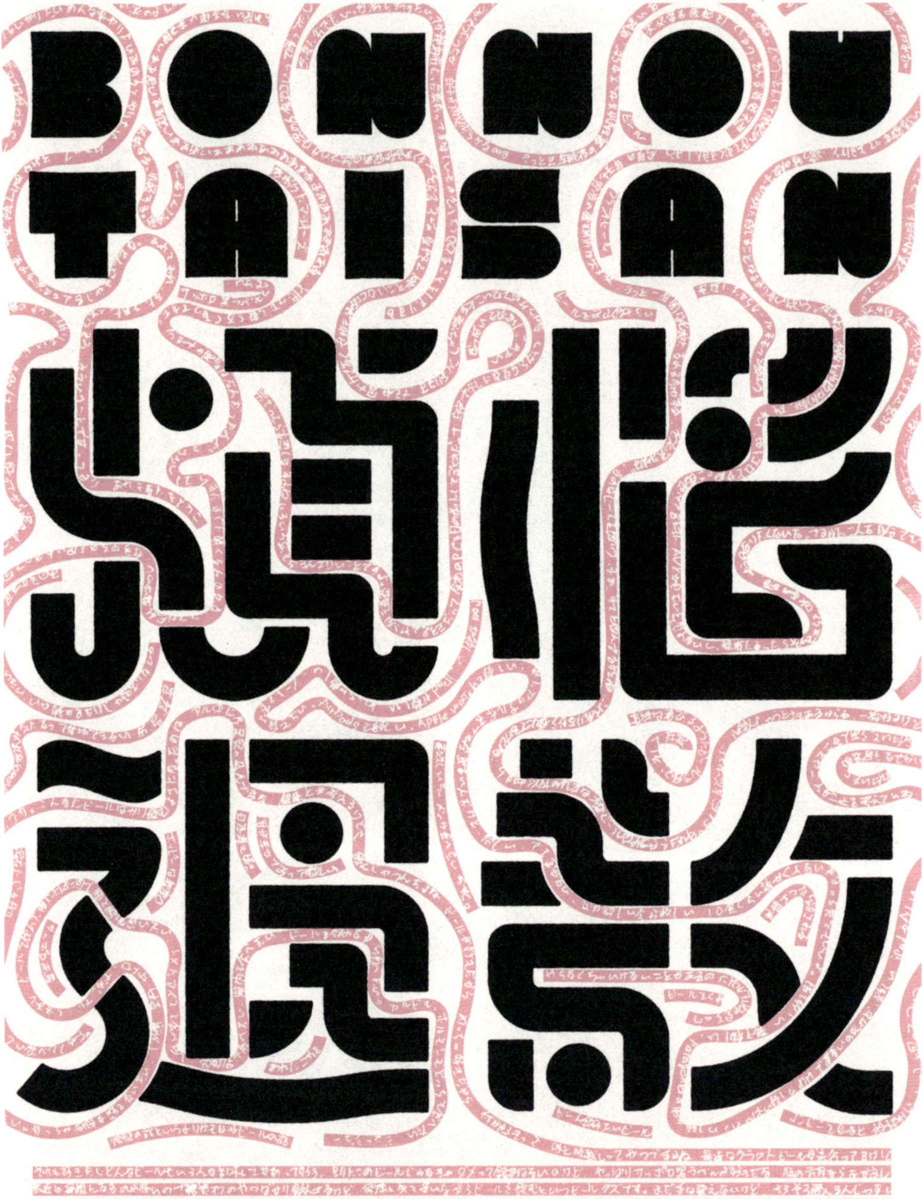
BONNOU
TAISAN

白と黒が反転する物語
つまり、オセロ。

いいね、オセロ。

涼しごと
suzushi-goto

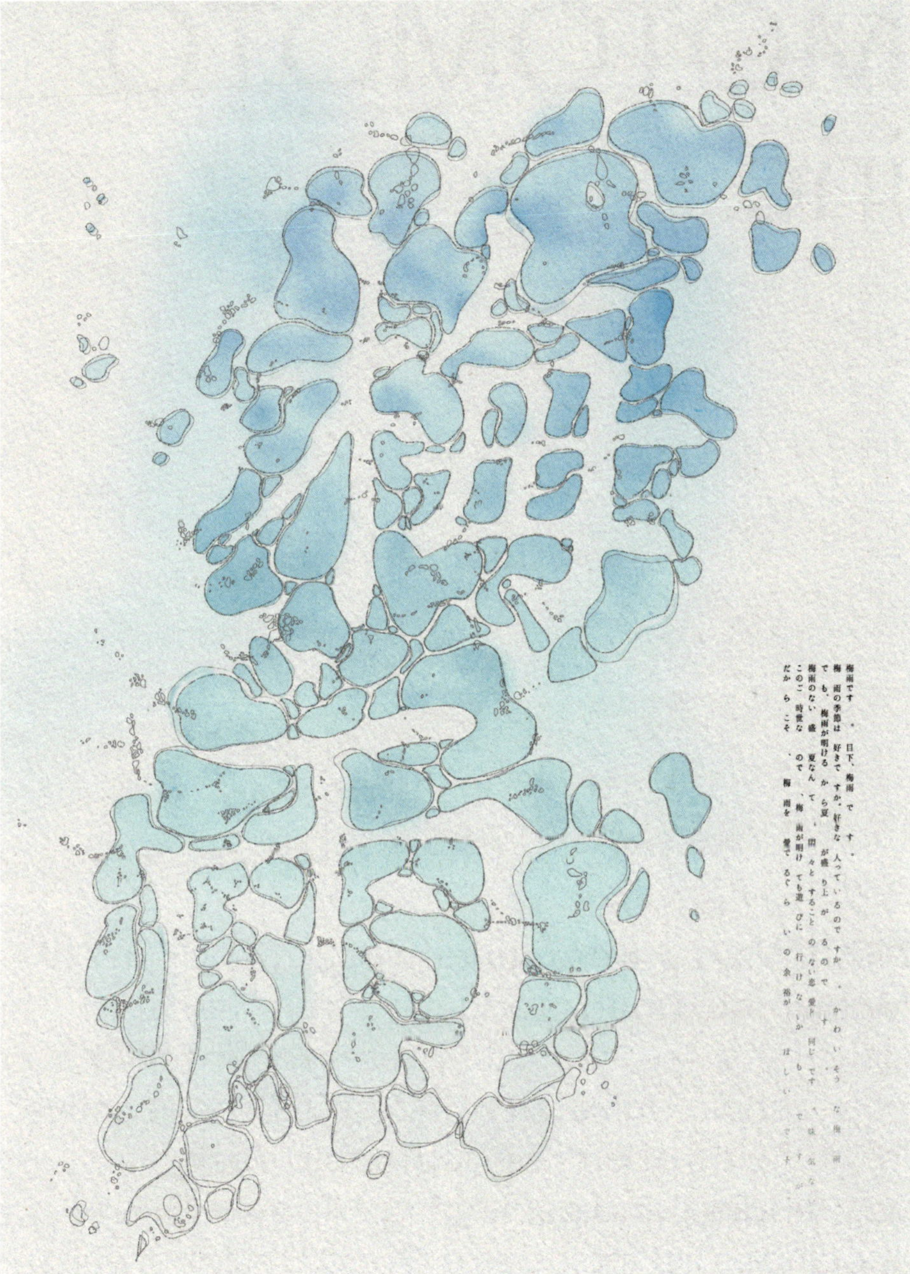
梅雨です。日下、梅雨です。
梅雨の季節は好きですか。好きな人っているのですか。かわいそうな梅雨。
でも、梅雨が明けるから夏が盛り上がるのです。
梅雨のない盛夏なんて、悶々とすることのない恋愛と同じです、味気ない。
このご時世なので、梅雨が明けても遊びに行けないかもですが。
だからこそ、梅雨を愛でるぐらいの余裕がほしいです。

MOTOMOTO inc.

MOTOMOTO was founded in 2013 by Kenichi Matsumoto upon graduating from Tama Art University. An associate professor at Tokyo Polytechnic University since 2020, he is active in the fields of branding, graphic design, way-finding, and packaging. His awards and accolades list includes a Good Design Award, The One Show Bronze, ADC Young Guns 8 Prize, and Japan Typography Yearbook Best Work recognition.

hugcoffee
company
https://hugcoffee.co
Wakasa Bldg. 1F
1-3-9 Ryogaecho
Aoi-ku Shizuoka
420-0032 Japan
+81(0)54-260-7578
11-1 Koyamachi
Aoi-ku Shizuoka
420-0852 Japan
+81(0)54-266-341
2-1 Minamicho
Suruga-ku Shizuoka
422-8067 Japan
1(0)54-286-1112

hugcoffee
company

https://hugcoffee.co

Wakasa Bldg. 1F
1-3-9 Ryogaecho
Aoi-ku Shizuoka
420-0032 Japan
+81(0)54-260-7578

11-1 Koyamachi
Aoi-ku Shizuoka
420-0852 Japan
+81(0)54-266-3418

2-1 Minamicho
Suruga-ku Shizuoka
422-8067 Japan
+81(0)54-286-1112

hugcoffee
company

https://hugcoffee.co

Wakasa Bldg. 1F
1-3-9 Ryogaecho
Aoi-ku Shizuoka
420-0032 Japan
+81(0)54-260-7578

11-1 Koyamachi
Aoi-ku Shizuoka
420-0852 Japan
+81(0)54-266-3418

2-1 Minamicho
Suruga-ku Shizuoka
422-8067 Japan
+81(0)54-286-1112

12.09 WED
/
12.25 FRI
Jewelry
Week 2020
TOKYO
NAGOYA
OSAKA
FUKUOKA

12.04 FRI
/
12.25 FRI
Jewelry
Week 2020
TOKYO
NAGOYA
OSAKA
FUKUOKA
and more...

Mu Design Room

Mu Design Room was founded by Takehiko Muramatsu, a graphic designer in Tokyo who was once artist Koichi Sato's assistant. He is also a member of the Japan Graphic Designers Association and Tokyo TDC.

グラフィックデザイナーのための
風土記
ふどき
FUDOKI
www.fudoki.tokyo
ワクワク
テクテク テクテク

グラフィックデザイナーのための
東京風土記
OK!
www.fudoki.tokyo
フフフフ
ハハハハハハハハハ
ハハハハハハハハハ
ハハハハハハッ

グラフィックデザイナーのための
TOKYO
FUDOKI
www.fudoki.tokyo
サー
スー

文学座
文化座
俳優座
民藝
青年座
東演
青年劇場
フリー
新劇交流プロジェクト公演2
美しきものの伝説
作＝宮本研／演出＝鵜山仁
六月十六日[木]―二十六日[日]二〇二二年
六本木・俳優座劇場

劇団青年座 第234回公演
残り火
作＝瀬戸山美咲
演出＝黒岩亮
そのとき、私の中の何かに火がついた。
出演＝山野史人・平尾仁・山本龍二・逢笠恵祐・須田祐介・麻生侑里・松熊つる松・安藤瞳・市橋恵
美術＝柴田秀子 照明＝中川隆一 音響＝城戸智行 衣裳＝竹原典子 舞台監督＝尾花真 製作＝森正敏・川上英四郎
入場料［全席指定］＝◉一般4500円（11月22日［木］19時開演のみ初日割引3000円）◉U25［25歳以下］3000円
前売開始＝◉10月11日［木］
お問い合わせ＝◉劇団青年座 〒151-0063 東京都渋谷区富ヶ谷1-53-12◎電話＝03-5478-8571◎FAX＝03-3465-0335◎E-mail＝info@seinenza.com◎http://seinenza.com
前売所＝◉劇団青年座 0120-291-481（チケット専用11時～18時・土日祝日除く）◉青年座ホームページ http://seinenza.com ◉チケットぴあ 0570-02-9999［Pコード489-201］◉ローソンチケット 0570-084-003［Lコード33054］◎0570-000-407（オペレーター対応10時～20時）◉イープラス http://eplus.jp
会場＝◉ザ・スズナリ 03-3469-0511 京王井の頭線・小田急線 下北沢駅北口より徒歩7分
11月22日［木］―12月2日［日］2018年
ザ・スズナリ

めめ
はな
Typoianchi 2017

N.G.inc.

Born in Tokyo, Hiroaki Nagai established N.G.inc. in 1989 after a working stint at Breakfast Inc. An emeritus professor of Tokyo Zokei University, he is also a member of the Japan Graphic Designers Association, Tokyo ADC, and Tokyo TDC.

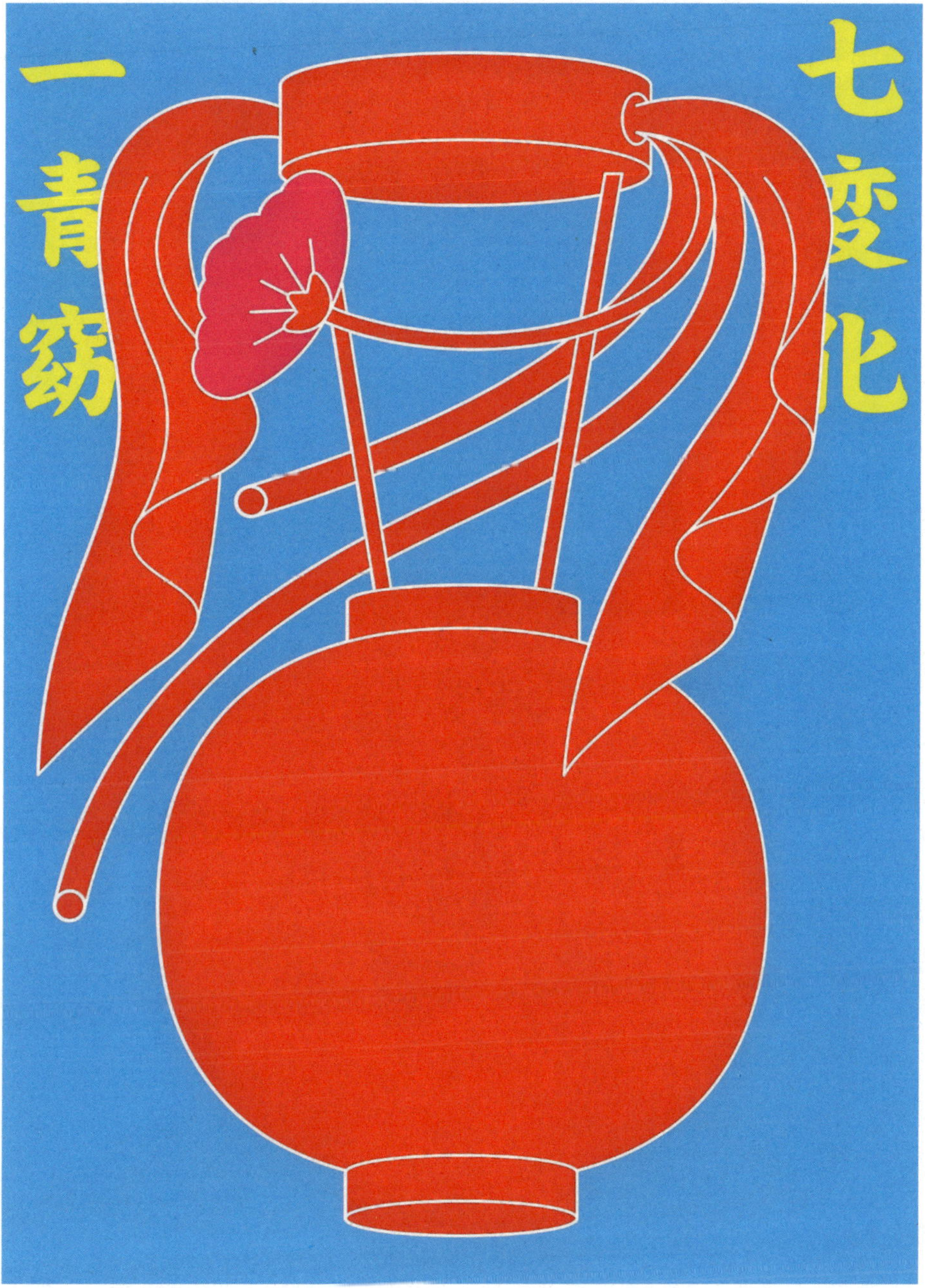
七变化
一青窈

七变化
一青窈

七変化
一青窈

邪祓

邪祓

邪祓

邪祓

(At Design 企划展)
(日本平面设计展)
(我可以)
Japan Graphic Design Exhibition - I'M POSSIBLE
2021.10/1 - 2022.1/9 @移动的头脑博物馆
10:00-19:00(周一休馆) 上海市黄浦区半淞园路388号越界・世博园 B4-1 主催：At Design, MUSEu&m
井口 皓太◎瓜生 太郎◎大河 紀◎柏木 美月◎佐々木 俊◎市東 基◎清水 彩香
田部井 美奈◎三重野 龍◎矢野 恵司◎GOO CHOKI PAR◎SHUTO OTSUKI

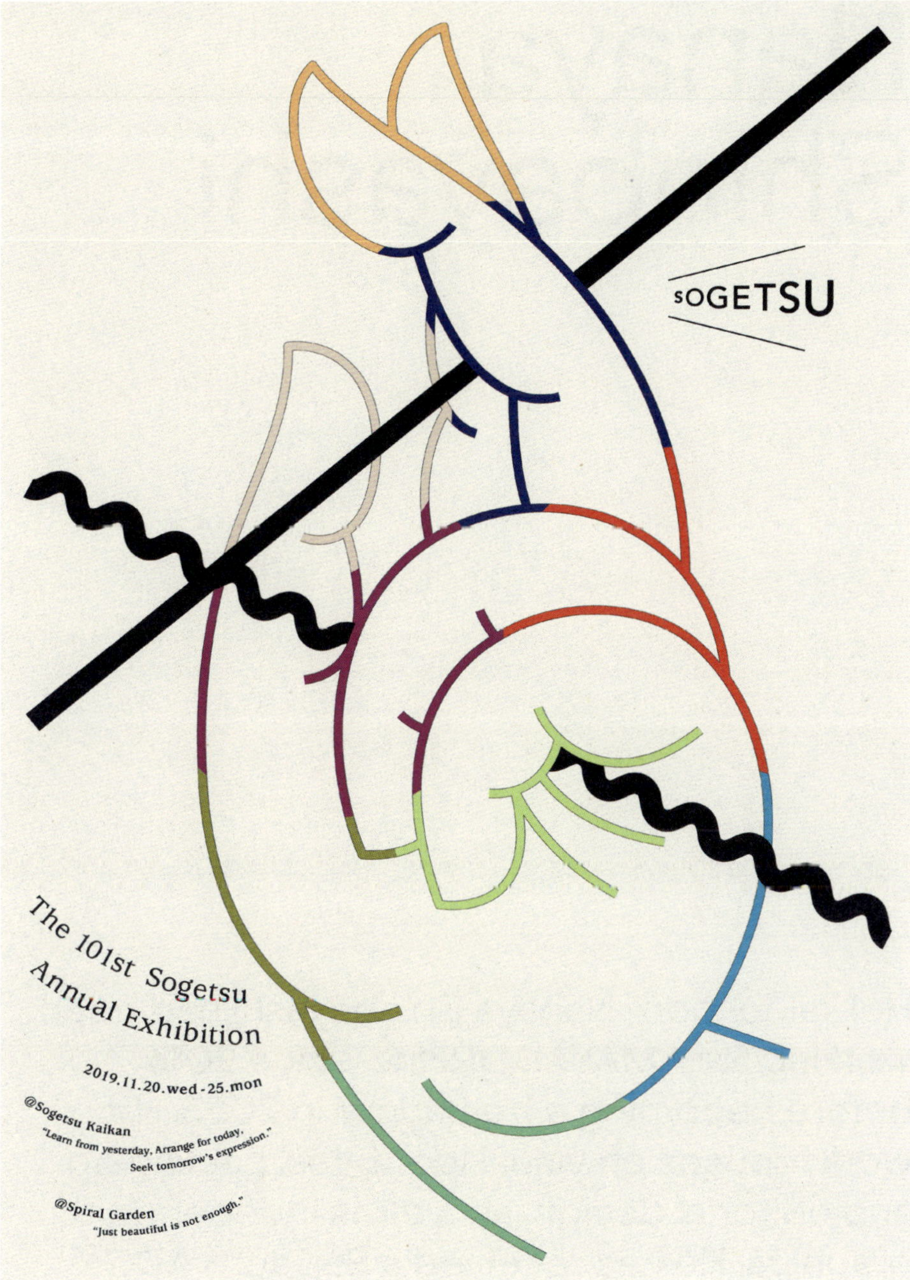
sOGETSU
The 101st Sogetsu
Annual Exhibition
2019.11.20.wed - 25.mon
@Sogetsu Kaikan
"Learn from yesterday, Arrange for today,
Seek tomorrow's expression."
@Spiral Garden
"Just beautiful is not enough."

Nanaya Shinbayashi

Hokkaido-born Nanaya Shinbayashi had been working for AMAYADORI Inc. since 2016 before becoming a freelancer in 2023. His work focuses on visual identities, packaging and editorial design, as well as independent graphics. He has received a Sapporo ADC Annual Competition and Award Grand Prix and Hokkaido Package Design Contest Grand Prix to name a few.

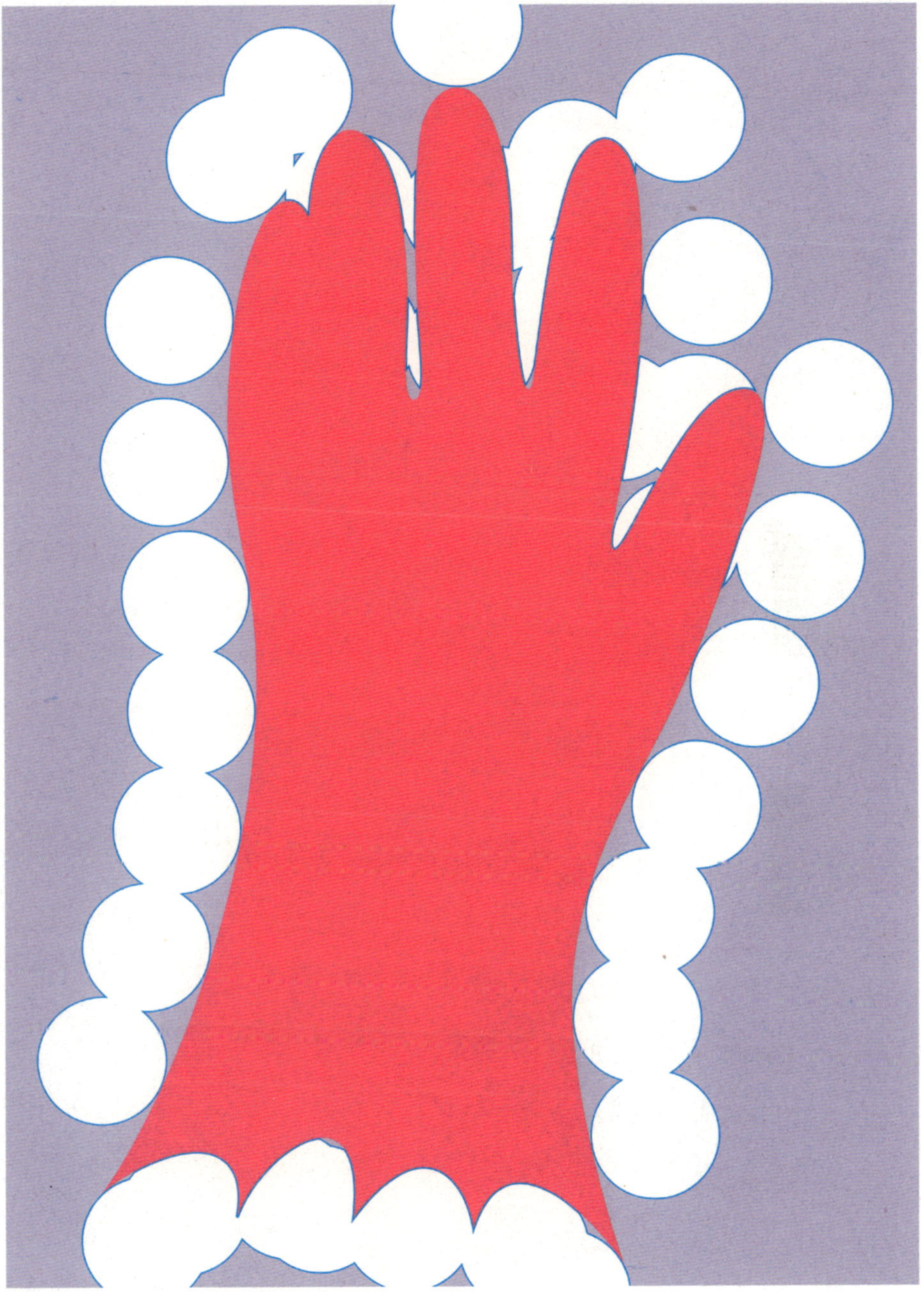

There is one banana
in my room.
The method for producing banana with discoloration-inhibited
flesh includes a process for soaking a peduncle and/or
a style-side tip end part of an unpeeled banana fruit in
a liquid inhibiting flesh discoloration.
กล้วย

There is one banana in my room.
The method for producing banana with discoloration-inhibited flesh includes a process for soaking a peduncle and/or a style-side tip end part of an unpeeled banana fruit in a liquid inhibiting flesh discoloration.
กล้วย

JAGDA HOKKAIDO
POSTER EXHIBITION 2022
'SAPPORO'

新林 七也 個展 脈
二〇二二年六月十一日から十九日
ギャラリークラック
10.00-19:00

Red RGB value [0-255]

Green RGB value [0-255]

METEOR SHOWER
AUG12, 10:00PM
METEOR SHOWER
METEOR SHOWER 2020
METEOR SHOWER
AUG12, 10:00PM
METEOR SHOWER
METEOR SHOWER

Inter cross
Creative
Center
ICC
キャッチコピー&ポスターデザインコンペティション
2021
※キャッチコピー部門の募集は終了いたしました。
8月上旬 募集期間 10.18(月) 17時まで
ポスターデザイン部門 募集中
ICC Copy & Poster design competition 2021

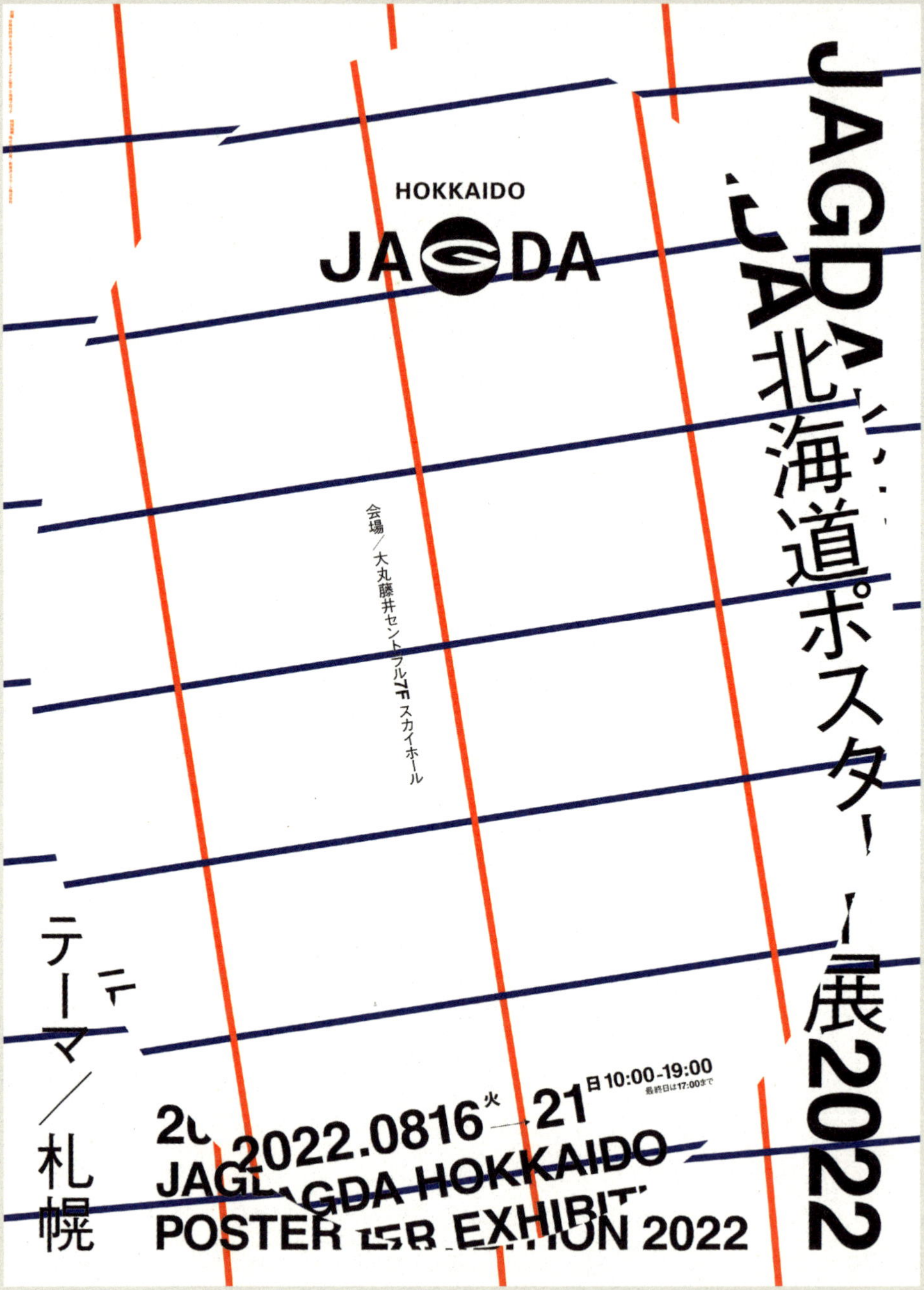
HOKKAIDO
JAGDA
JAGDA北海道ポスター展2022
会場／大丸藤井セントラル7F スカイホール
テーマ／札幌
2022.0816火—21日 10:00-19:00
最終日は17:00まで
JAGDA HOKKAIDO
POSTER EXHIBITION 2022

Naonori Yago

Born in Shizuoka, Naonori Yago is an art director and graphic designer who has won awards from the Tokyo and New York ADCs, D&AD, Cannes Lions, and The One Show to name a few. She graduated from the Department of Visual Communication Design at Musashino Art University in 2009.

casa tree

casa tree

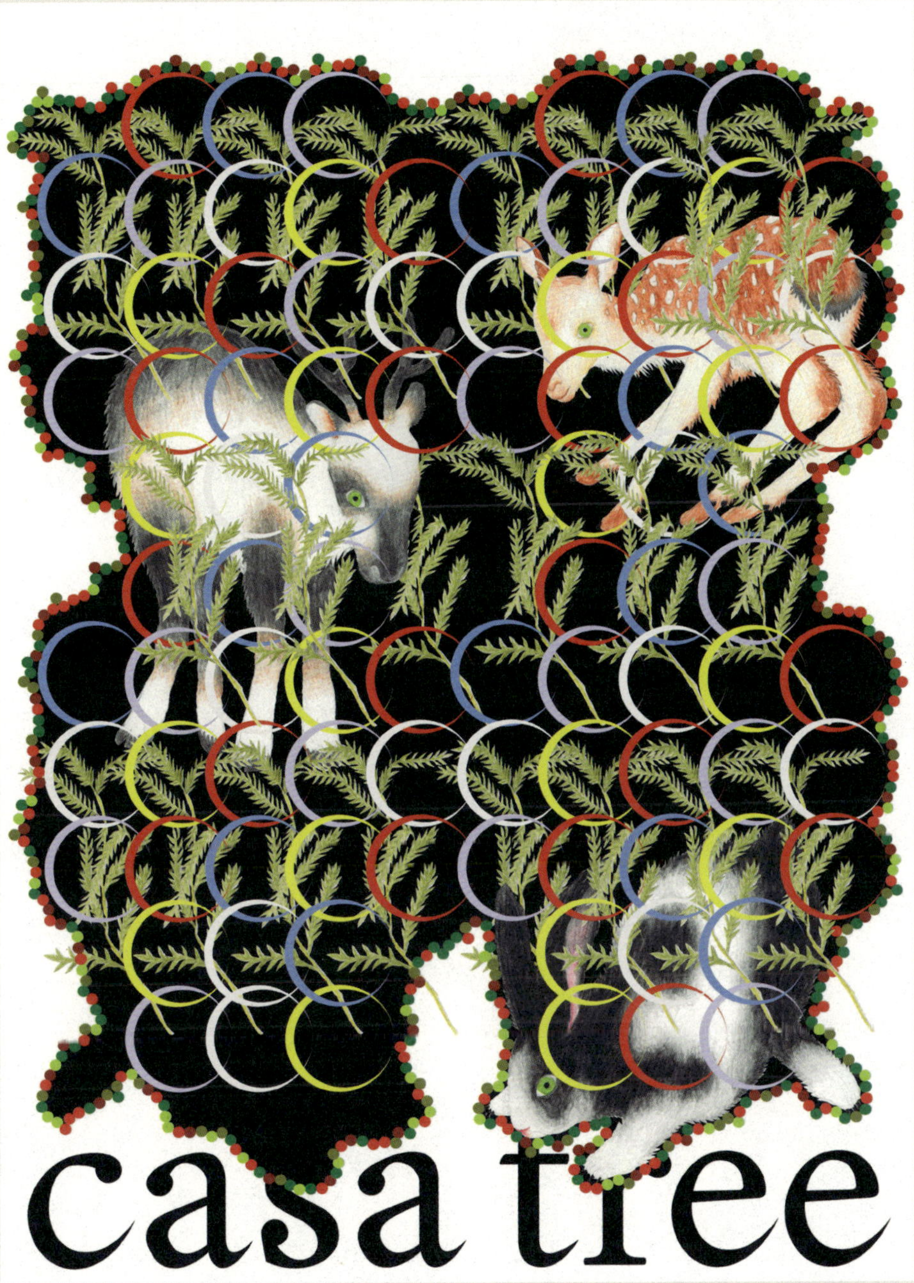
casa tree

HAKUHODO
DY
GROUP
GLOBAL
PURPOSE
OPEN BRIEF

Polarno

Polarno is a design company founded by Kentaro Sagara. It explores the possibilities of design with the aim to create something new, beautiful, and meaningful.

Open
Tokyo Kougei University
Open Campus 2022
0619 (sun) 0717 (sun) 0819 (fri) 20 (sat)

Open
Tokyo Kougei University
Open Campus 2022
0619 (sun) 0717 (sun) 0819 (fri) 20 (sat)

Open
Tokyo Kougei University
Open Campus 2022
0619 (sun) 0717 (sun) 0819 (fri) 20 (sat)

Open
Tokyo Kougei University
Open Campus 2022
0619 (sun) 0717 (sun) 0819 (fri) 20 (sat)

Open
Tokyo Kougei University
Open Campus 2022

TOKYO GARDEN THEATER 20210612 Saturday
MIYAMOTO HIROJI
JUUOUMUJIN
20210612
on Birthday
BirthdayLIVE "MIYAMOTO HIROJI JUUOUMUJIN"

TOKYO GARDEN THEATER 20210612 Saturday
MIYAMOTO
HIROJI
JUUOU
MUJIN
20210612
on Birthday
Birthday LIVE "MIYAMOTO HIROJI JUUOUMUJIN"

TOKYO GARDEN THEATER 20210612 Saturday
宮本浩次
縦横無尽
BirthdayLIVE "MIYAMOTO HIROJI JUUOUMUJIN"

TOKYO GARDEN THEATER 20210612 Saturday
宮本浩次
縦横無尽
BirthdayLIVE "MIYAMOTO HIROJI JUUOUMUJIN"

新しい風、新しい日本酒、新潟から。
King of Modern Light from Echigo
純米大吟醸
KING OF MODERN LIGHT

新しい風、新しい日本酒、新潟から。
KING OF MODERN LIGHT

新しい風、新しい日本酒、新潟から。
純米吟醸
KING OF MODERN LIGHT

新しい風、新しい日本酒、新潟から。
King of Modern Light from Echigo
純米大吟醸
KING OF MODERN LIGHT

REFLECTA, Inc.

Mariko Okazaki is a Tokyo-born graphic designer who worked at various design studios upon graduating from Keio University and Gerrit Rietveld Academie. After becoming independent in 2018, she founded REFLECTA in 2022. Through the cultural realms of contemporary art, the performing arts, and architecture, she explores design solutions rooted in observation and conceptual thinking.

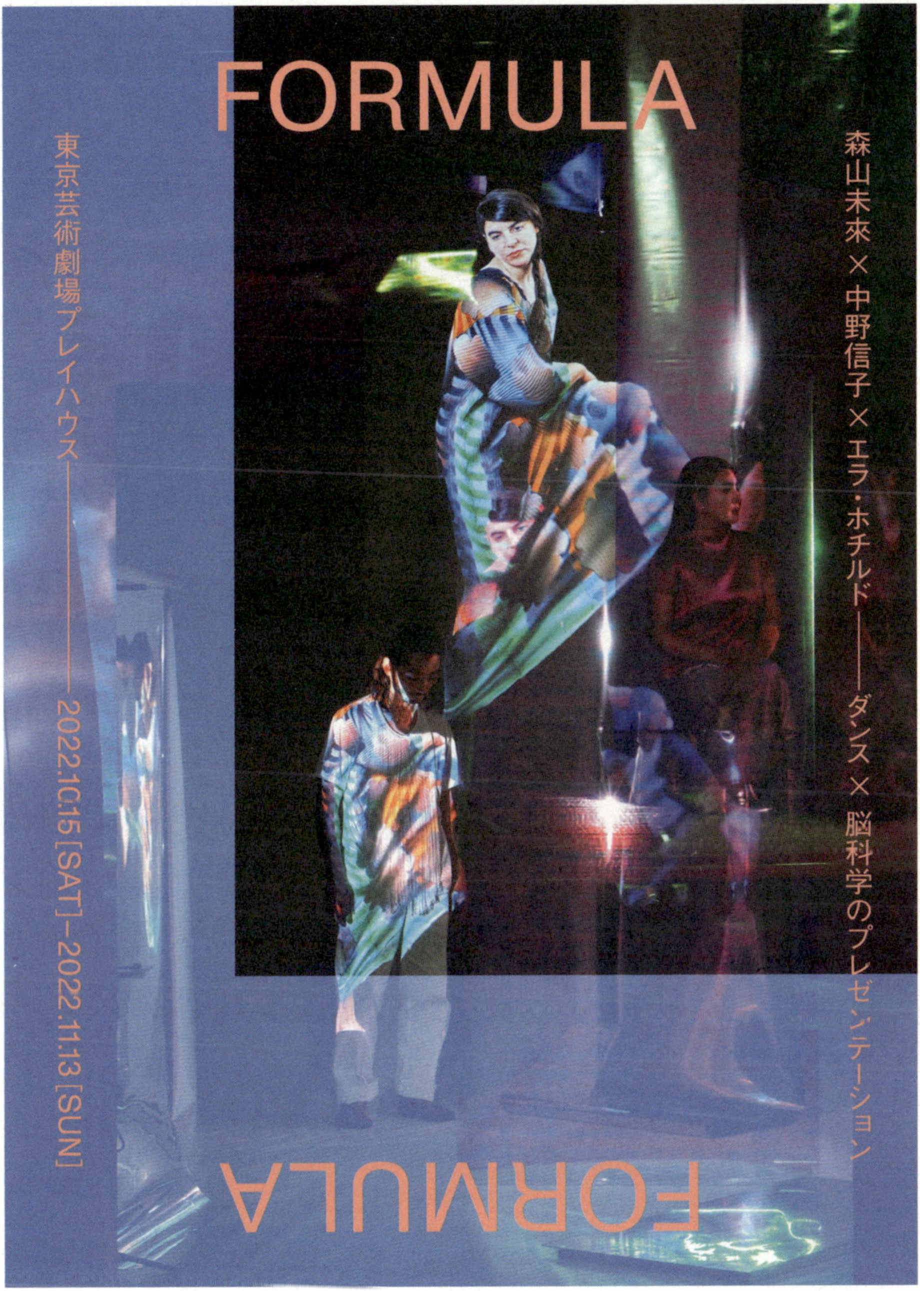
FORMULA
森山未來 × 中野信子 × エラ・ホチルド——ダンス × 脳科学のプレゼンテーション
東京芸術劇場プレイハウス——2022.10.15 [SAT]–2022.11.13 [SUN]
FORMULA

PIPILOTTI
RIST
YOUR EYE
IS MY
ISLAND
PIPILOTTI RIST ／ピピロッティ・リスト
YOUR EYE IS MY ISLAND
あなたの眼はわたしの島／
beyond 2020
prohelvetia
April 6 [Tue.] – June 13 [Sun.], 2021
The National Museum of Modern Art, Kyoto
2021年4月6日[火]–6月13日[日]
京都国立近代美術館［岡崎公園内］
［開館時間］午前9時30分－午後5時／［休館日］月曜日／［主催］京都国立近代美術館、京都新聞／［後援］在日スイス大使館／［協賛］クヴァドラ／［協力］株式会社長谷ビル、国立新美術館、ユニバーサル・ビジネス・テクノロジー株式会社／［助成］スイス・プロ・ヘルヴェティア財団／［企画協力］Hauser & Wirth、一色事務所／［観覧料］一般1200［1000］円、大学生500［400］円
／［前売券の主な販売場所］チケットぴあ、ローソンチケット
か主要プレイガイド、コンビニエンスストアなど／新型コロナウイルス感染予防のため、開館時間・休館日は変更になる場合があります。ご来館前に当館ホームページなどで最新情報をご確認ください。／［お問合せ］京都国立近代美術館　〒606-8344 京都市左京区岡崎円勝寺町／TEL：075-761-4111／https://www.momak.go.jp

PIPILOTTI RIST
YOUR EYE IS MY ISLAND
PIPILOTTI RIST / ピピロッティ・リスト
YOUR EYE IS MY ISLAND
あなたの眼はわたしの島
swiss arts council
prohelvetia
August 7 [Sat.]–October 17 [Sun.], 2021 / 2021年8月7日[土]——10月17日[日]
Contemporary Art Gallery, Art Tower Mito / 水戸芸術館現代美術ギャラリー
水戸芸術館
ART TOWER MITO
[Open Hours] 10:00–18:00 / Closed on Mondays and days following national holidays / [Organized by] Mito Arts Foundation and The National Museum of Modern Art, Kyoto / [Supported by] Embassy of Switzerland in Japan / [Sponsored by] Kvadrat / [Cooperated by] Hase Building Co., Ltd., The National Art Center, Tokyo, Mori Art Museum, Universal Business Technologies Corporation, Suntory Holdings Limited / [With the support of] The Swiss Arts Council Pro Helvetia / [Project coordinated by] Hauser & Wirth, Yoshiko Isshiki Office

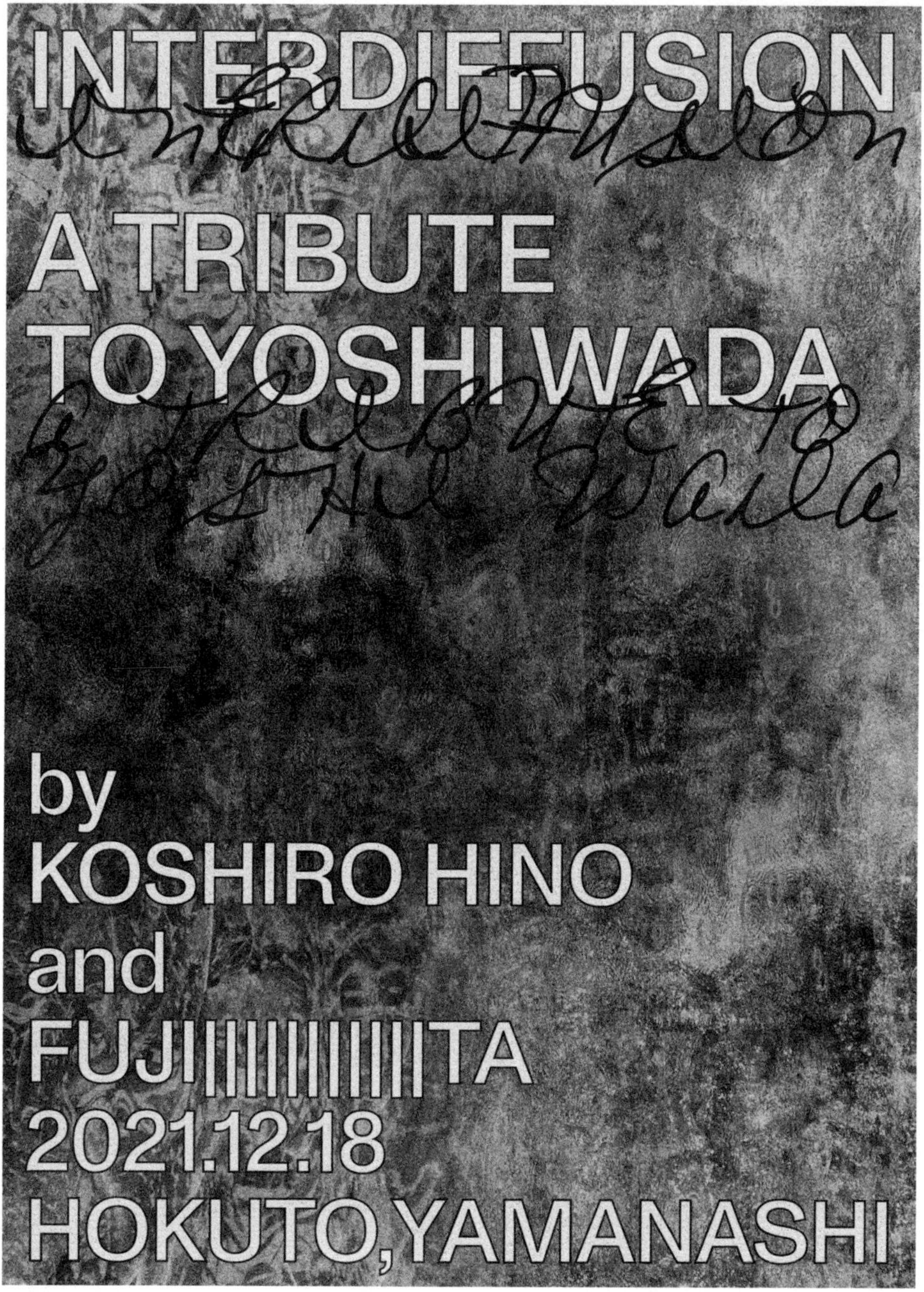
INTERDIFFUSION
A TRIBUTE
TO YOSHI WADA
by
KOSHIRO HINO
and
FUJI|||||||||||TA
2021.12.18
HOKUTO, YAMANASHI

Planned and Curated by Mariko Okazaki
Supported by Rondade
Syntactic Forest
Mariko Okazaki Graphic Designer
Naoyuki Hata Photographer
Sawada Hashimura Architects
2020.12.09(Wed)–12.27(Sun)
Alternative Space The White
NASA LAUNCH,OPER.DIR.
CAPE CANAVERAL
K.H.DEBUS,CHAIR.
JOINT ATLAS SPACE
FLIGHT TEST WORKING
GROUP
COL.H.MYERS,CHAIR
GROUND
INSTRUMENTATION
REVIEW COMMITTEE

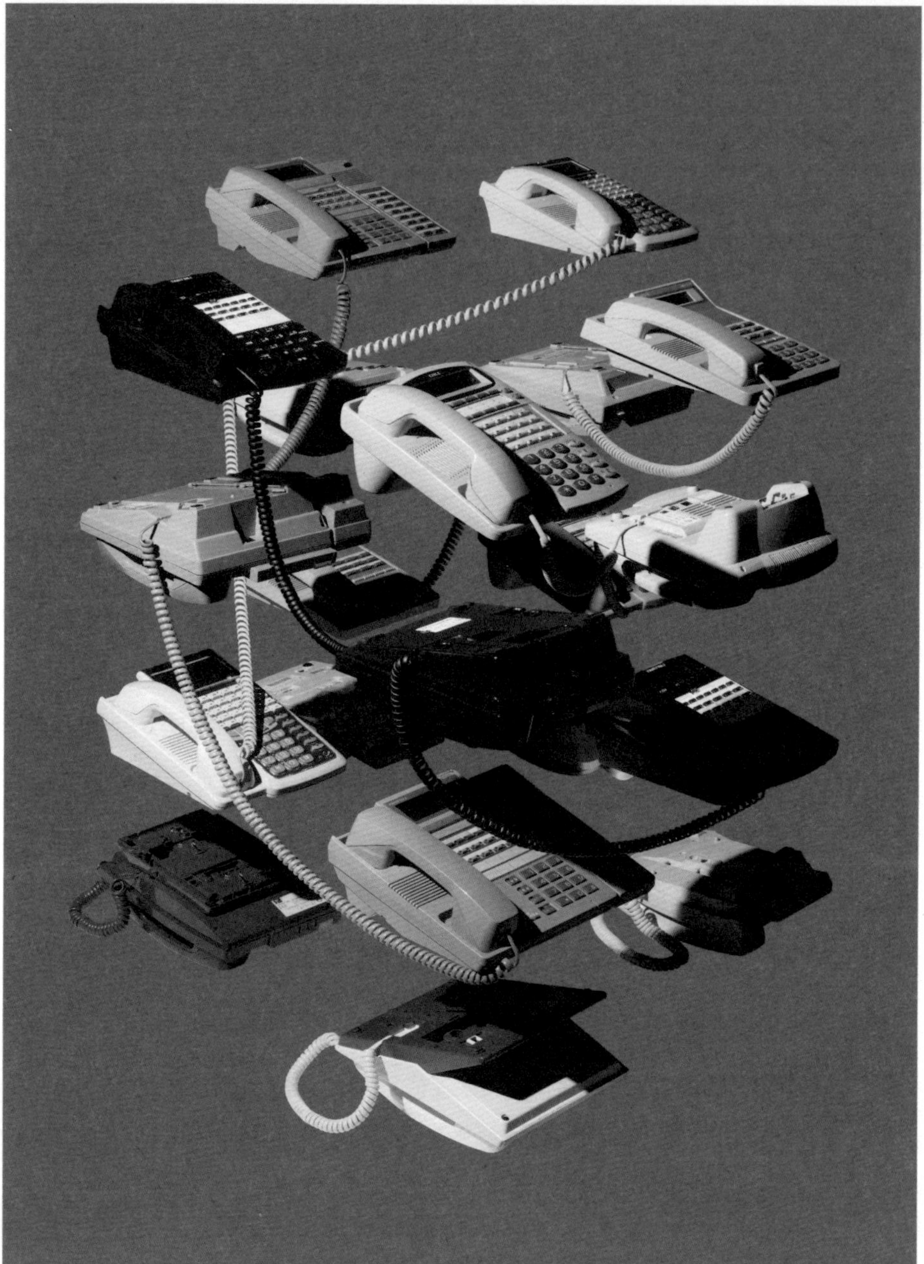

LANDSCAPE GOES DOMESTIC
BY ULTRA STUDIO
2021.10.9 (SAT.)–2021.10.22 (FRI.)
AT THE 5TH FLOOR

Ryotaro Hirosaki

Born in 1996, Ryotaro Hirosaki was working at a Japanese graphic design office for three years before becoming independent. He currently creates posters and illustrations of people and plants.

She is beautiful like a flower.

FLOWERS

FLOWER
Examination
of the colors and shapes
with flower motifs.

FLOWER

FLOWERS
Examining the visualization
of flowers by composing shapes

THE FLOWER

This is an expression of a flower that adds line expression to a simple color surface.

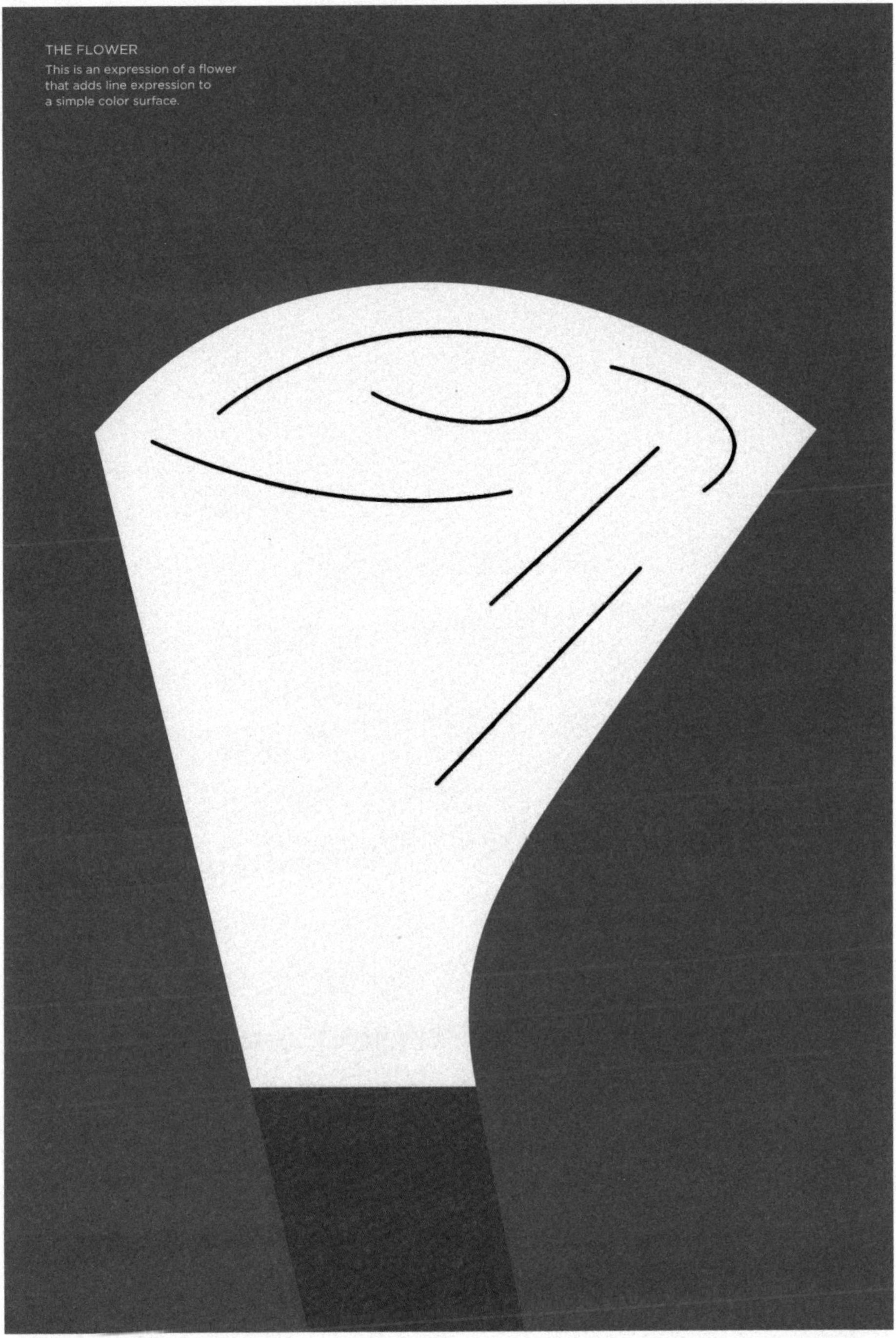
THE FLOWER
This is an expression of a flower
that adds line expression to
a simple color surface.

Ryuichi Kawajiri

Ryuichi Kawajiri is a Hokkaido-born graphic designer based in Sapporo. Since 2023, he has been freelancing under the name "Kawa" for clients in fashion, music, exhibitions, and the like. His work has been recognised with a JAGDA New Designer Award and Taiwan International Graphic Design Award Grand Prix to name a few.

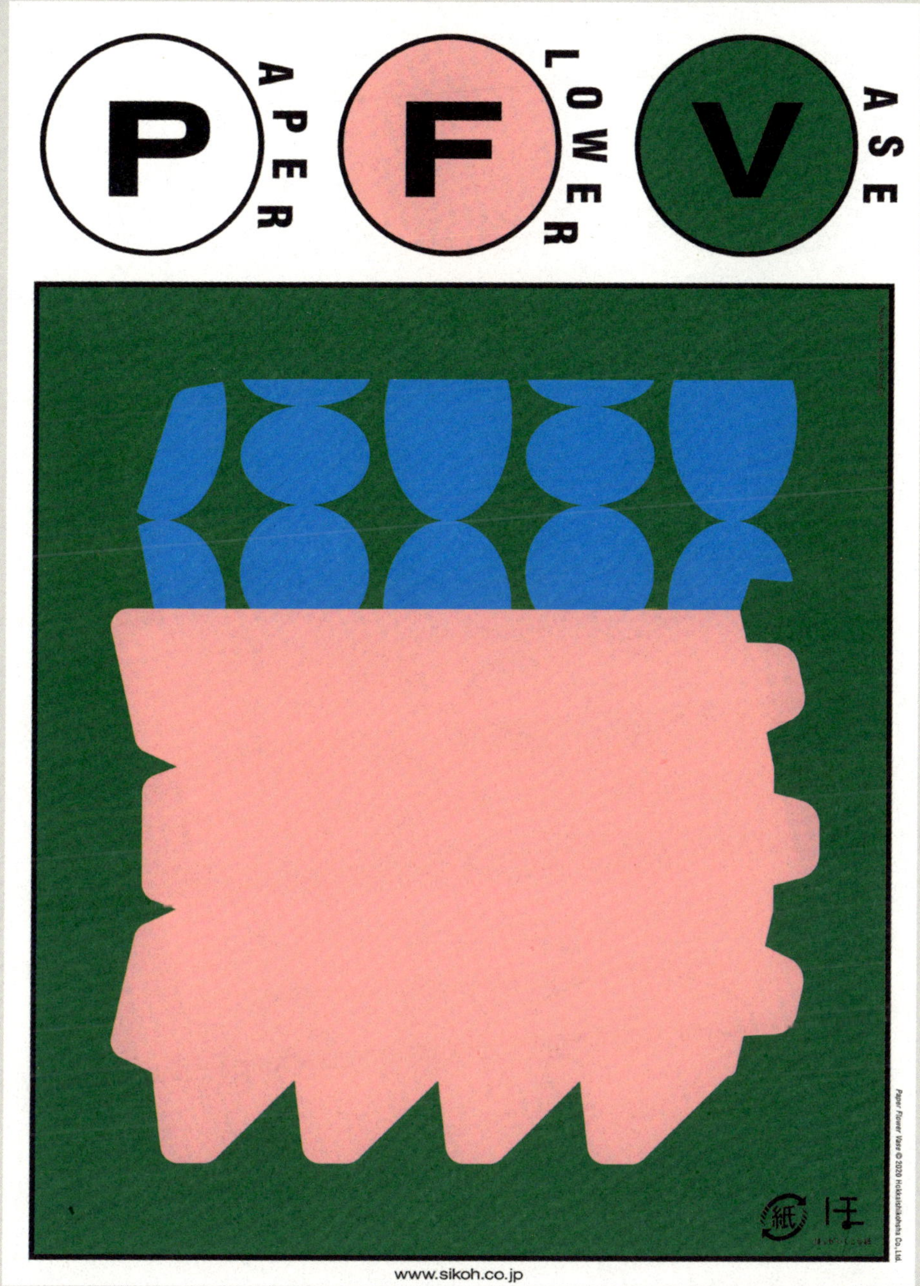
P APER
F LOWER
V ASE
紙 ほ
Paper Flower Vase © 2020 Hokkaishikohsha Co., Ltd.
www.sikoh.co.jp

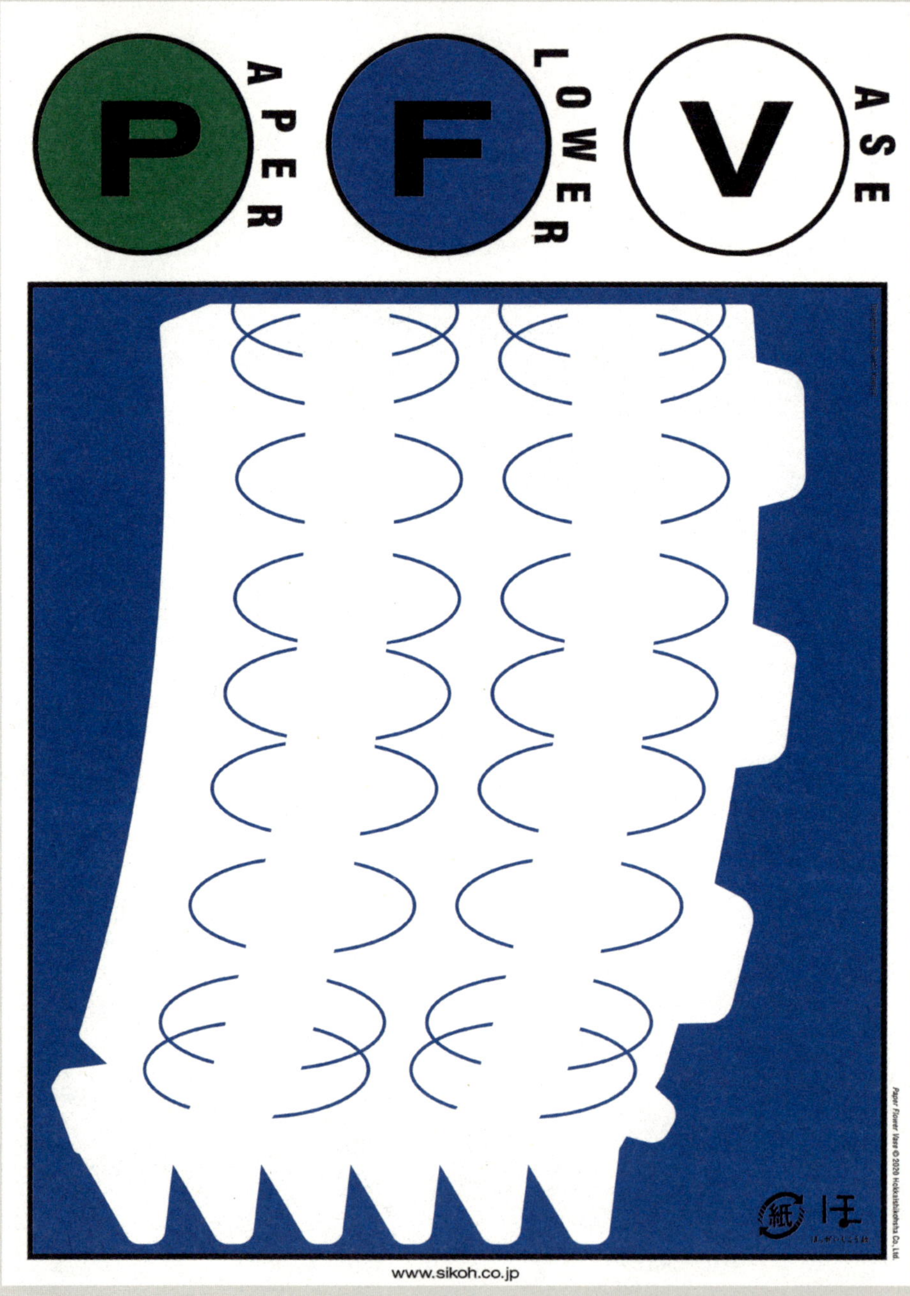
P
APER
F
LOWER
V
ASE
Paper Flower Vase © 2020 Hokkaishikohsha Co., Ltd.
www.sikoh.co.jp

P
APER
F
LOWER
V
ASE
Paper Flower Vase © 2020 Hokkaishikohsha Co., Ltd.
紙
ほ
ほっかいしこう社
www.sikoh.co.jp

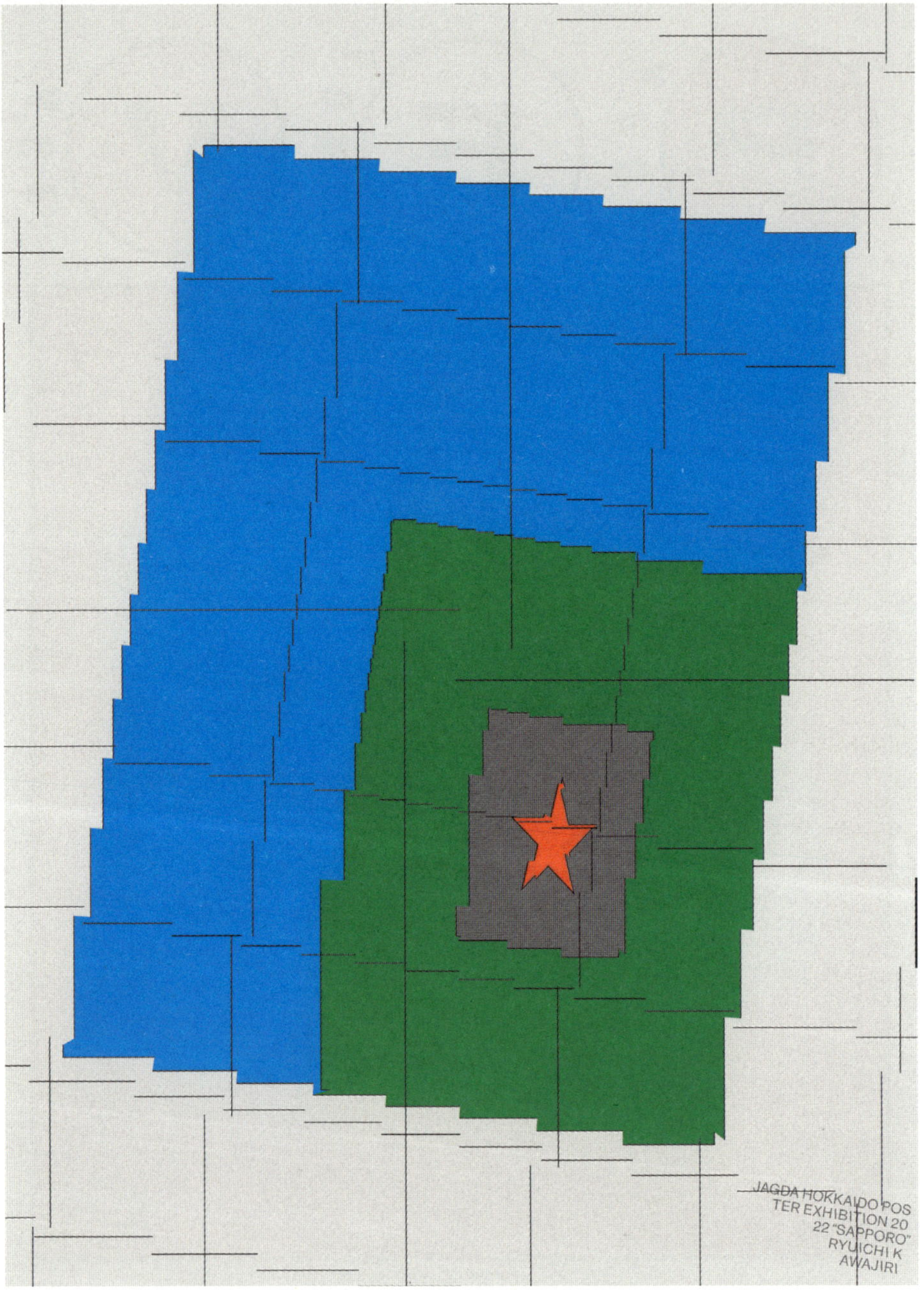
JAGDA HOKKAIDO POS
TER EXHIBITION 20
22 "SAPPORO"
RYUICHI K
AWAJIRI

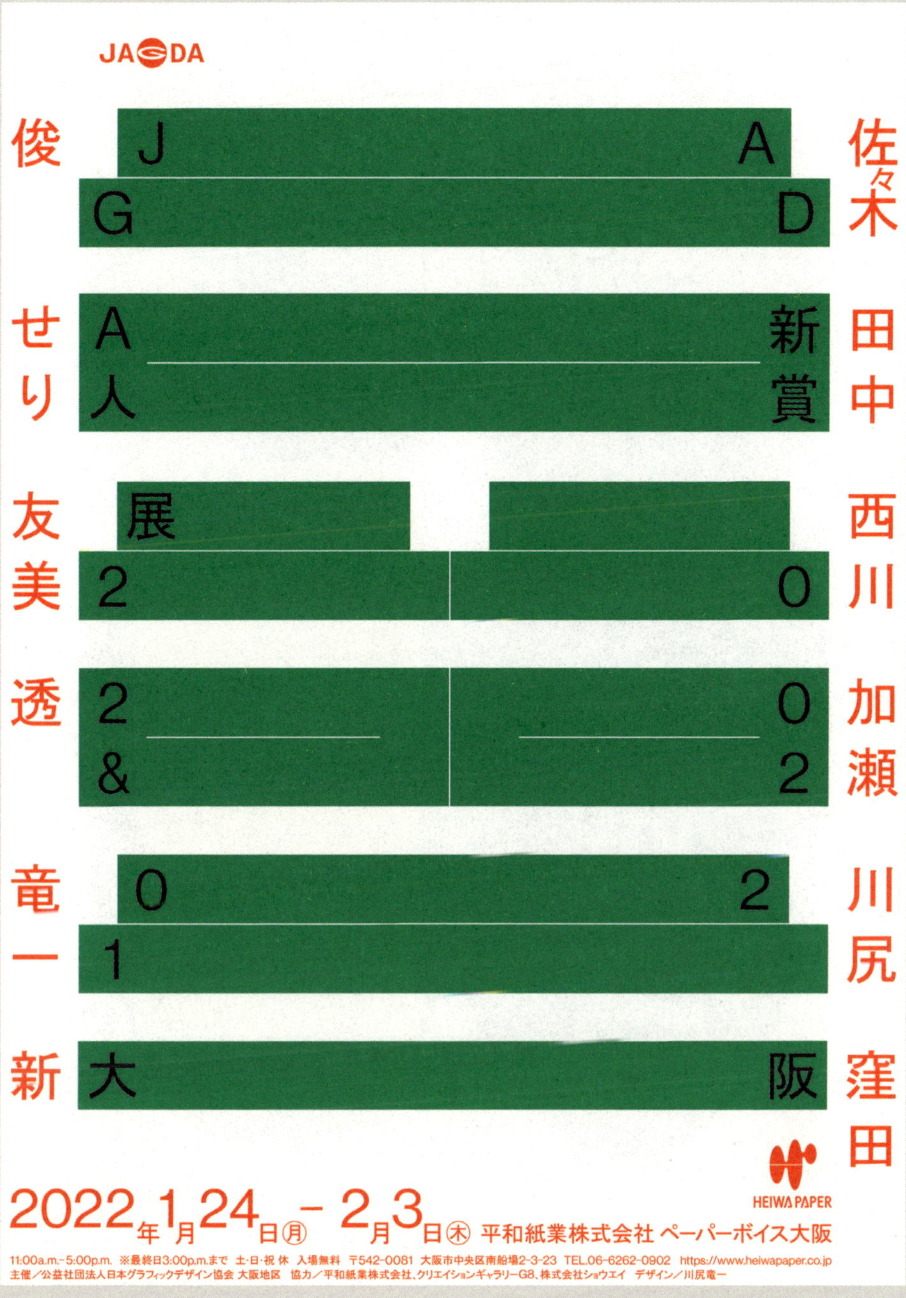
JAGDA
俊
J
A
佐々木
G
D
せり
A
新
田中
人
賞
友美
展
西川
2
0
透
2
0
加瀬
&
2
竜一
0
2
川尻
1
新
大
阪
窪田
HEIWA PAPER
2022年1月24日㈪ – 2月3日㈭ 平和紙業株式会社 ペーパーボイス大阪
11:00a.m.–5:00p.m. ※最終日3:00p.m.まで 土・日・祝 休 入場無料 〒542-0081 大阪市中央区南船場2-3-23 TEL.06-6262-0902 https://www.heiwapaper.co.jp
主催／公益社団法人日本グラフィックデザイン協会 大阪地区 協力／平和紙業株式会社、クリエイションギャラリーG8、株式会社ショウエイ デザイン／川尻竜一

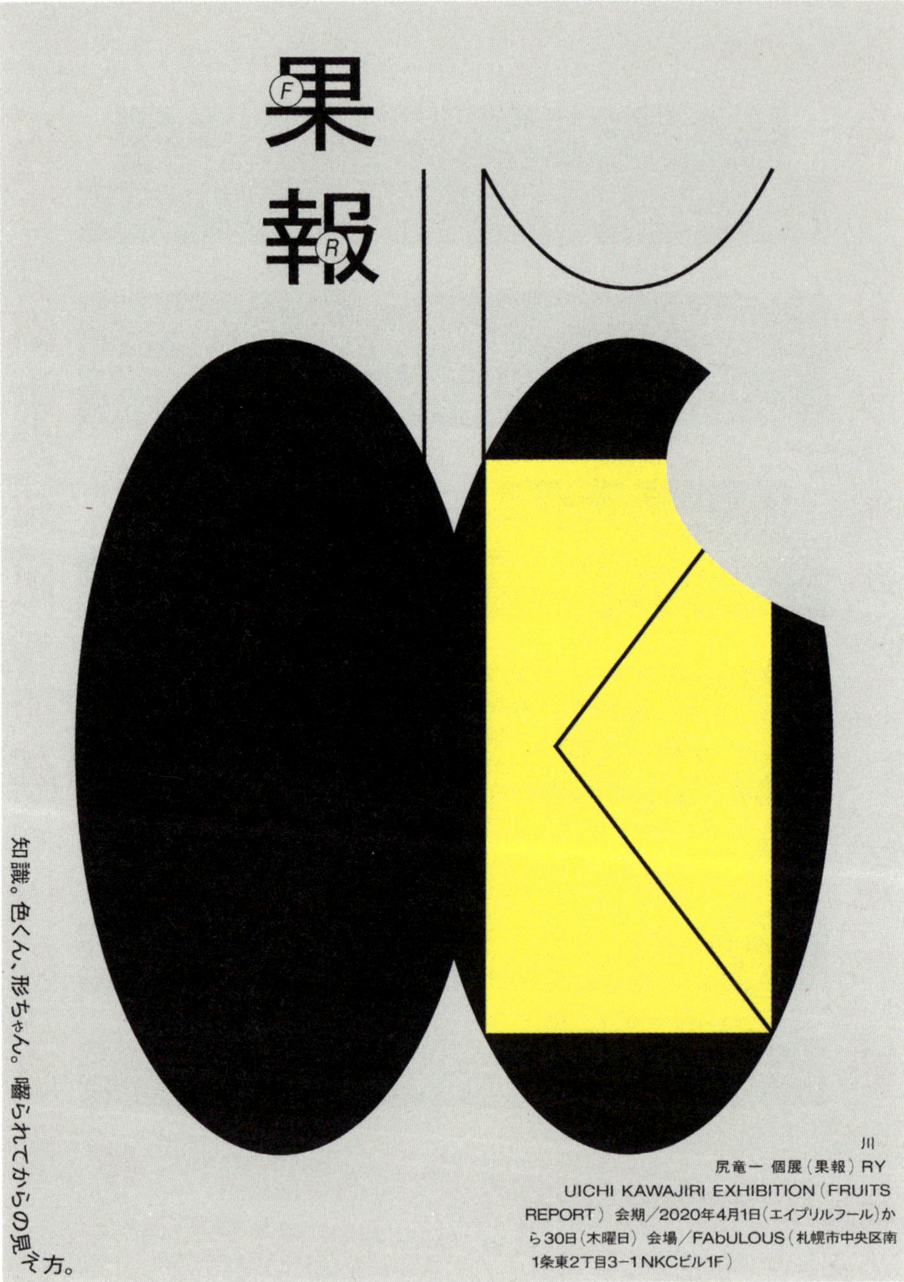
果報
F
R
知識。色くん、形ちゃん。齧られてからの見え方。
川
尻竜一 個展（果報）RY
UICHI KAWAJIRI EXHIBITION（FRUITS
REPORT） 会期／2020年4月1日（エイプリルフール）か
ら30日（木曜日） 会場／FAbULOUS（札幌市中央区南
1条東2丁目3−1 NKCビル1F）

果 F
R 報
知識。色くん、形ちゃん。囓られてからの見え方。
川
尻竜一 個展（果報）RY
UICHI KAWAJIRI EXHIBITION（FRUITS
REPORT） 会期／2020年4月1日（エイプリルフール）か
ら30日（木曜日） 会場／FAbULOUS（札幌市中央区南
1条東2丁目3−1 NKCビル1F）

合
理
〇三年〇三月一三日　場
所
約）予（ntiti.info@gmail.com）約
予
要　ム　二円体　図
）ヅ　画
名　ル
五　ナヂ　一竜尻川
ンチチビル
住（大阪市浪速区戎本町2-1-20）所
員定　円〇〇〇二　金料

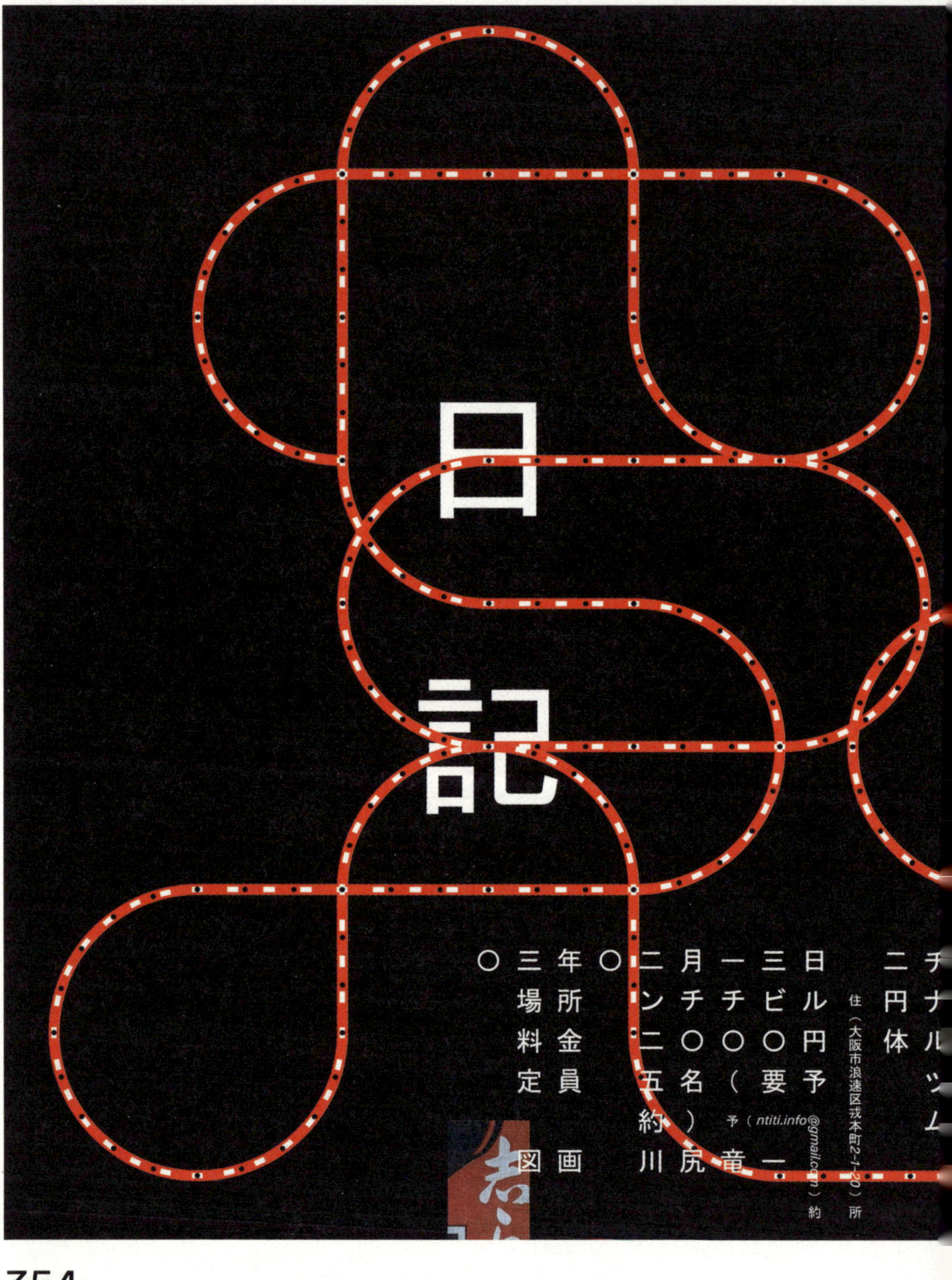
日
記
〇三年〇二月一三日
場所　ンチチビル
料金　二〇〇〇円
定員　五名（要予
約）
予（ntiti.info@gmail.com）約
住（大阪市浪速区戎本町2-1-20）所
図画　川尻竜一
ニチ
円ナ
体ル
ツ
ム

合理

日記

音楽

七円体

合
理
〇一年
一〇月
場所
ンチチ物体
図画
住（大阪市浪速区戎本町2-1-20）所
料金
二〇〇〇円

Sato Design

Sato Design was founded in 2012 by Tottori-born Daisuke Sato, a graphic designer who has worked at various design offices and advertising agencies upon graduating from Seian University of Art and Design.

第37回人文機構シンポジウム
この世のキワ
自然と超自然のはざま
Boundaries of the 'natural' and 'supernatural'
2019.11.23 SAT.
13:00-16:30（開場12:30）
場所：グランフロント大阪北館タワーC8階
ナレッジキャピタルカンファレンスルームタワーC RoomC01+02
参加費：無料 ※要事前申込（定員200名、先着順、定員に達し次第締切り）
ジル・クック（大英博物館 学芸員） 黒川正剛（太成学院大学 教授）
小松和彦（国際日本文化研究センター 所長） 木場貴俊（国際日本文化研究センター プロジェクト研究員）
山中由里子（国立民族学博物館 教授）
●申込方法
Webサイト内の受付フォーム、もしくは往復ハガキにてお申し込みください。
https://www.nihu.jp/ja/event/symposium/37
●問い合わせ先
第37回人文機構シンポジウム事務局（一般財団法人 千里文化財団内）
TEL:06-6877-8893（平日9:00-17:00） Mail:sympo@senri-f.or.jp
主催：大学共同利用機関法人 人間文化研究機構 後援：文部科学省
人間文化研究機構
国立民族学博物館
National Museum of Ethnology
人間文化研究機構 基幹研究プロジェクト
REGNUM IMAGINARIUM
RI
REALM OF THE MARVELOUS AND UNCANNY
特別展「驚異と怪異——想像界の生きものたち」関連
11月26日（火）まで 場所：国立民族学博物館 特別展示館

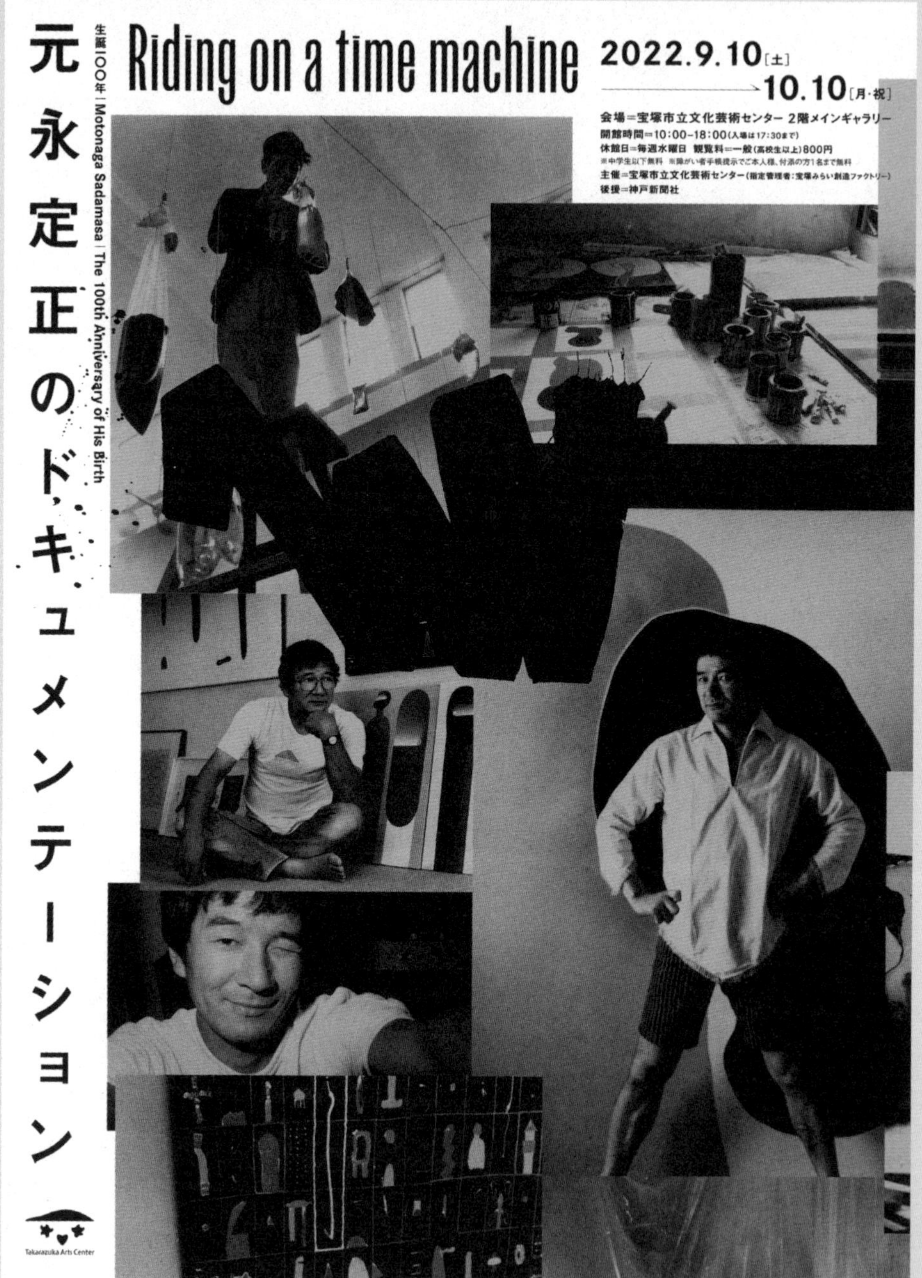
元永定正のドキュメンテーション
生誕100年 | Motonaga Sadamasa | The 100th Anniversary of His Birth
Riding on a time machine
2022.9.10［土］
→10.10［月·祝］
会場＝宝塚市立文化芸術センター 2階メインギャラリー
開館時間＝10:00–18:00（入場は17:30まで）
休館日＝毎週水曜日 観覧料＝一般（高校生以上）800円
※中学生以下無料 ※障がい者手帳提示でご本人様、付添の方1名まで無料
主催＝宝塚市立文化芸術センター（指定管理者：宝塚みらい創造ファクトリー）
後援＝神戸新聞社
Takarazuka Arts Center

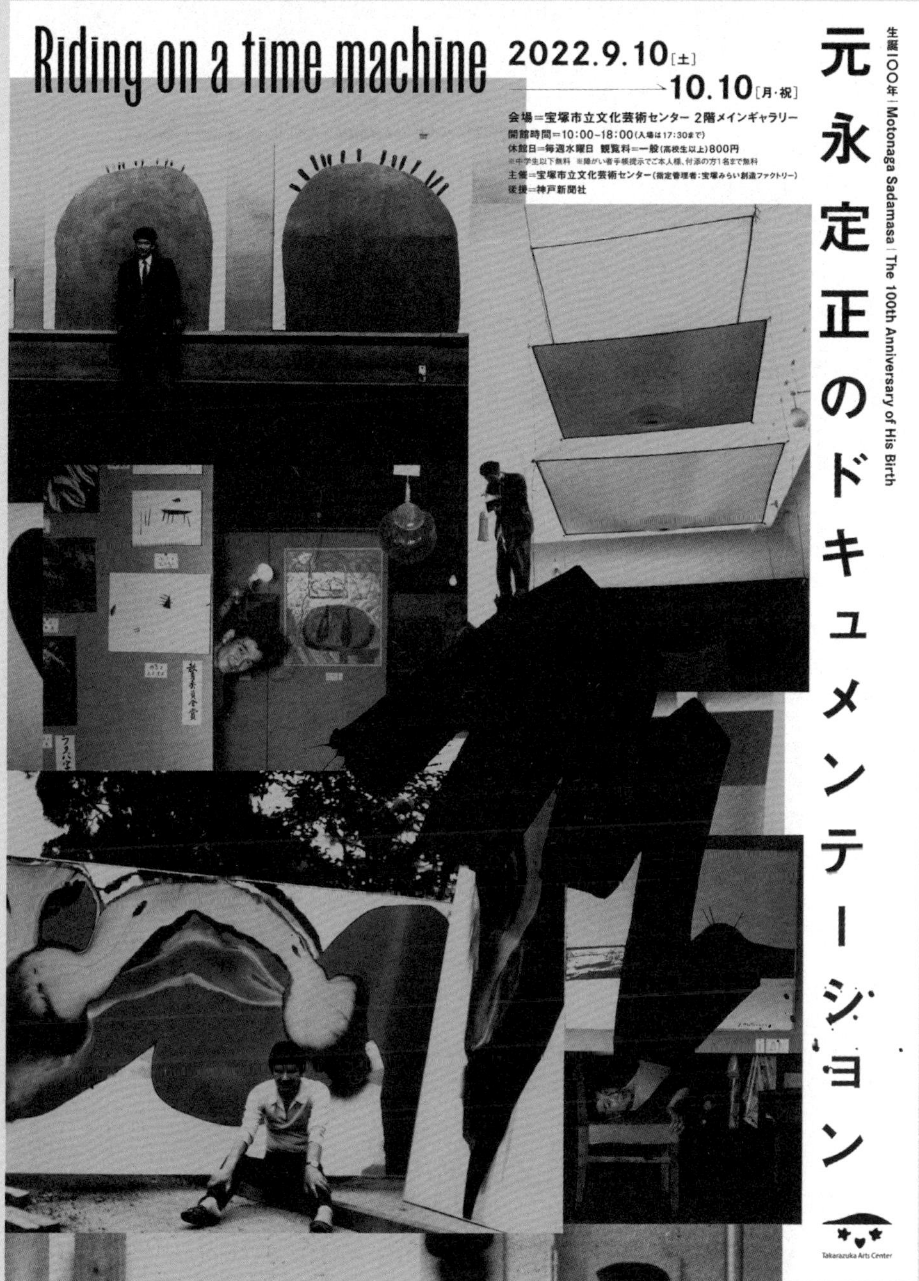
Riding on a time machine
2022.9.10［土］
→10.10［月·祝］
会場＝宝塚市立文化芸術センター 2階メインギャラリー
開館時間＝10：00–18：00（入場は17：30まで）
休館日＝毎週水曜日 観覧料＝一般（高校生以上）800円
※中学生以下無料 ※障がい者手帳提示でご本人様、付添の方1名まで無料
主催＝宝塚市立文化芸術センター（指定管理者：宝塚みらい創造ファクトリー）
後援＝神戸新聞社
元永定正のドキュメンテーション
生誕100年 | Motonaga Sadamasa | The 100th Anniversary of His Birth
Takarazuka Arts Center

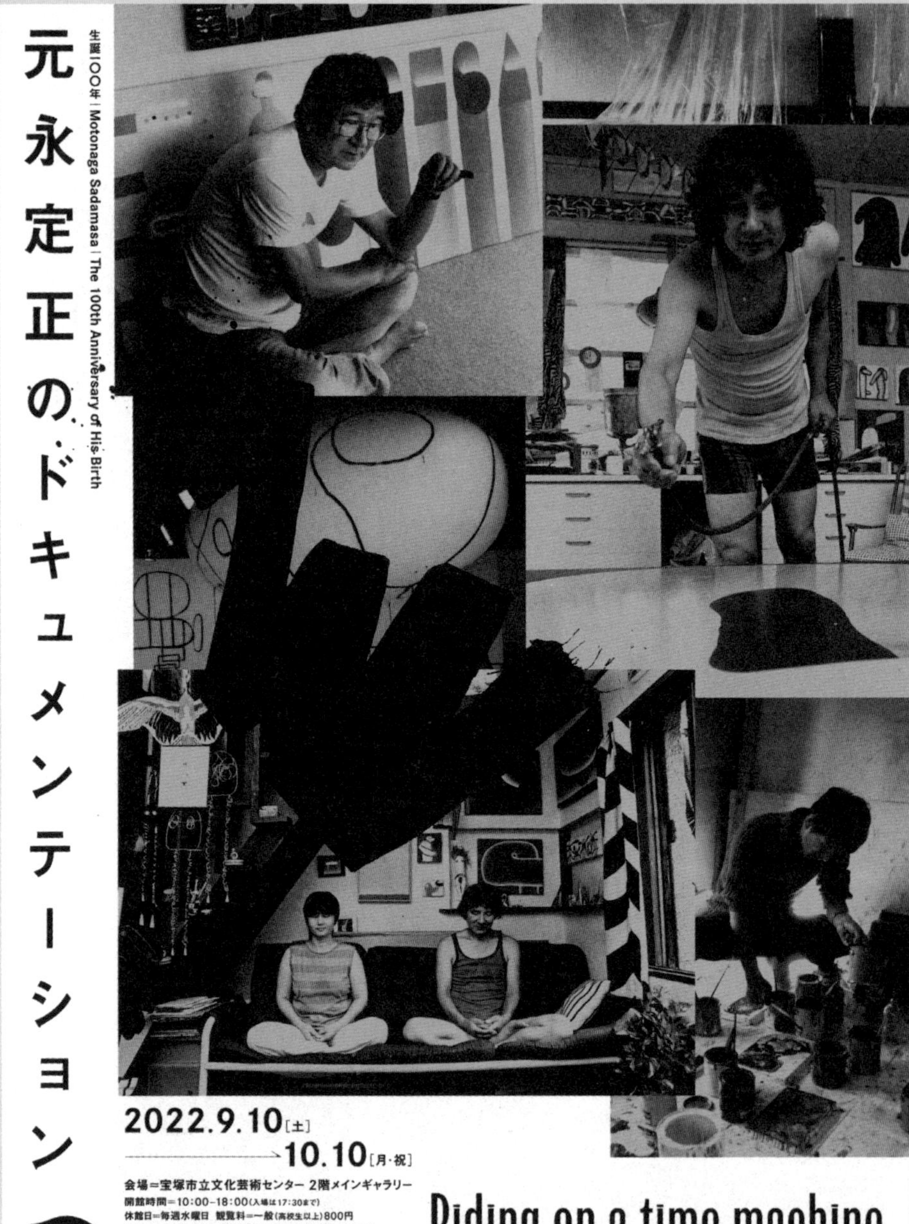

生誕100年 | Motonaga Sadamasa | The 100th Anniversary of His Birth
元永定正のドキュメンテーション
2022.9.10[土]
→10.10[月·祝]
会場＝宝塚市立文化芸術センター 2階メインギャラリー
開館時間＝10:00–18:00(入場は17:30まで)
休館日＝毎週水曜日 観覧料＝一般(高校生以上)800円
※中学生以下無料 ※障がい者手帳提示でご本人様、付添の方1名まで無料
主催＝宝塚市立文化芸術センター(指定管理者：宝塚みらい創造ファクトリー)
後援＝神戸新聞社
Takarazuka Arts Center
Riding on a time machine

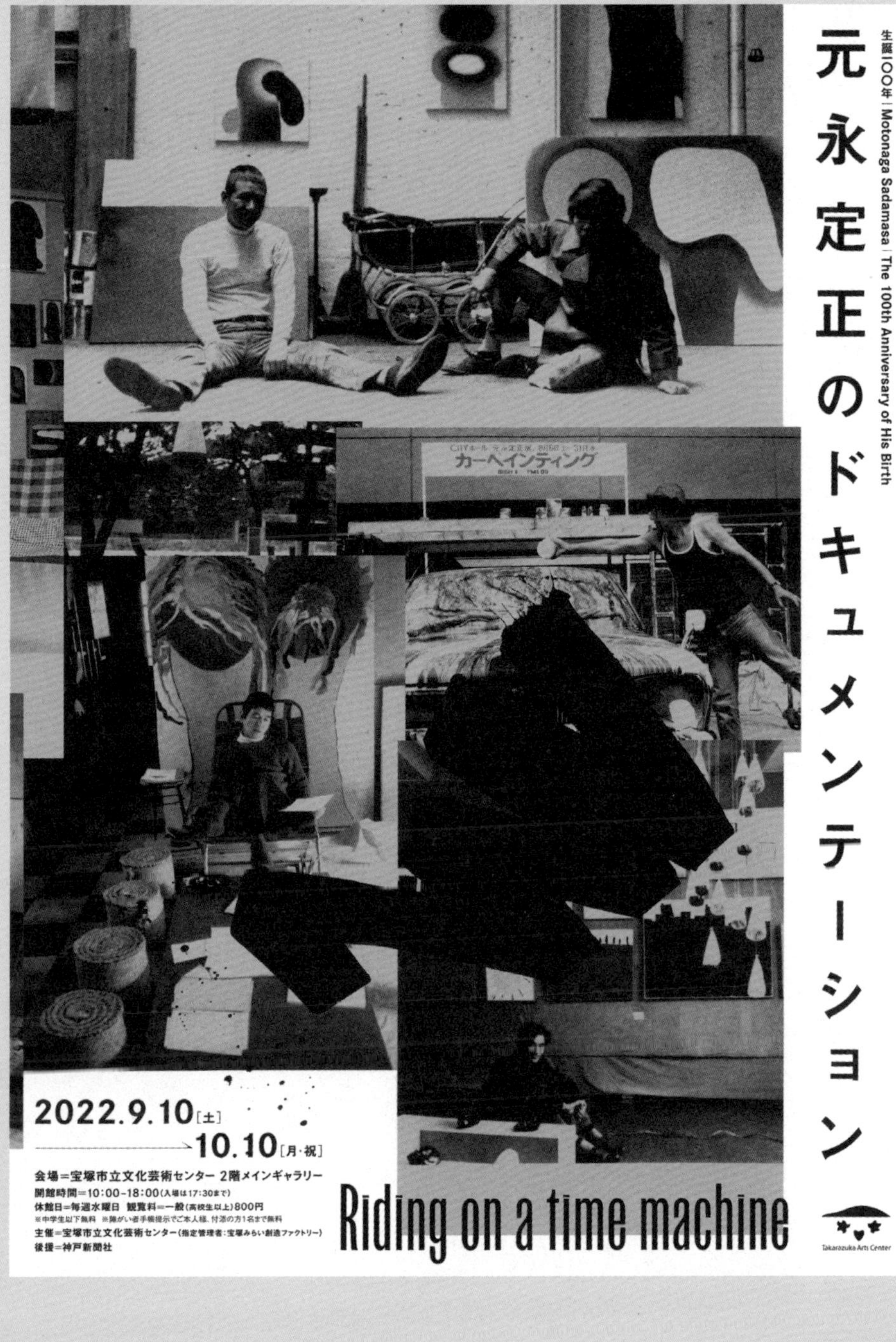
生誕100年 | Motonaga Sadamasa | The 100th Anniversary of His Birth
元永定正のドキュメンテーション
カーペインティング
2022.9.10［土］
→10.10［月・祝］
会場＝宝塚市立文化芸術センター 2階メインギャラリー
開館時間＝10:00–18:00（入場は17:30まで）
休館日＝毎週水曜日　観覧料＝一般（高校生以上）800円
※中学生以下無料　※障がい者手帳提示でご本人様、付添の方1名まで無料
主催＝宝塚市立文化芸術センター（指定管理者：宝塚みらい創造ファクトリー）
後援＝神戸新聞社
Riding on a time machine
Takarazuka Arts Center

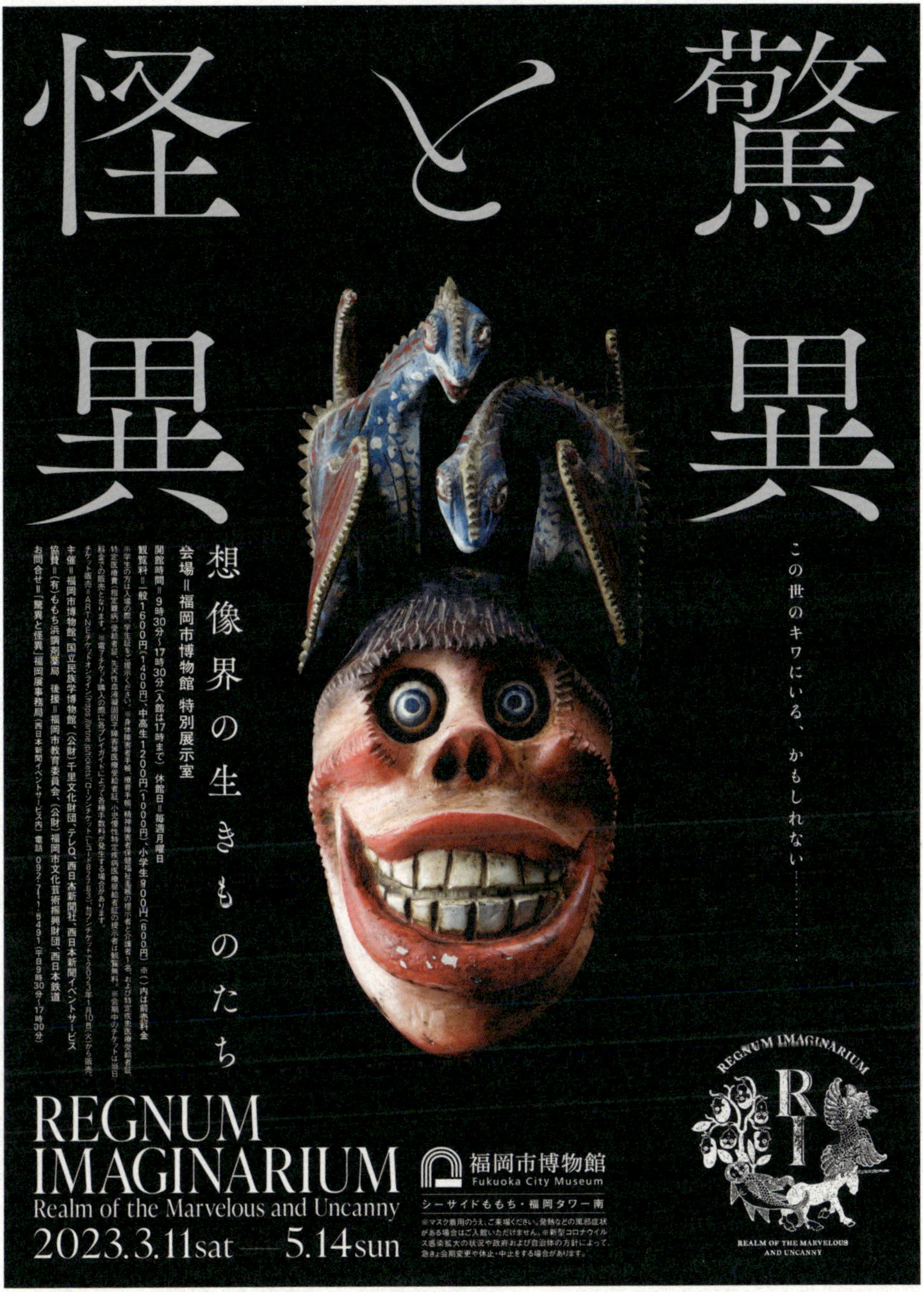
驚異と怪異
想像界の生きものたち
この世のキワにいる、かもしれない……
会場＝福岡市博物館 特別展示室
開館時間＝9時30分～17時30分（入館は17時まで） 休館日＝毎週月曜日
観覧料＝一般1600円（1400円）、中高生1200円（1000円）、小学生900円（600円） ※（）内は前売料金
主催＝福岡市博物館、国立民族学博物館、（公財）千里文化財団、テレQ、西日本新聞社、西日本新聞イベントサービス
協賛＝（有）ももち浜調剤薬局 後援＝福岡市教育委員会、（公財）福岡市文化芸術振興財団、西日本鉄道
お問合せ＝「驚異と怪異」福岡展事務局（西日本新聞イベントサービス内） 電話 092-711-5491（平日9時30分～17時30分）
REGNUM IMAGINARIUM
Realm of the Marvelous and Uncanny
2023.3.11sat — 5.14sun
福岡市博物館
Fukuoka City Museum
シーサイドももち・福岡タワー南
※マスク着用のうえ、ご来場ください。発熱などの風邪症状がある場合はご入館いただけません。※新型コロナウイルス感染拡大の状況や政府および自治体の方針によって、急きょ会期変更や休止・中止をする場合があります。
REGNUM IMAGINARIUM
RI
REALM OF THE MARVELOUS AND UNCANNY

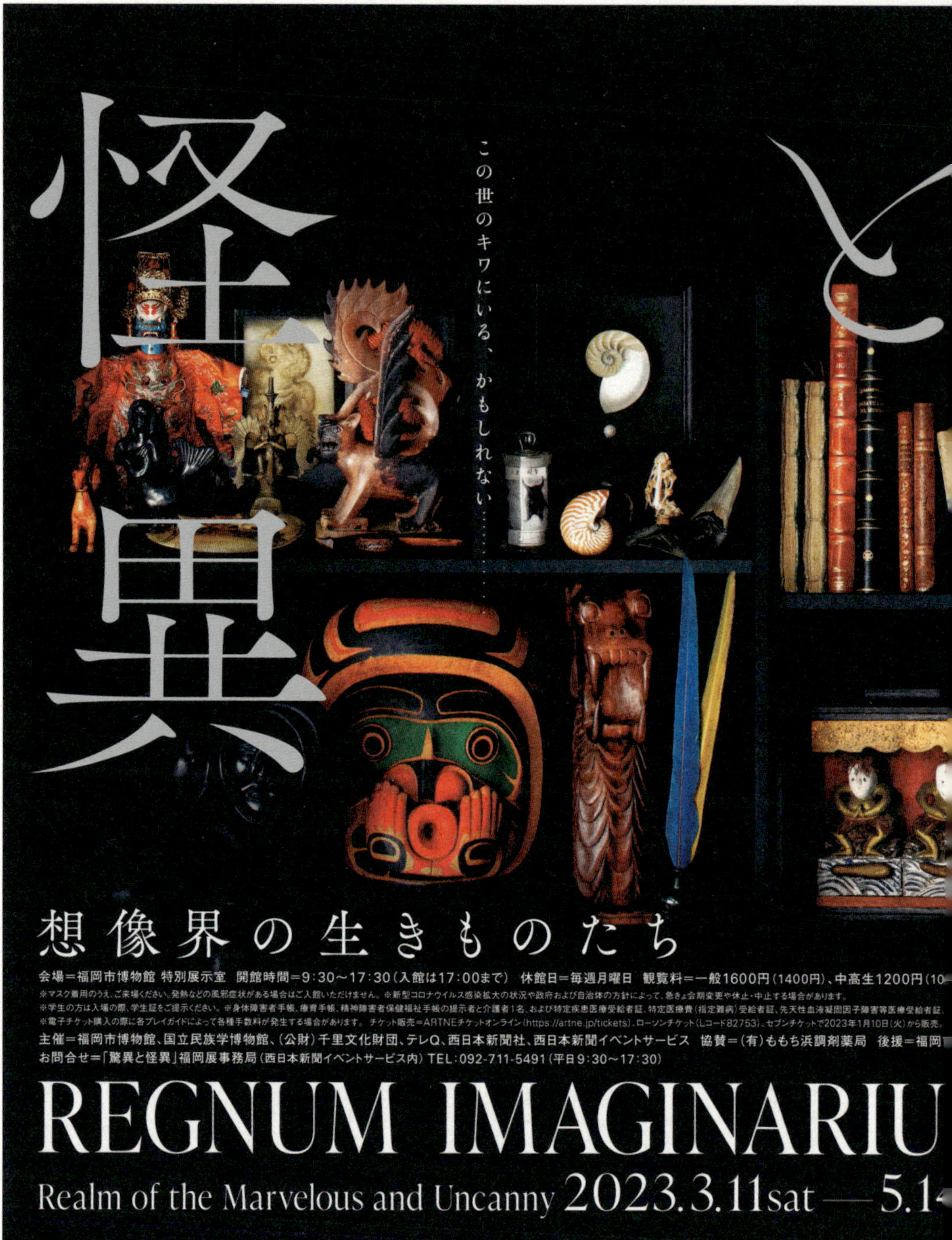
と
怪異
この世のキワにいる、かもしれない……
想像界の生きものたち
会場＝福岡市博物館 特別展示室　開館時間＝9：30～17：30（入館は17：00まで）　休館日＝毎週月曜日　観覧料＝一般1600円（1400円）、中高生1200円（10
※マスク着用のうえ、ご来場ください。発熱などの風邪症状がある場合はご入館いただけません。※新型コロナウイルス感染拡大の状況や政府および自治体の方針によって、急きょ会期変更や休止・中止する場合があります。
※学生の方は入場の際、学生証をご提示ください。※身体障害者手帳、療育手帳、精神障害者保健福祉手帳の提示者と介護者1名、および特定疾患医療受給者証、特定医療費（指定難病）受給者証、先天性血液凝固因子障害等医療受給者証、
※電子チケット購入の際に各プレイガイドによって各種手数料が発生する場合があります。　チケット販売＝ARTNEチケットオンライン（https://artne.jp/tickets）、ローソンチケット（Lコード82753）、セブンチケットで2023年1月10日（火）から販売。
主催＝福岡市博物館、国立民族学博物館、（公財）千里文化財団、テレQ、西日本新聞社、西日本新聞イベントサービス　協賛＝（有）ももち浜調剤薬局　後援＝福岡
お問合せ＝「驚異と怪異」福岡展事務局（西日本新聞イベントサービス内）TEL：092-711-5491（平日9：30～17：30）
REGNUM IMAGINARIU
Realm of the Marvelous and Uncanny 2023.3.11sat — 5.1

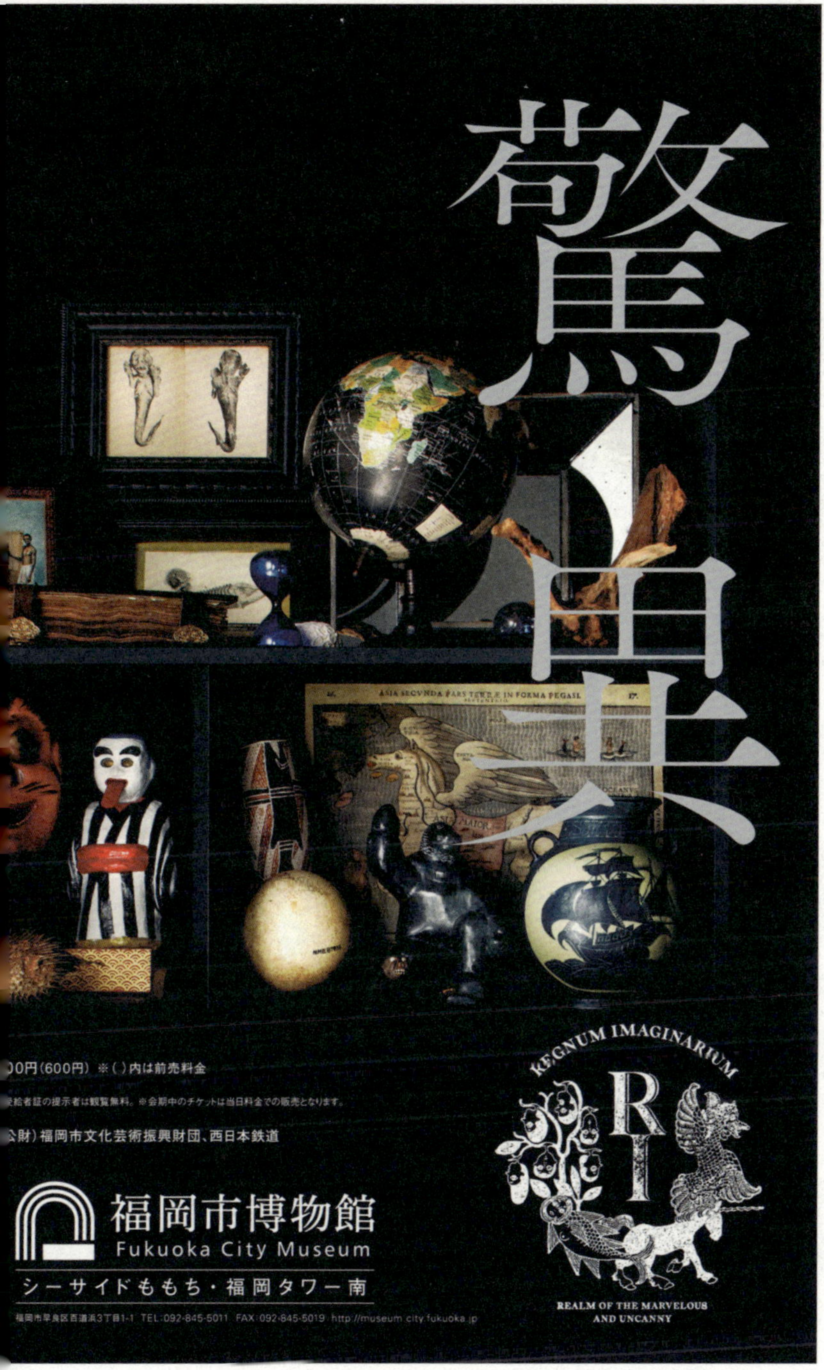
驚異
0円(600円) ※( )内は前売料金
給者証の提示者は観覧無料。※会期中のチケットは当日料金での販売となります。
公財)福岡市文化芸術振興財団、西日本鉄道
福岡市博物館
Fukuoka City Museum
シーサイドももち・福岡タワー南
福岡市早良区百道浜3丁目1-1 TEL:092-845-5011 FAX:092-845-5019 http://museum.city.fukuoka.jp
REGNUM IMAGINARIUM
RI
REALM OF THE MARVELOUS
AND UNCANNY

SPICE CURRY
ムジャラ
मसाले करी मुजरा
カレー＆スパイス料理 ムジャラ
京都市京都府下京区高辻通大宮西入坊門町 832 イツワマンション 1階
大宮駅もしくは四条大宮から徒歩約 5 分 電話 080-9161-1191
営業日・営業時間はホームページかツイッターで確認してください
不定休
2016.7.25mon
11:30 OPEN
www.mujara.net

インド料理をベースにしたオリジナ
ルスパイスカレーのお店で夜はカ
フェバー営業しますスパイスをあて
にゆっくりくつろいでください
SPICE CURRY
ムジャラ
मसाले करी मुजरा
京都市京都府下京区高辻通
大宮西入坊門町832
イツワマンション 1階
2016.7.25mon
11:30 OPEN
ホールスパイスたっぷりのランチは日替わりでカレー1品、おかずが4品、じっくり仕込んだピクルス、塩漬けなどを一皿に盛り付けています。店主自ら改装した店内は異空間、ヘンテコな音楽が流れる空間に仕上げました。ドリンクのみのオーダーも可能です。
営業日・営業時間は
ホームページかツイッター
で確認してください
www.mujara.net
電話 080-9161-1191
大宮駅
文
堀川高辻
高辻通
ムジャラ
大宮駅もしくは
四条大宮から
徒歩約5分

SPICE CURRY
ムジャラ
मसाले करी मुजरा
インド料理をベースとしたオリジナルスパイスカレーのお店で夜はカフェバー営業しますスパイスをあてにゆっくりくつろいでください
大宮駅もしくは四条大宮から徒歩約5分
大宮駅
堀川高辻
高辻通
ムジャラ
2016.7.25mon
11:30 OPEN
カレー&スパイス料理 ムジャラ
京都市京都府下京区高辻通大宮西入坊門町832 イツワマンション 1階
不定休
営業日・営業時間はホームページかツイッターで確認してください
www.mujara.net
電話 080-9161-1191

SPICE CURRY
ムジャラ
मसाले करी मुजरा
インド料理をベースにしたオリジナルスパイスカレーのお店で夜はカフェバー営業します スパイスをあてにゆっくりくつろいでください ホールスパイスたっぷりのランチは日替わりでカレー1品、おかずが4品、じっくり仕込んだピクルス、塩漬けなどを一皿に盛り付けています。店主自ら改装した店内は異空間、ヘンテコな音楽が流れる空間に仕上げました ドリンクのみのオーダーも可能です
カレー&スパイス料理 ムジャラ
京都市京都府下京区高辻通
大宮西入坊門町 832
イツワマンション 1階
2016.7.25mon
11:30 OPEN
営業日・営業時間は
ホームページかツイッター
で確認してください
www.mujara.net
電話 080-9161-1191
大宮駅
堀川高辻
高辻通
ムジャラ

Satomi Okubo

Satomi Okubo specialises in branding, product and service design, as well as design and communication planning. A fan of cats, tipples, and researching cuisine, she is also pursuing her interest in educational content for children through picture books and workshops. She has received many awards for her work, including a Gold Cannes Lion, New York ADC Gold Prize, D&AD Graphite Pencil, Dentsu Award for Best Design, and Good Design Award.

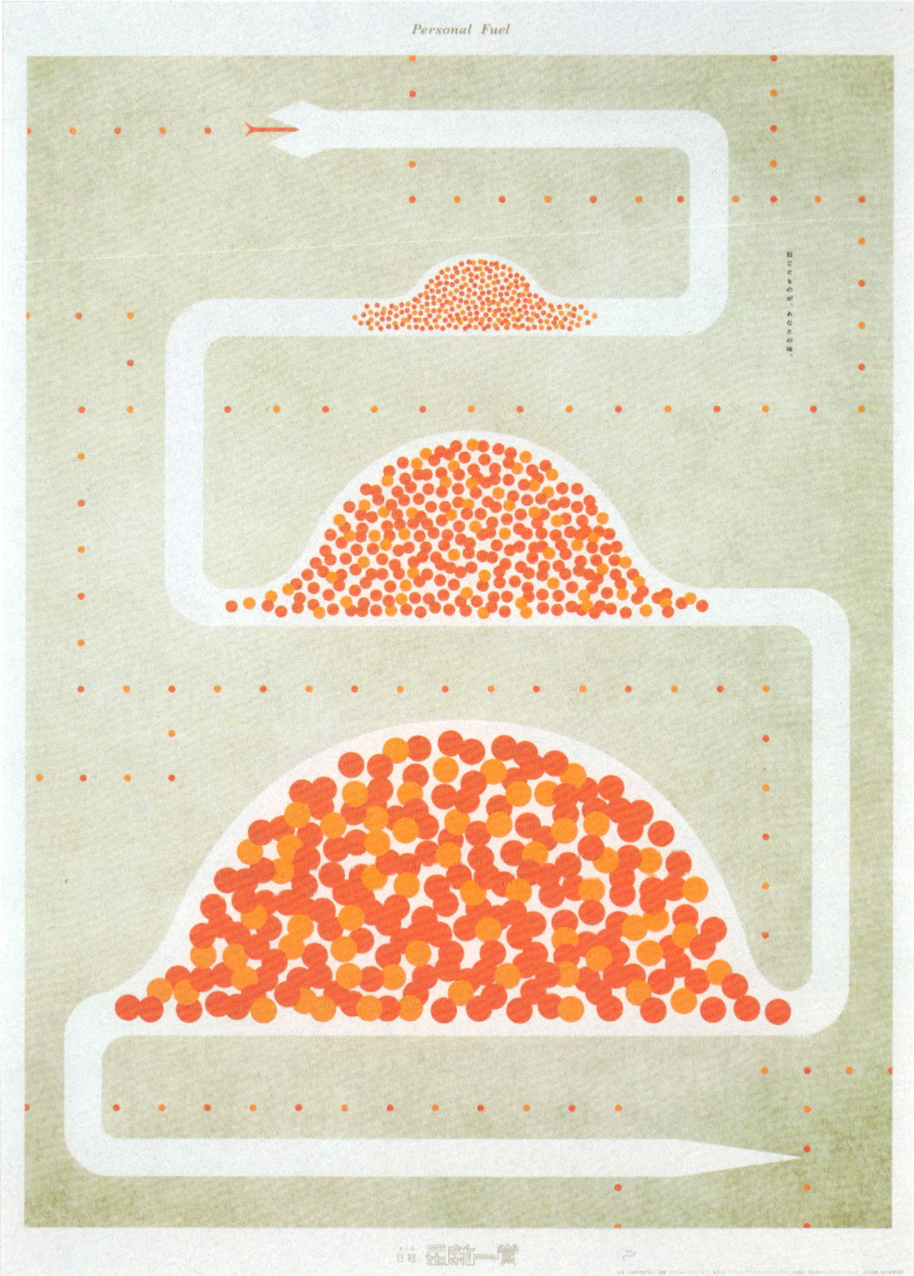
Personal Fuel
信じたものが、あなたの味。

Personal Fuel
みんなが心をひとつにしたら、きっとつまらない。
日経

Personal Fuel
どこにもない味は、どこにでもある味から生まれる。

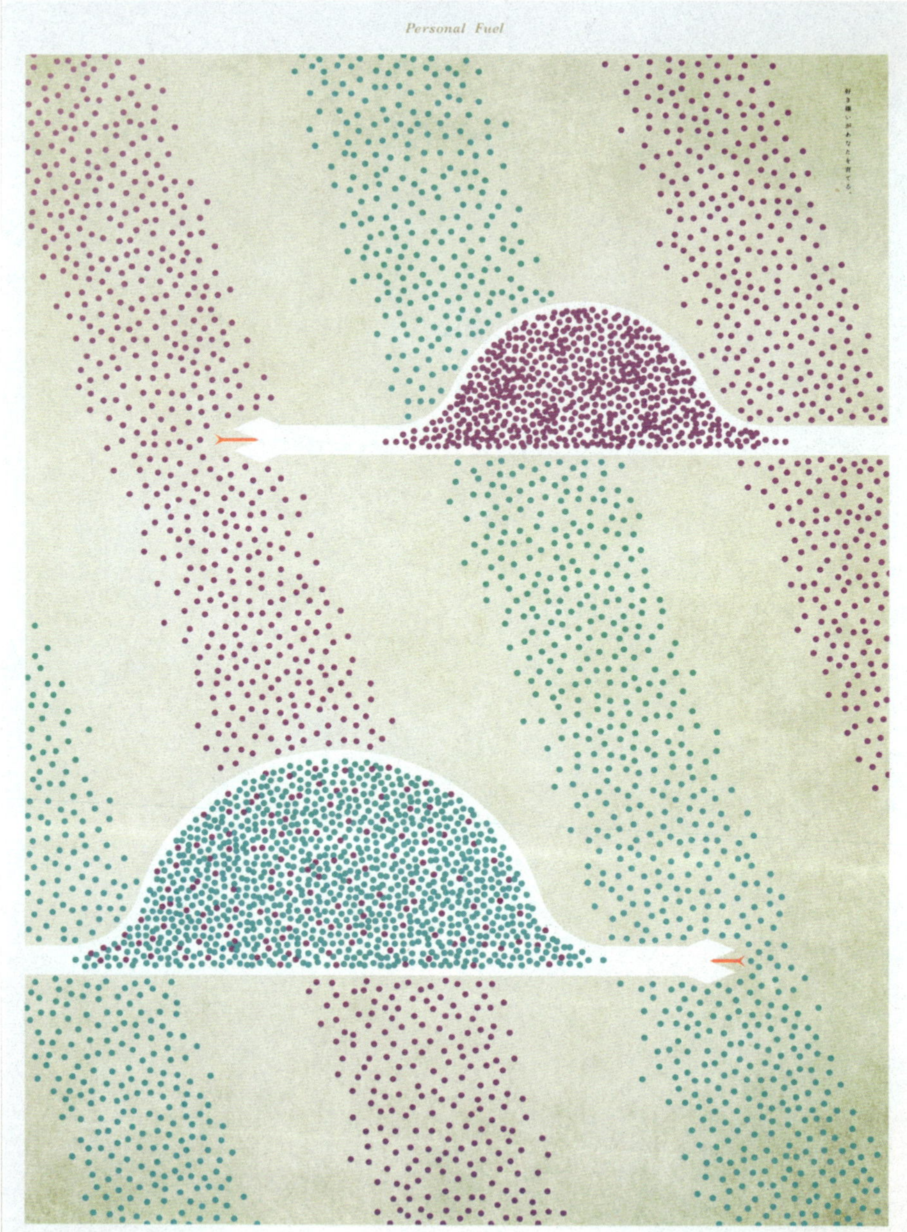
Personal Fuel
好き嫌いがあなたを育てる。

Personal Fuel
あなたのふつうは、みんなのふしぎ。
日経

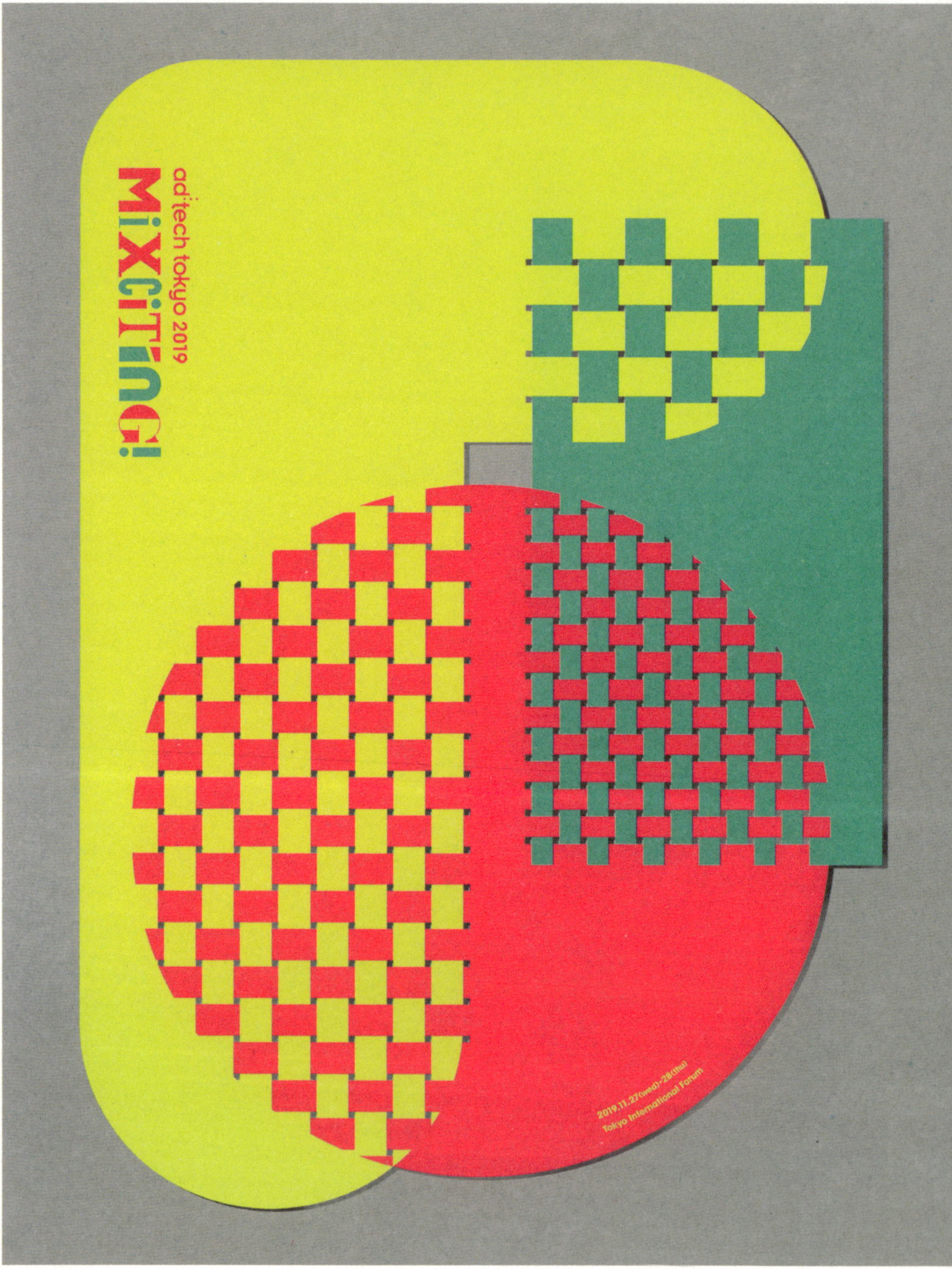

ad:tech tokyo 2019
MiXCiTinG!
2019.11.27(wed)-28(thu)
Tokyo International Forum

ad:tech tokyo 2019
MiXCiTinG!
2019.11.27(wed)-28(thu)
Tokyo International Forum

ad:tech tokyo 2019
MiXCiTiNG!
2019.11.27(wed)-28(thu) Tokyo International Forum

ad:tech tokyo 2019
MiXCiTinG!
2019.11.27(wed)-28(thu)
Tokyo International Forum

Shoichi Maehara

Born in Tokyo, Shoichi Maehara graduated from Tama Art University with a focus in graphic design. After working stints at Dentsu Tec and Draft, he began freelancing in 2019. In 2022, he became a recipient of the JAGDA New Designer Award.

四国大会 2022
Hanaike Battle
Shikoku Round 2022
2022/10/16 START 12:00
高知県立高知追手前高等学校 芸術ホール
全国高校生花いけバトル 四国大会 2022
Follow us!
LIVE配信
大会詳細情報
全国高校生
花いけバトル
グロリくん

沖縄大会 2022
Hanaike Battle
Okinawa Round 2022
2022/11/5 OPEN12:15 START 13:00
アイム・ユニバース てだこホール（小ホール）
【大会の花】 ストレリチア
全国高校生花いけバトル 沖縄大会2022
Follow us!
LIVE配信
大会詳細情報
全国高校生
花いけバトル
ストリ

北海道大会 2022
Hanaike Battle
Hokkaido Round 2022
2022/11/13 START 12:00
モエレ沼公園　ガラスのピラミッド
全国高校生花いけバトル 北海道大会 2022
Follow us!
LIVE配信
大会詳細情報
全国高校生花いけバトル
アルストリオ

やまびこ
第3号
響きあう
やまびこ
YAMABIKO

やまびこ
第3号
響きあうやまびこ
YAMABIKO

やまびこ
第4号
響きあうやまびこ
YAMABIKO ACADEMY
YAMABIKO

YAMABIKO
やまびこ
第4号
響きあう
やまびこ

東京ミッドタウン・デザインハブ・
キッズ・ワークショップ 2022
Tokyo Midtown Design Hub Kids Workshop 2022
Dates: Sat 13 August –Sun 21 August 2022
Venue: Tokyo Midtown Design Hub (Midtown Tower 5F)
Organizer: Tokyo Midtown Design Hub
Booking Required https://designhub.jp/
DESIGN
HUB
2022.8.13 SAT-8.21 SUN
TOKYO
MIDTOWN
DESIGN HUB
KIDS
WORKSHOP
2022

東京ミッドタウン・デザインハブ・
キッズ・ワークショップ2022
Tokyo Midtown Design Hub Kids Workshop 2022
Dates: Sat 13 August - Sun 21 August 2022
Venue: Tokyo Midtown Design Hub (Midtown Tower 5F)
Organizer: Tokyo Midtown Design Hub
Booking Required https://designhub.jp/
Tokyo Midtown
DESIGN
HUB
2022.8.13 SAT-8.21 SUN
TOKYO MIDTOWN DESIGN HUB KIDS WORKSHOP 2022

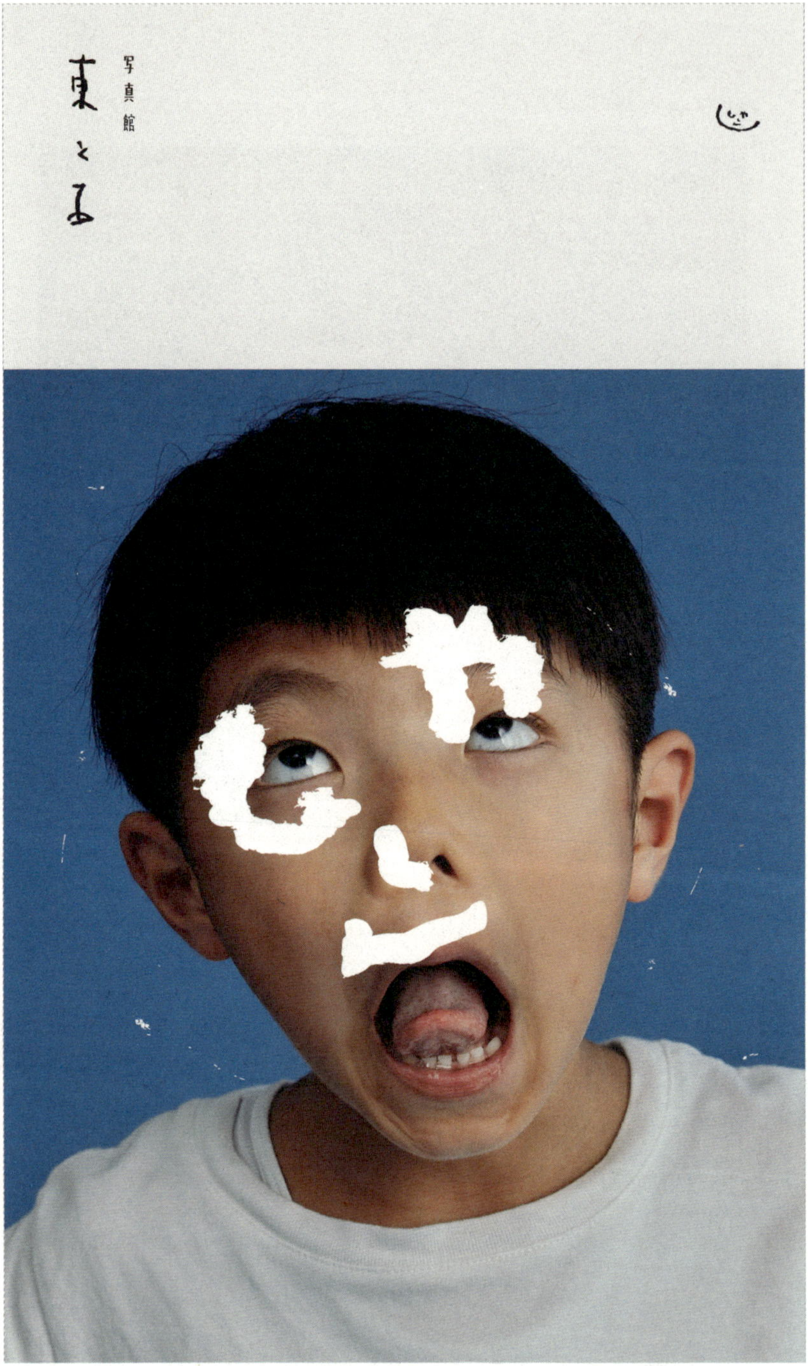
東とる
写真館

写真館

東とま

SORA KASA KIT
MY FIRST
UMBRELLA
Ca Et La

SORA
KASA KIT
MY FIRST
UMBRELLA
Ca Et La

Shunsuke Suzuki

Born in 2002, Shunsuke Suzuki creates art revolving around the theme of his inner self while working for an advertising production company in Tokyo.

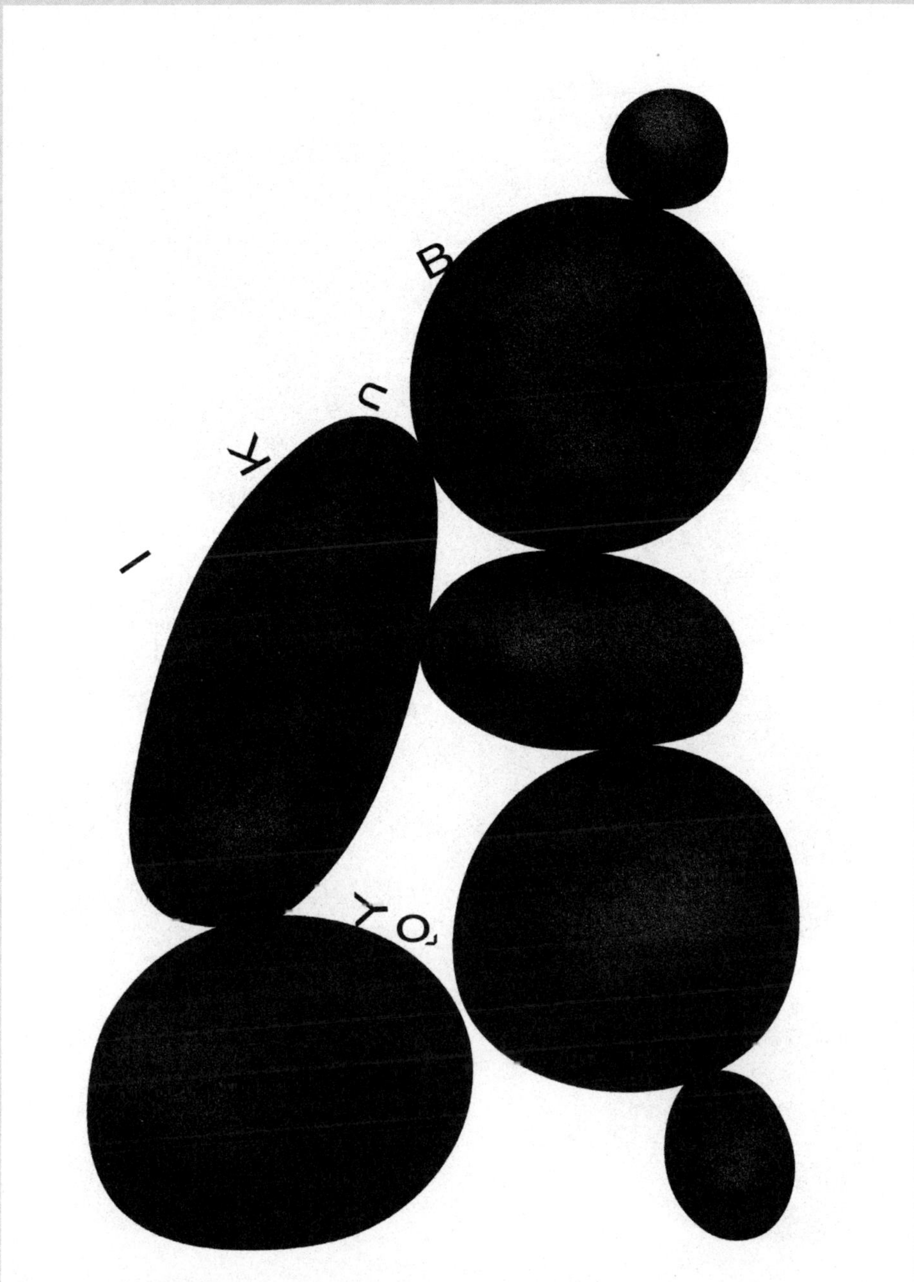

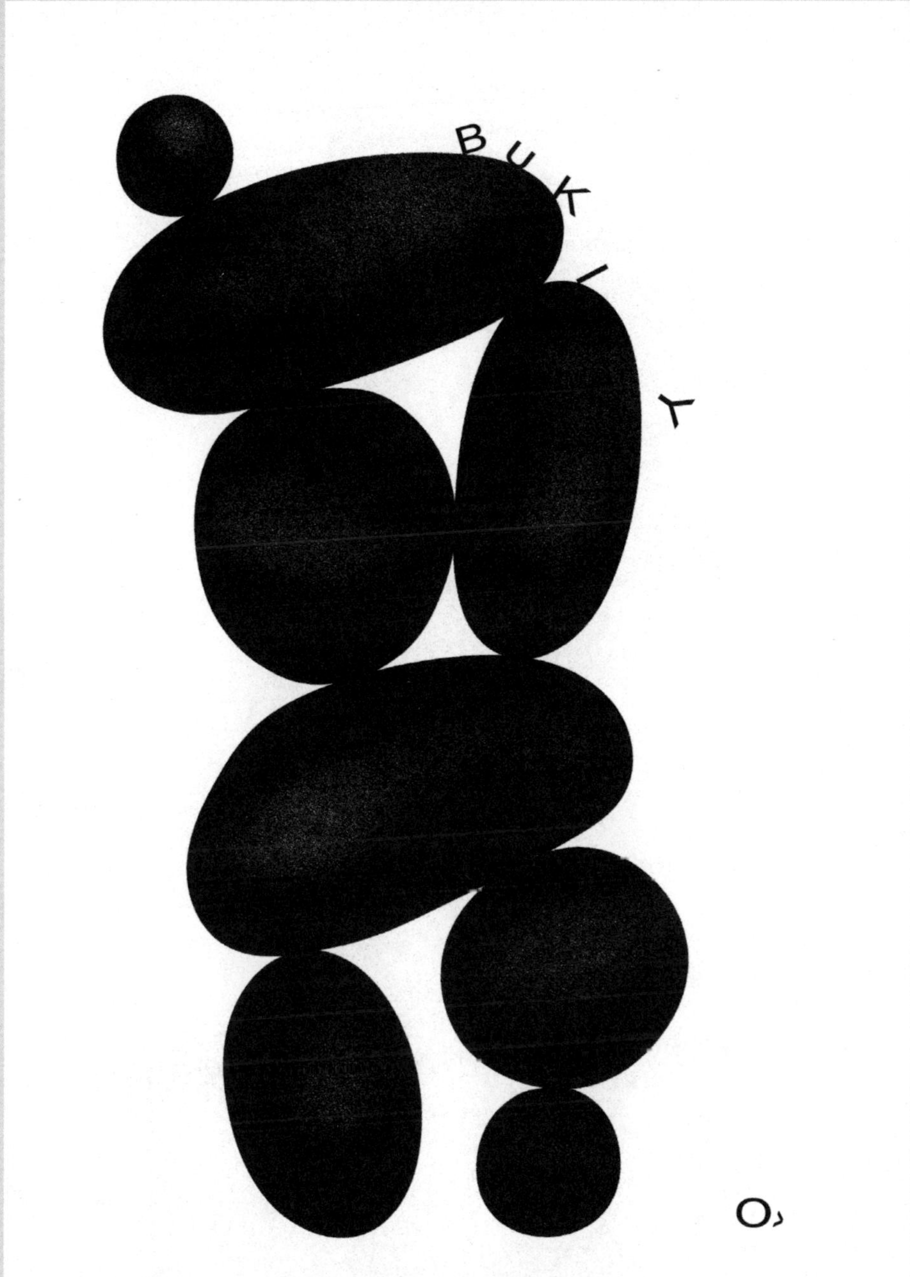
B U K I Y

まだ
自を　分
らな知　い

まだ
自を分
らな知い

よくばる

Tree
When human beings try to live
more humanly, their figure closely
resembles the powerful nature.

Tree
When human beings try to live
more humanly, their figure closely
resembles the powerful nature.

Sitoh inc.

Sitoh inc. is a Tokyo-based consulting firm that focuses on communication design. Through creativity, the team is dedicated to extracting the context that maximises a company's philosophy and principles in building up a corporate stance that best embodies its world-view.

TRAILS
O
0 — 0 : 900Steps

TRAILS 1
1 — 1: 500 Steps

TRAILS 2
2 — 2: 500 Steps

TRAILS 3
3—3: 600Steps

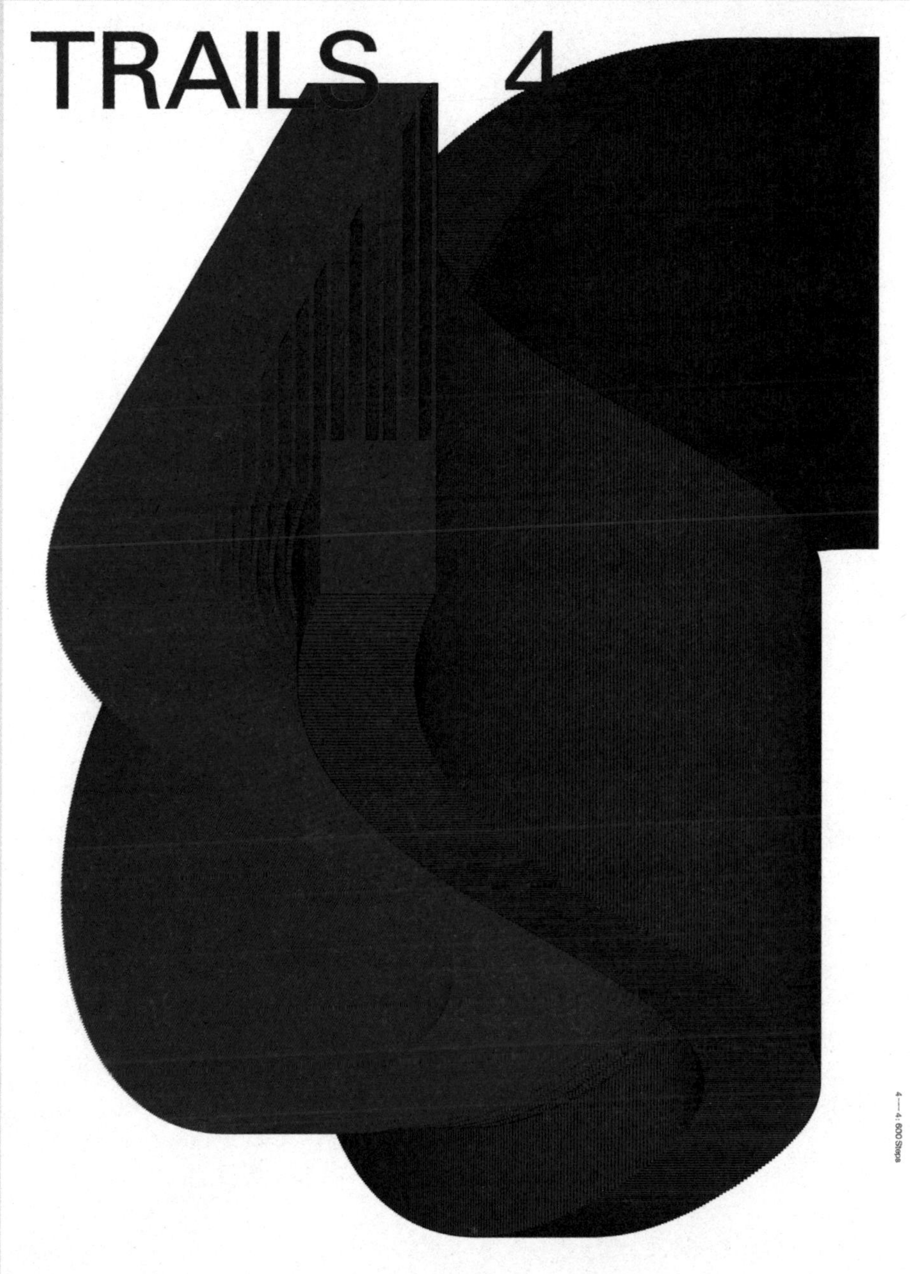
TRAILS
4
4 — 4: 600 Steps

THE FRAGMENT ASSEMBLY, shatter HAIR & MAKEUP
B1 3-4-9 JINGUMAE, SHIBUYA-KU, TOKYO 150-0001 03-6447-5495 SHATTER.TOKYO
OPEN WEEKDAY 11:00-20:00 / SATURDAY & SUNDAY 10:00-19:00 / TUESDAY CLOSED
6 30
Grand
Opening 11A.M.

THE FRAGMENT ASSEMBLY, shatter HAIR & MAKEUP
B1 3-4-9 JINGUMAE, SHIBUYA-KU, TOKYO 150-0001 03-6447-5495 SHATTER.TOKYO
OPEN WEEKDAY 11:00-20:00 / SATURDAY & SUNDAY 10:00-19:00 / TUESDAY CLOSED
7/02
Reception
Party 18P.M.

Strange
of
Japan
support Japanese artists and craftworkers who
aesthetics. The qualification criteria are
tists and their work to inherit and value
tradition, yet to think outside the box.
We will meet person-to-person with each artist,
in order to select
Art Work
Wood Turning

Art Work
Wood Turning | Yonehara
Strange
of
Japan
STRANGE OF JAPAN is a project to discover and support Japanese artists and craftworkers who carry high aesthetics. The qualification criteria are for the artists and their work to inherit and value Japanese tradition, yet to think outside the box. We will meet person-to-person with each artist, prize them on the personal level in order to select and offer the clients the very best.

för ägg ITOIGAWA | 2116 Hiraushi, Itoigawa-shi, Niigata, 941-0047 Open: 10:00-18:00 Close: Wed, Thu / för ägg JOETSU | elmar 1F 113, 3-8-8 Nishihon-cho, Joetsu-shi, Niigata, 942-0004 Open: 10:00-20:00 / www.f-agg.com @foragg_official

I'M POS
S
I
B
LE
GRAPHIC DESIGN BY

DESIGNS FOR
TRAVEL BOA
RD

DESIGNS FOR
TRAVEL EXPE
ERIENCE

THE GATE by SUNDAY MOUNTAIN

GA

STUDIO WONDER Co.,Ltd.

STUDIO WONDER's designs are characterised by the creation and development of images from concepts and keywords. The studio offers a wide range of creative and consultation services spanning branding, packaging, way-finding, and motion graphics — centred on originality.

春物 予約会
2023 1.16 mon → 2.28 tue
PARCOカードもしくはポケパル払いで対象の予約商品が
最大10％OFF!!
詳細はこちら →
札幌PARCO

daughter,
MOTHER,

daughter,
MOTHER

20
札幌 PARCO
22
PCS WRAP
PARCO CULTURE SUPERMARKET
03.19 SAT
→
03.21 MON

PARCO
CULTURE
SUPERMARKET
NO.2
(VOLUME UP)
パルコ
カルチャースーパーマーケット
2022
09.17 sat - 09.19 mon
11:00-20:00
AT
SAPPORO
PARCO7F
SPACE7

SOFT SERVE ICE CREAM
OMELETTE RICE
SANDWICH
珈琲
食事
PARFAIT
BEEF STEW
COFFEE

PUDDING
GOOD TIME
HAMBURG STEAK
CURRY
NEAPOLITAN
TEA

Susukino Kissa
CAFE AND RESTAURANT
Purple Dahlia
sk
珈琲
食事
SANDWICH
BEEF STEW
COFFEE
SOFT SERVE ICE CREAM
GOOD TIME
PARFAIT
TEA
HAMBURG STEAK
CURRY RICE
OMELETTE RICE
PUDDING
NEAPOLITAN

珈琲
食事
PUDDING
HAMBURG
STEAK
CURRY
BEEF
STEW
RICE
OMELETTE
TEA
COFFEE
SOFT
SERVE
ICE
CREAM
GOOD
TIME
NEAPOLITAN
SANDWICH
PARFAIT
薄野喫茶 パープルダリア
CAFE AND RESTAURANT
Purple Dahlia

CAFE AND RESTAURANT
Purple Dahlia sk
Susukino Kissa
BEEF STEW
PARFAIT
HAMBURG STEAK
CURRY RICE
OMELETTE
SANDWICH
TEA
COFFEE
PUDDING
GOOD TIME
SOFT SERVE ICE CREAM
NEAPOLITAN
珈琲
食事

EYES SAY
SOMETHING
JAGDA HOKKAIDO
POSTER EXHIBITION 2016

EYES SAY
SOMETHING
JAGDA HOKKAIDO
POSTER EXHIBITION 2016

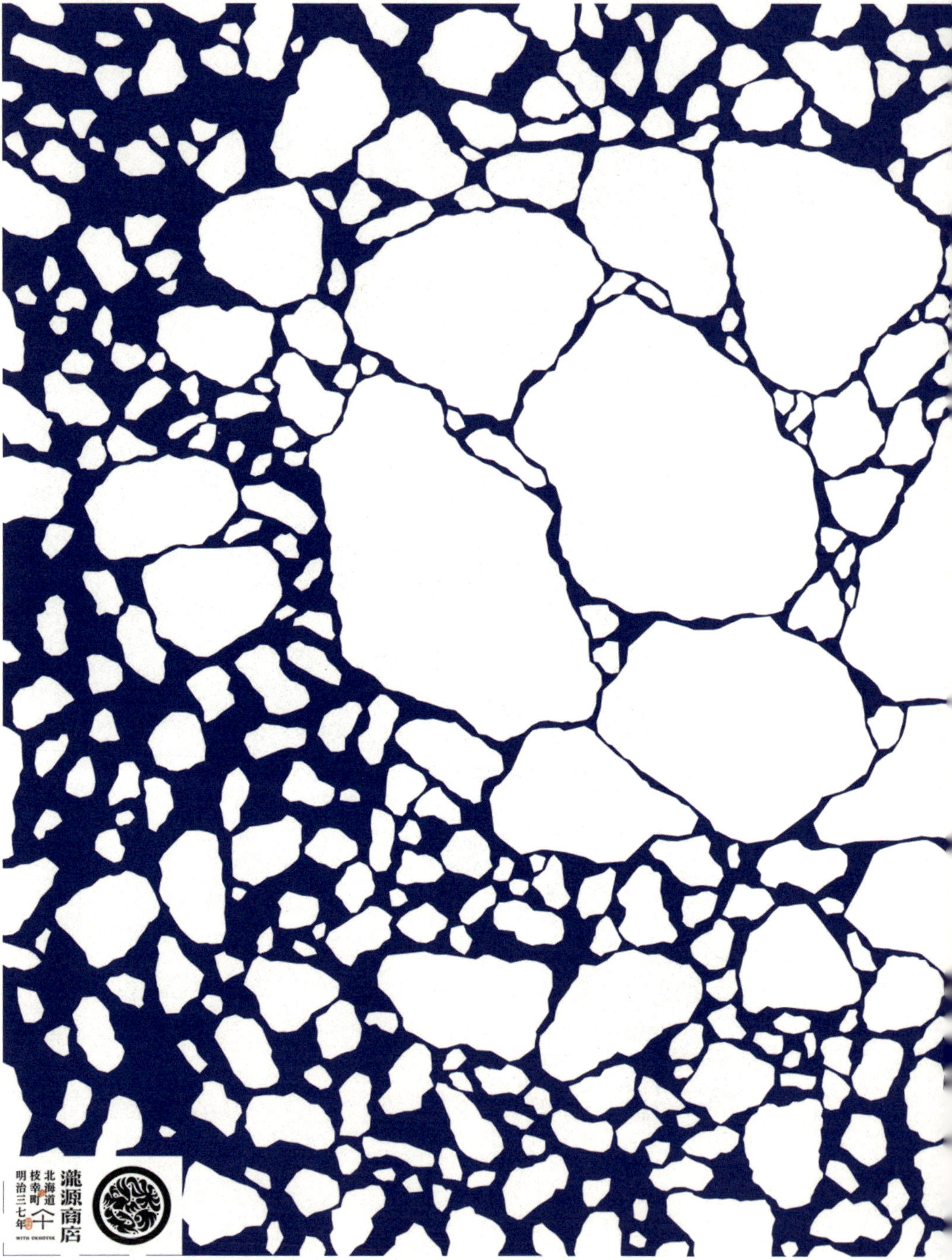
瀧源商店
北海道
枝幸町
明治三七年
WITH OKHOTSK

オホーツク、
生きた流氷の恵。

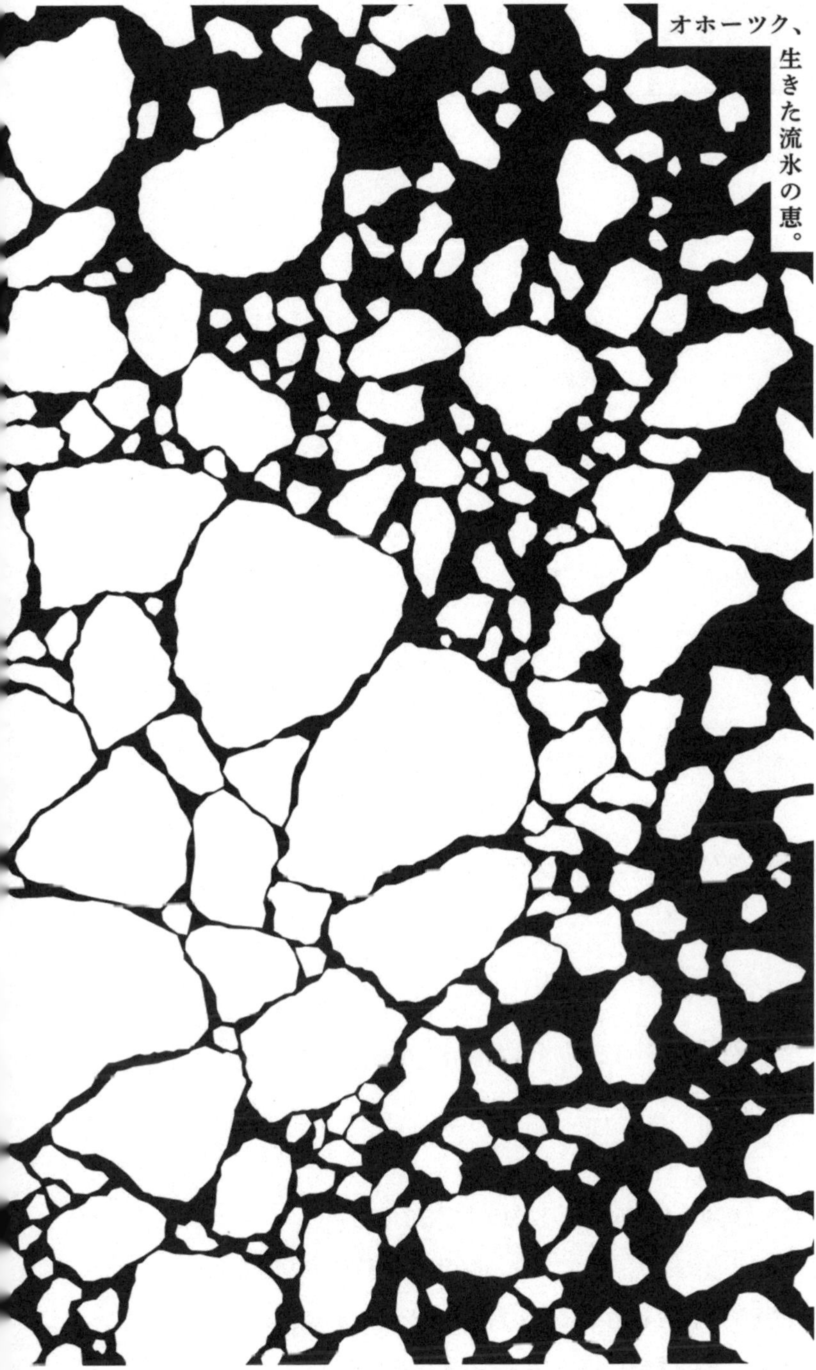

STUDY LLC.

STUDY LLC. in Tokyo was founded by Shizuoka-born Takahiro Eto, who graduated with a Ph.D. from Tama Art University in 2010. He enjoys experimenting with graphic design and expressions in various fields.

TAKAHIRO ETO EXHIBITION
BETWEEN SYMBOLS AND ILLUSTRATIONS
2018.10.7SUN–10.24WED TOKYO POLYTECHNIC UNIVERSITY

TAKAHIRO ETO Para-GRAPH
6-23 OCT. 2020
TOKYO POLYTECHNIC UNIVERSITY

TAKAHIRO ETO Para-GRAPH
6-23 OCT. 2020
TOKYO POLYTECHNIC UNIVERSITY

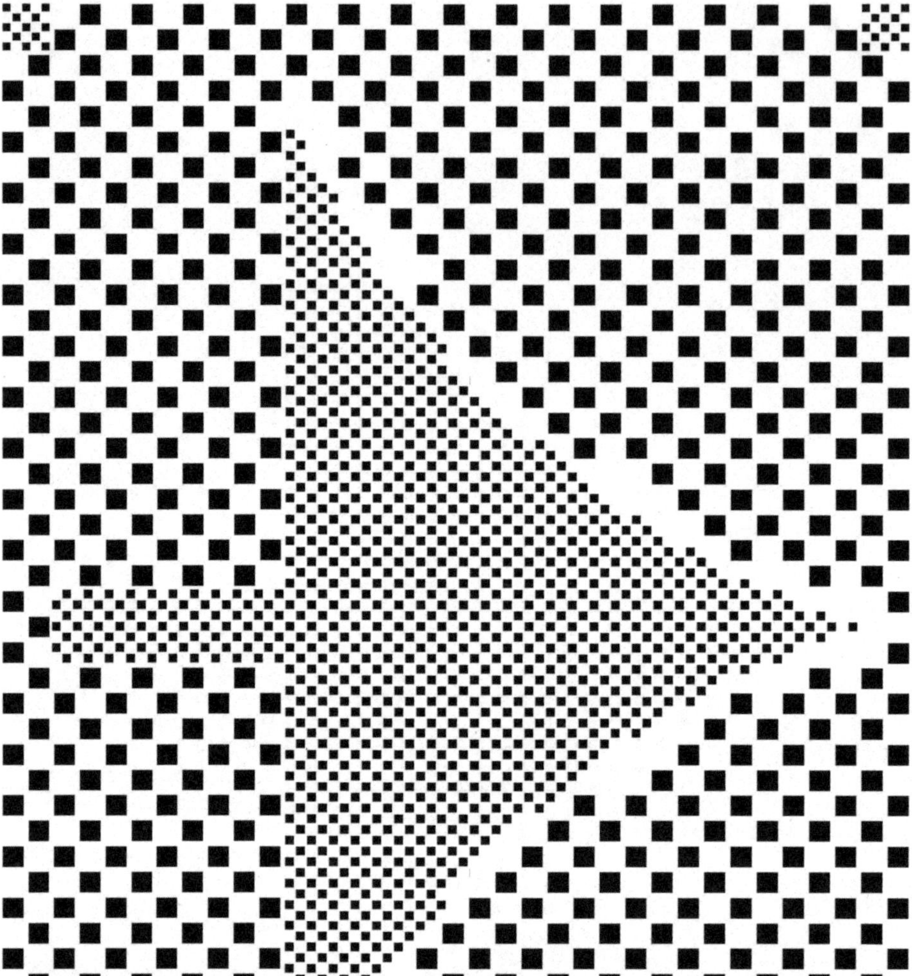

58CM
42CM

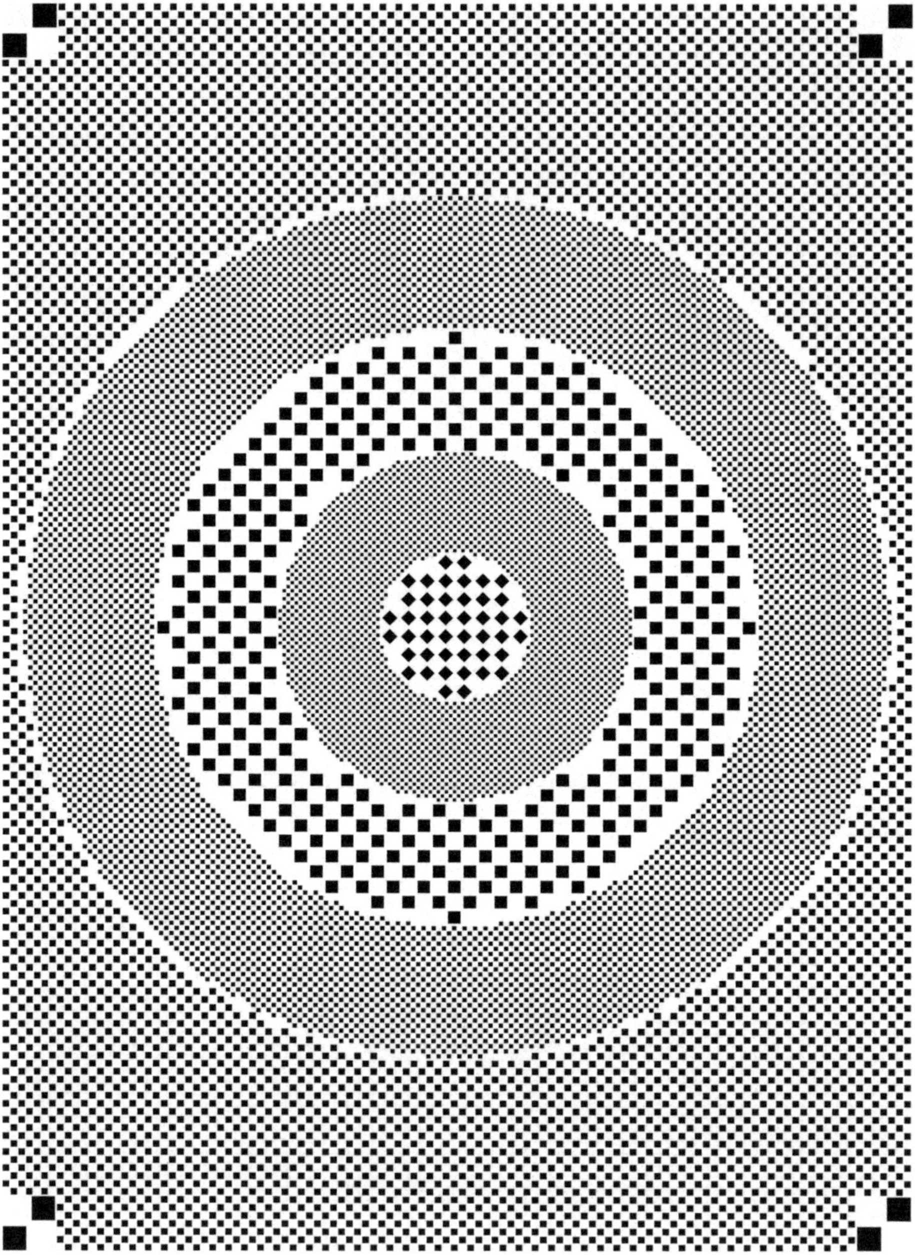

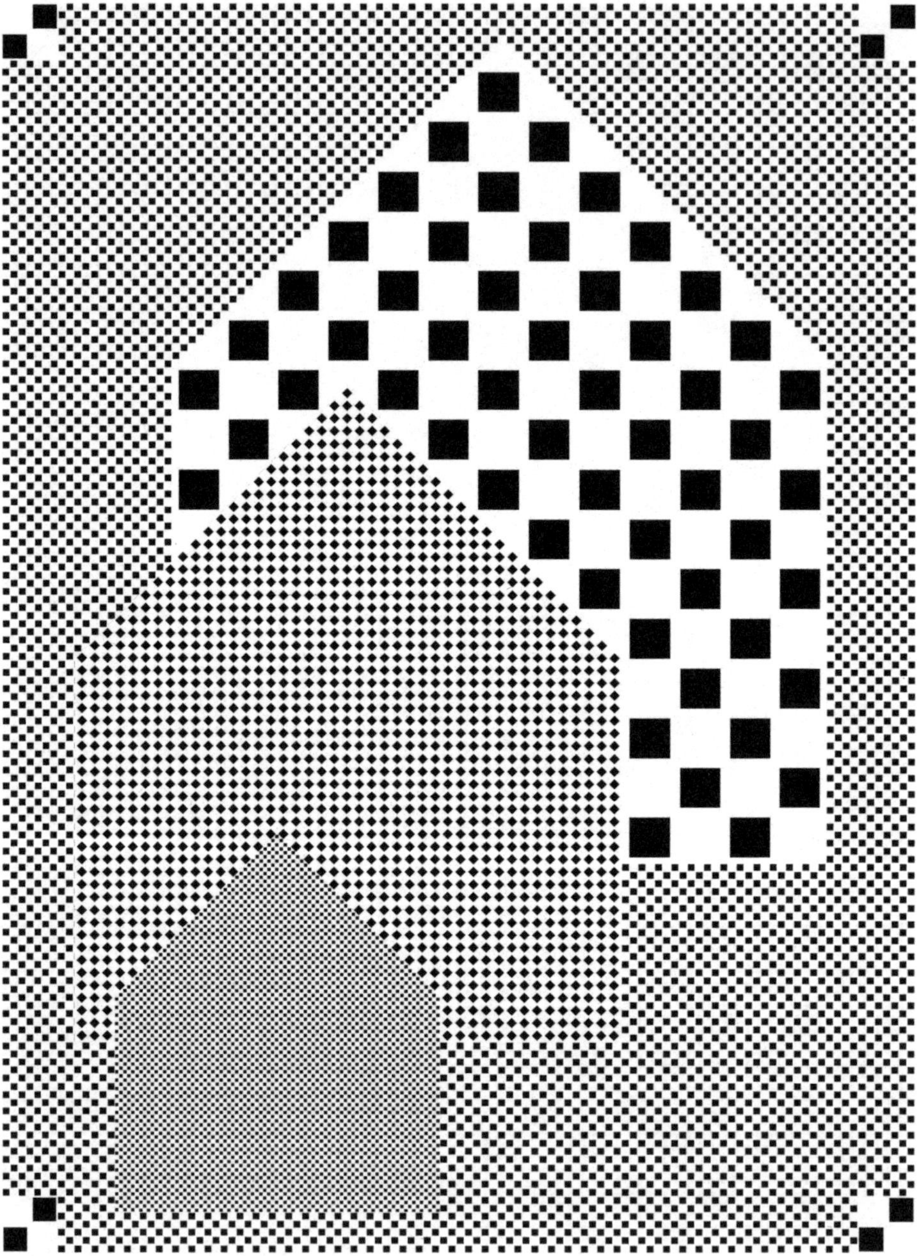

Tadashi Ueda

Born in Nara in 1988, Tadashi Ueda is a Tokyo-based freelance graphic designer.

鏘！
飛吧！！
咻
曲
1931
球
蘇正生安全
上二壘！
啪！
KANO

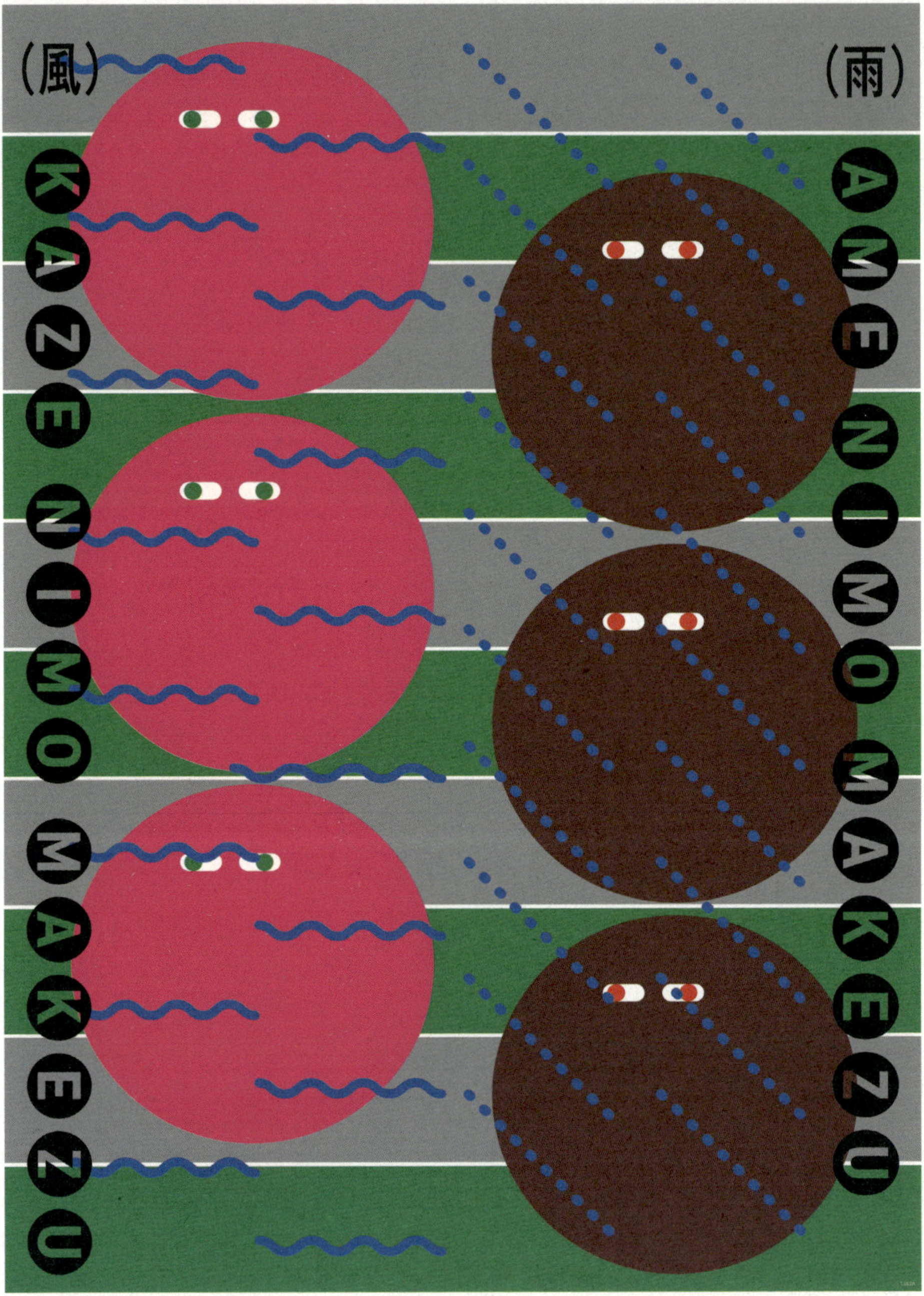
(風)
(雨)
KAZE NIMO MAKEZU
AME NIMO MAKEZU

Alexander Medel Calderón
Tadashi Ueda
握
手

石の上でも雑念
2021.9 ⇒ 2022.1
石の上にも三年という言葉をどう思いますか？
「三年って長くない？一年で良くない？」
「いやいや、三年いるとようやく見えてくものがあるんだよ。」
「そもそも何で石の上にいなきゃいけないの？」
ことわざ一つでも、いろいろな意見が出てきますよね。
そうなんですよ。この世界で生きていて思ったのは、考えは人それぞれということ。
自分が面白いと思うことが決して、他の人が良いと思うとは限らないのです。
でも、実際には自分は面白いと思う事実があります。
それはどうしたって、変えることが難しいですよね。
自分の面白いと思うことや、なぜ良いと感じたのか、誰かの意見に左右されずに、まずは共有することから
始めたいと思います。
松宮ブンカ・ラボ

Rising From A Night's Sleep
夜の眠りからの目覚め
Present Works Milwaukee, WI, USA
日本人たちによる展示
Observations of the Everyday in Japanese Graphic Design
日本のグラフィックデザインにおける日常の考察
7月12日(日)から8月3日(月)まで
July 12–
August 3, 2015
Opening Reception: Sunday, July 12, 6-9 PM
PRESENT WORKS × Gurafiku
Designed by Tadashi Ueda.

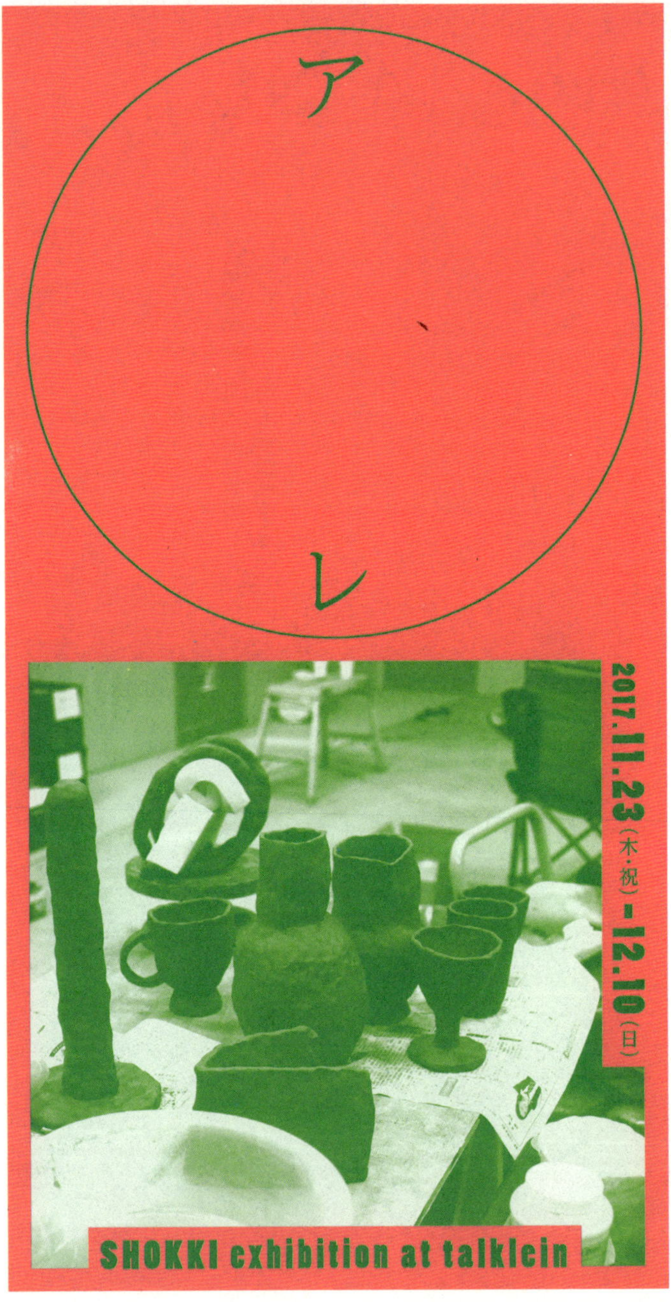
ア
レ
2017.11.23（木·祝）- 12.10（日）
SHOKKI exhibition at talklein

LUCK3月企画
LUCK014
ムムム
3月14日(火)〜4月2日(日)
小林聖也
11:00 OPEN 19:00 CLOSE
小指
水内実歌子
LUCK

Yamato Kitazono

Yamato Kitazono is a working designer and Aichi University of the Arts Graduate School of Fine Arts 2023 alumnus.

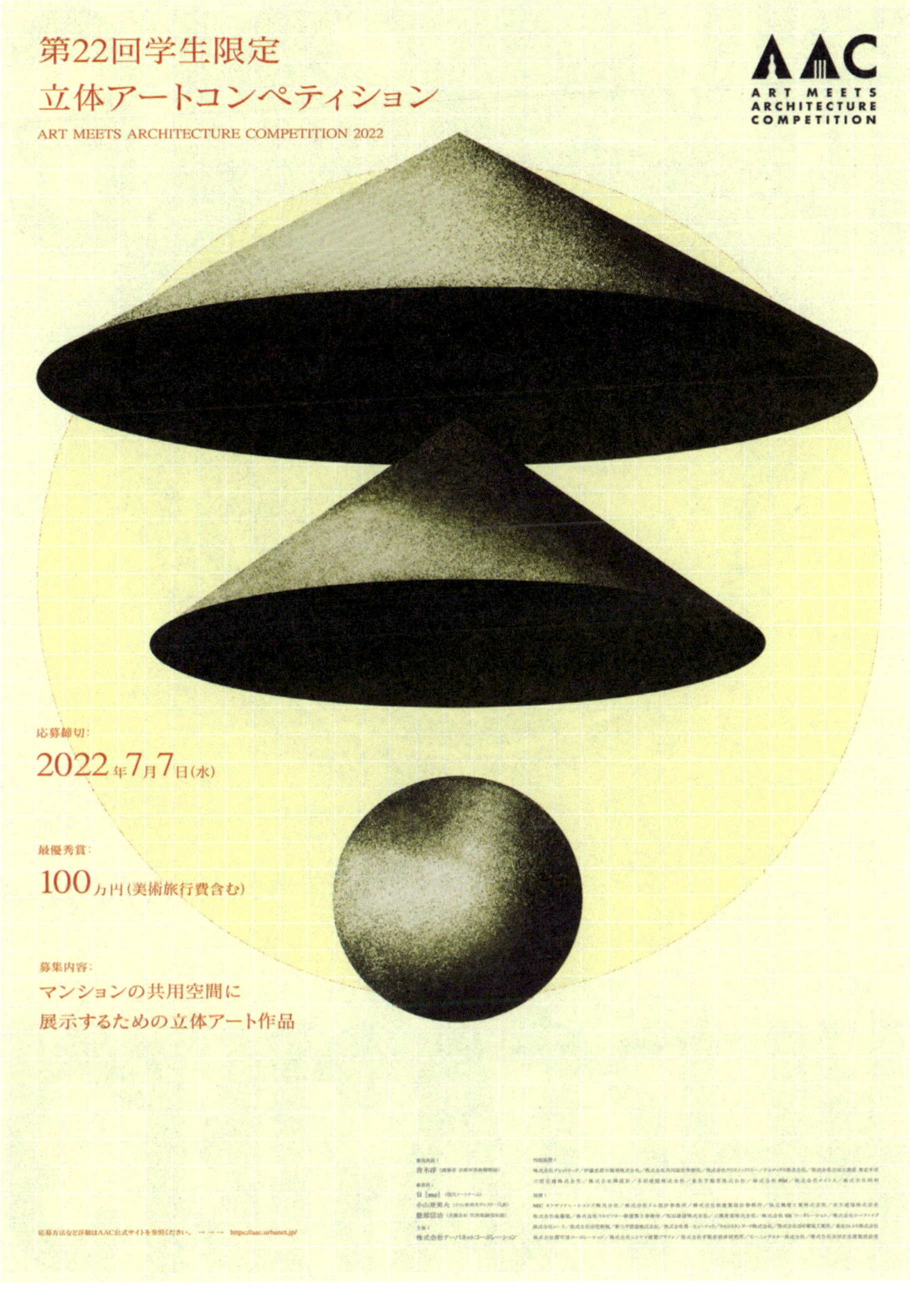

第22回学生限定
立体アートコンペティション
ART MEETS ARCHITECTURE COMPETITION 2022
AAC
ART MEETS ARCHITECTURE COMPETITION
応募締切:
2022年7月7日(水)
最優秀賞:
100万円(美術旅行費含む)
募集内容:
マンションの共用空間に
展示するための立体アート作品
応募方法など詳細はAAC公式サイトを参照ください。 → → → https://aac.urbanet.jp/
青木淳
目［mé］
株式会社アーバネットコーポレーション

INVISIBLE
You cannot see a person's true humanity.
INVISIBLE HUMANITY IPT 2021
HUMANITY

INVISIBLE HUMANITY IPT 2021
You cannot see a person's true humanity.

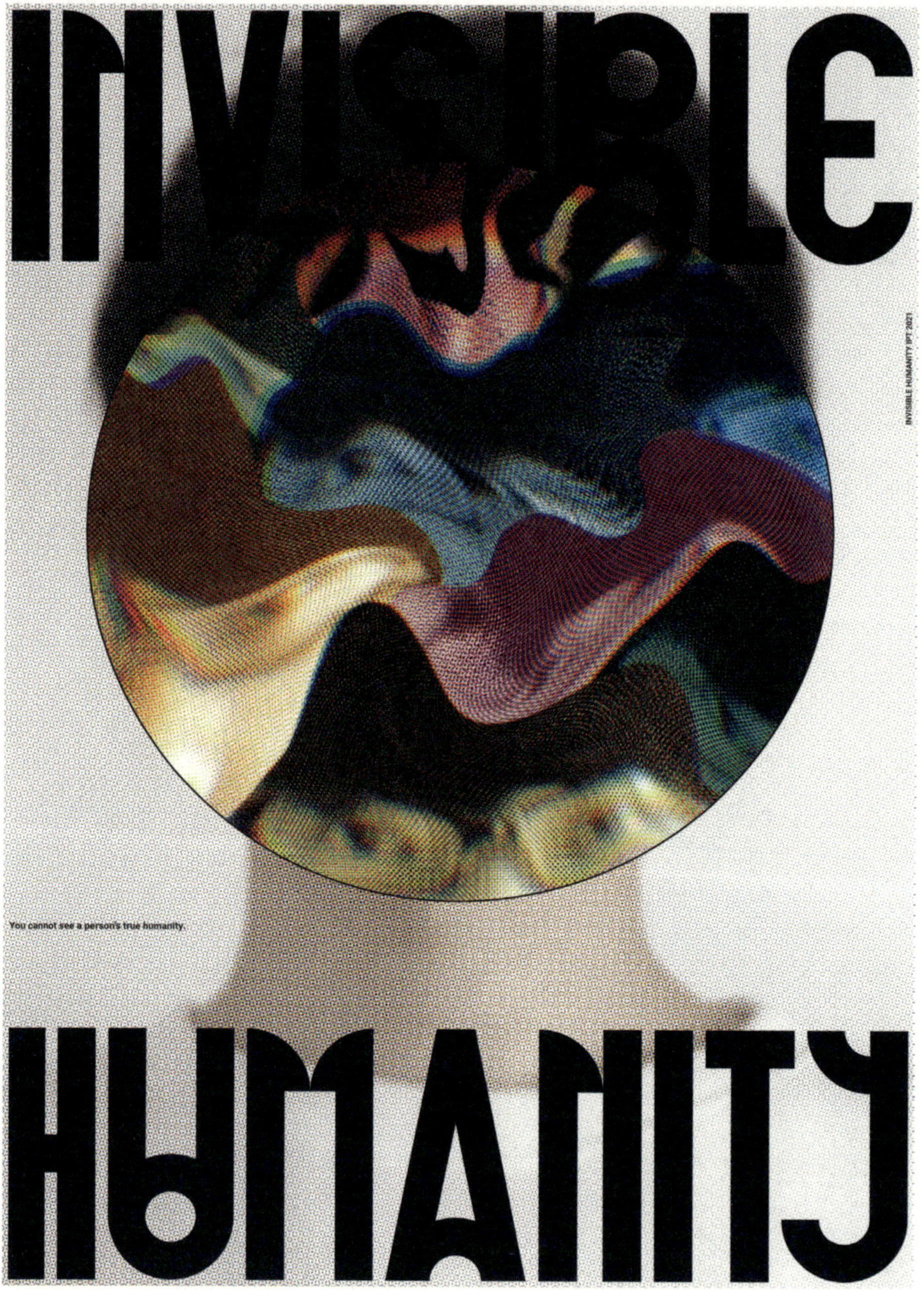
INVISIBLE
INVISIBLE HUMANITY IPT 2021
You cannot see a person's true humanity.
HUMANITY

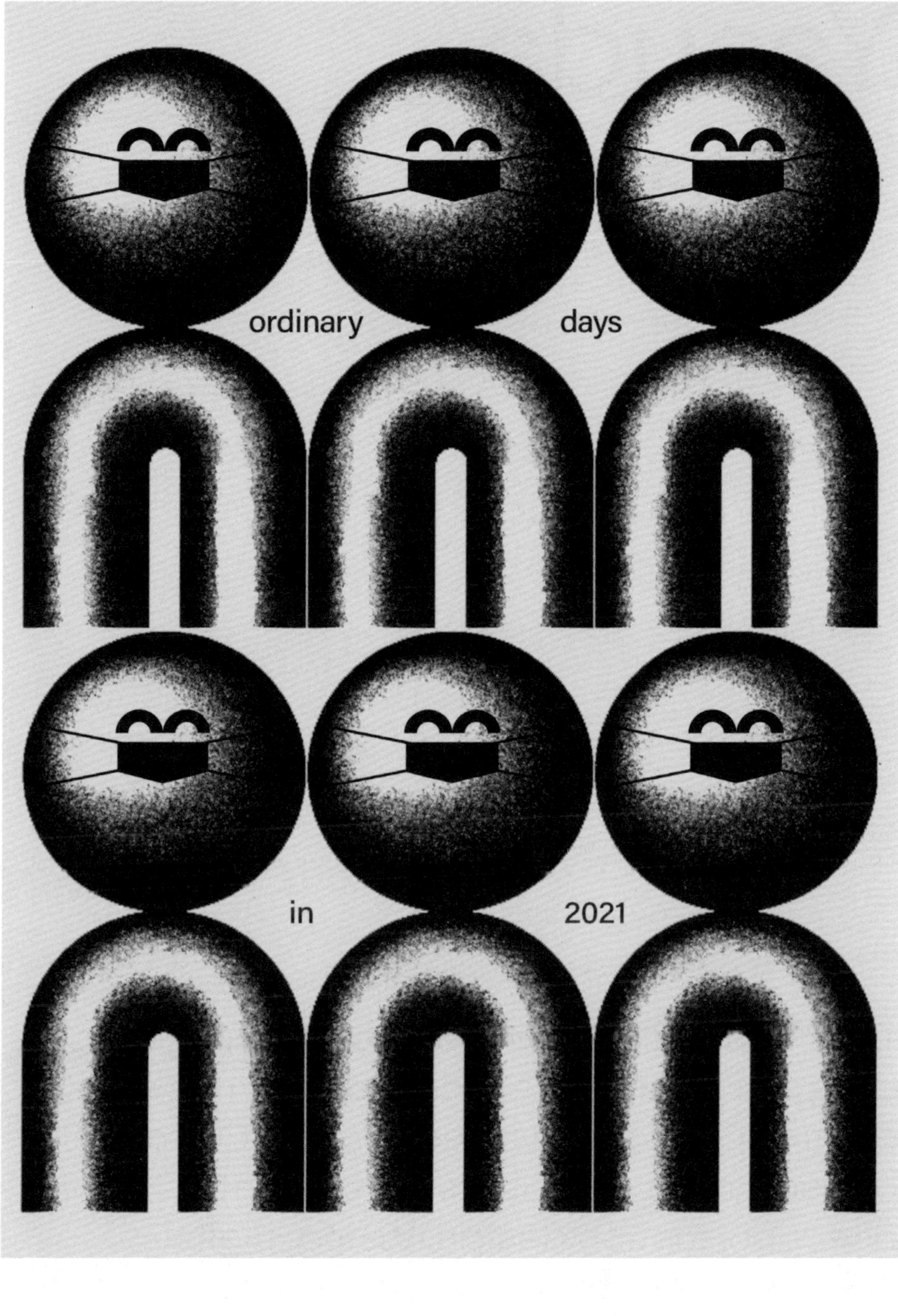
ordinary
days
in
2021

Yasuda Takahiro

Tokyo-based art director and graphic designer Takahiro Yasuda is also a member of the CEKAI creative association. On top of visual design, he is also proficient in film direction, motion design, VJ-ing, digital creative direction, and product design. His clients list includes NIKE, Red Bull, Goldwin, NHK, FamilyMart, and Google.

MYG PICTURES PRESENTS
IN ASSOCIATION WITH SPACEBUTE, HELIXES AND CEKAI
A MYG CREW PRODUCTION
AFTERGLOWS
A FILM BY TAICHI KIMURA
KENTEZ ASAKA
MEGUMI
AKIRA KOIEYAMA
KEIKO TAKESHITA
EXECUTIVE PRODUCER HIROKI SHIROTA, KENSUKE KIDANI, RYUNOSUKE SHIMURA
DIRECTOR OF PHOTOGRAPHY SEIYA UEHARA
CASTING BY KO IWAGAMI, YOKO YAMASHITA, KAIJU INC
MUSIC BY THOM YARDLEY, D.A.N.
WRITTEN BY RYOSUKE ASANO, YASUHIRO KIM
EDITED BY KENICHI HIRAI
PRODUCED BY TAKUMA HIRAMATSU, YUTARO TAGAWA
DIRECTED BY TAICHI KIMURA

B
elt
F
urniture
Daisuke Motogi · 元木 大輔
DDAA LAB Exhibition
Belt Furniture · ベルトファニチャー展
Venue · 会場 : HAPPA · ハッパ
1F 2-30-6, Kamimeguro, Meguro-ku,
Tokyo, Japan · 東京都 目黒区 上目黒
二丁目 三十番地 六号 一階 Date · 会期 :
June 24th Thu. - 27th Sun. · 六月二十四日(木) 〜 二十七日(日)
Open · 時間 : P.M.12 - P.M.19 · 午後十二時 〜 午後十九時

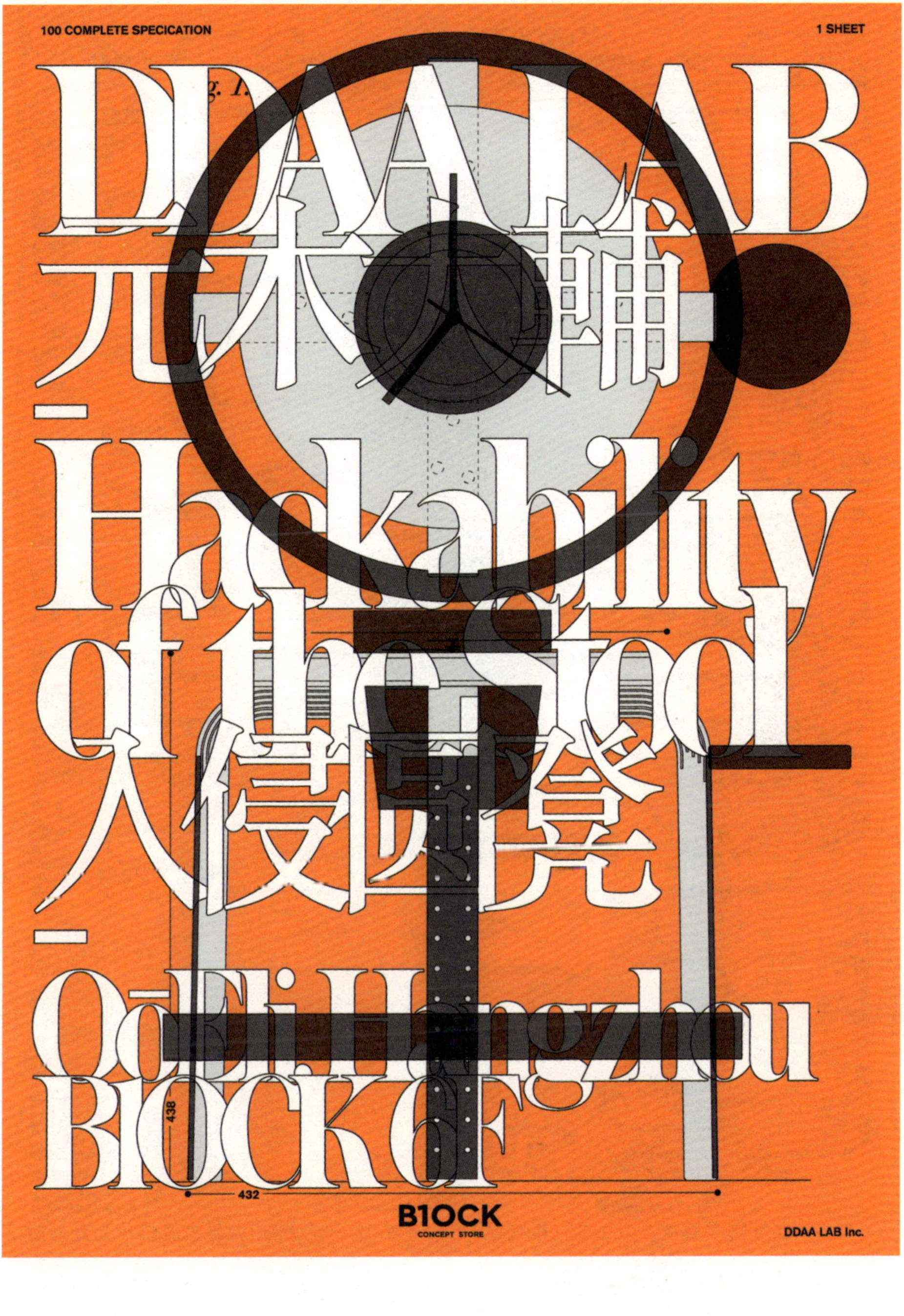
100 COMPLETE SPECICATION
1 SHEET
DDAA LAB
元木大輔
Hackability
of the Stool
OōEli Hangzhou
BlOCK 6F
438
432
B1OCK
CONCEPT STORE
DDAA LAB Inc.

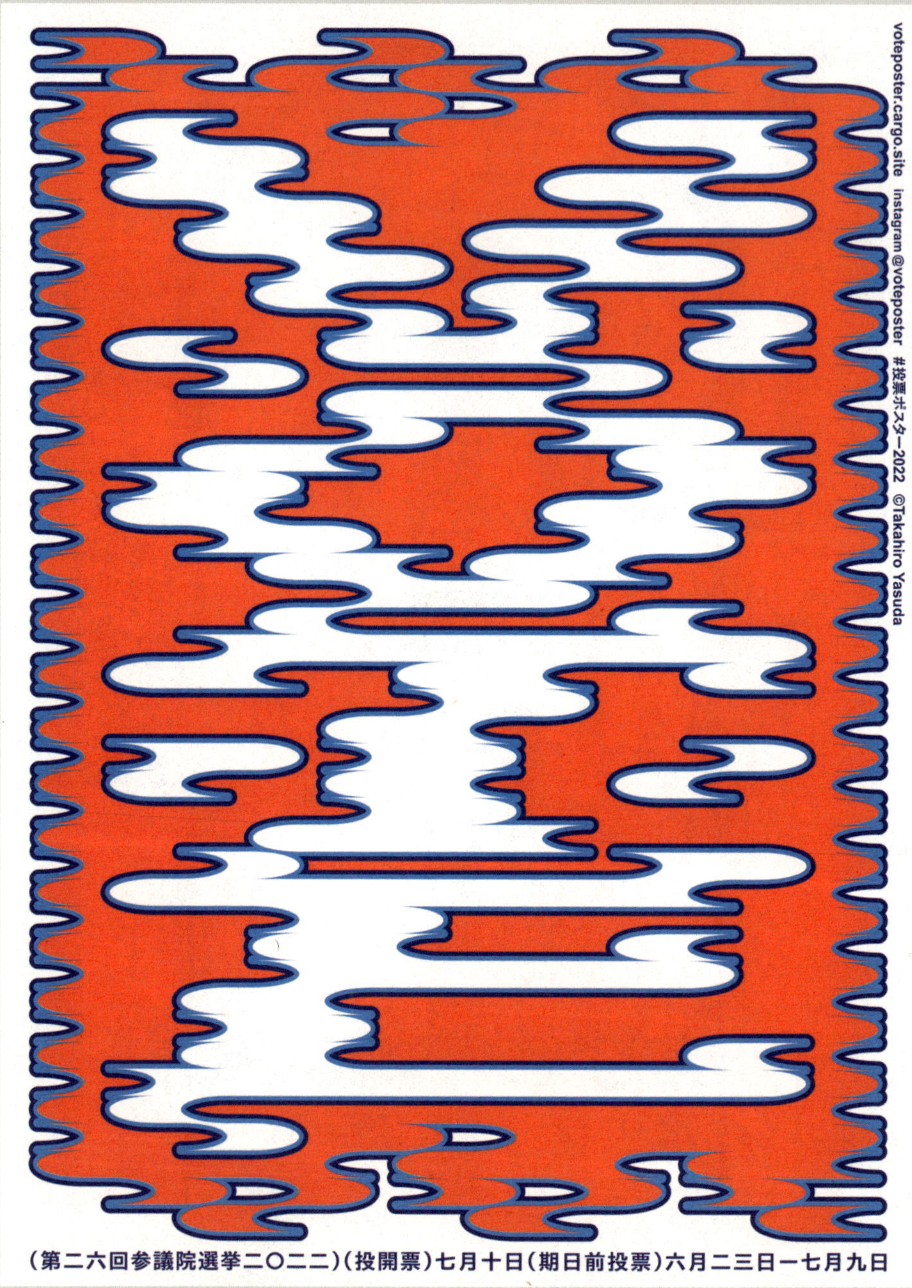
voteposter.cargo.site instagram@voteposter #投票ポスター2022 ©Takahiro Yasuda
（第二六回参議院選挙二〇二二）（投開票）七月十日（期日前投票）六月二三日ー七月九日

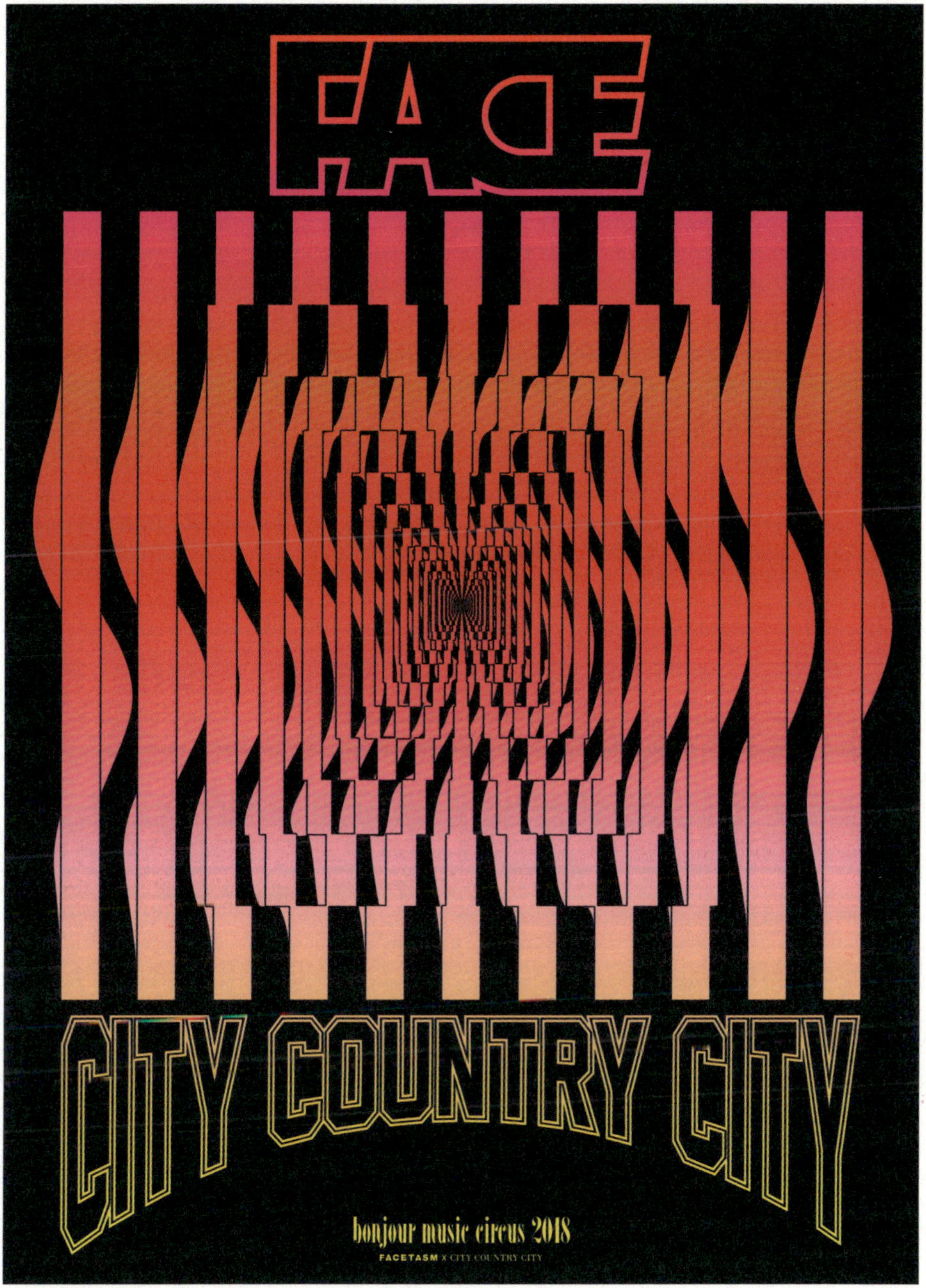
FACE
CITY COUNTRY CITY
bonjour music circus 2018
FACETASM X CITY COUNTRY CITY

EXPERIMENTAL
CREATIONS
EXPERIMENTAL CREATIONS 2017 TOKYO 16TH —— 22ND OCTOBER 12:00-20:00
ARAKAWA GRIP NEW SHOWROOM "TIERS" 5-7-12-1F JINGUMAE, SHIBUYA-KU, TOKYO
AMAM | Kairi Eguchi | oog design studio | STUDIO BYCOLOR | studio yumakano | Kunikazu Hamanishi | broom | Yu Matsuda, Yuichiro Tani | Jun Murakoshi Produced by Yumi Ueno

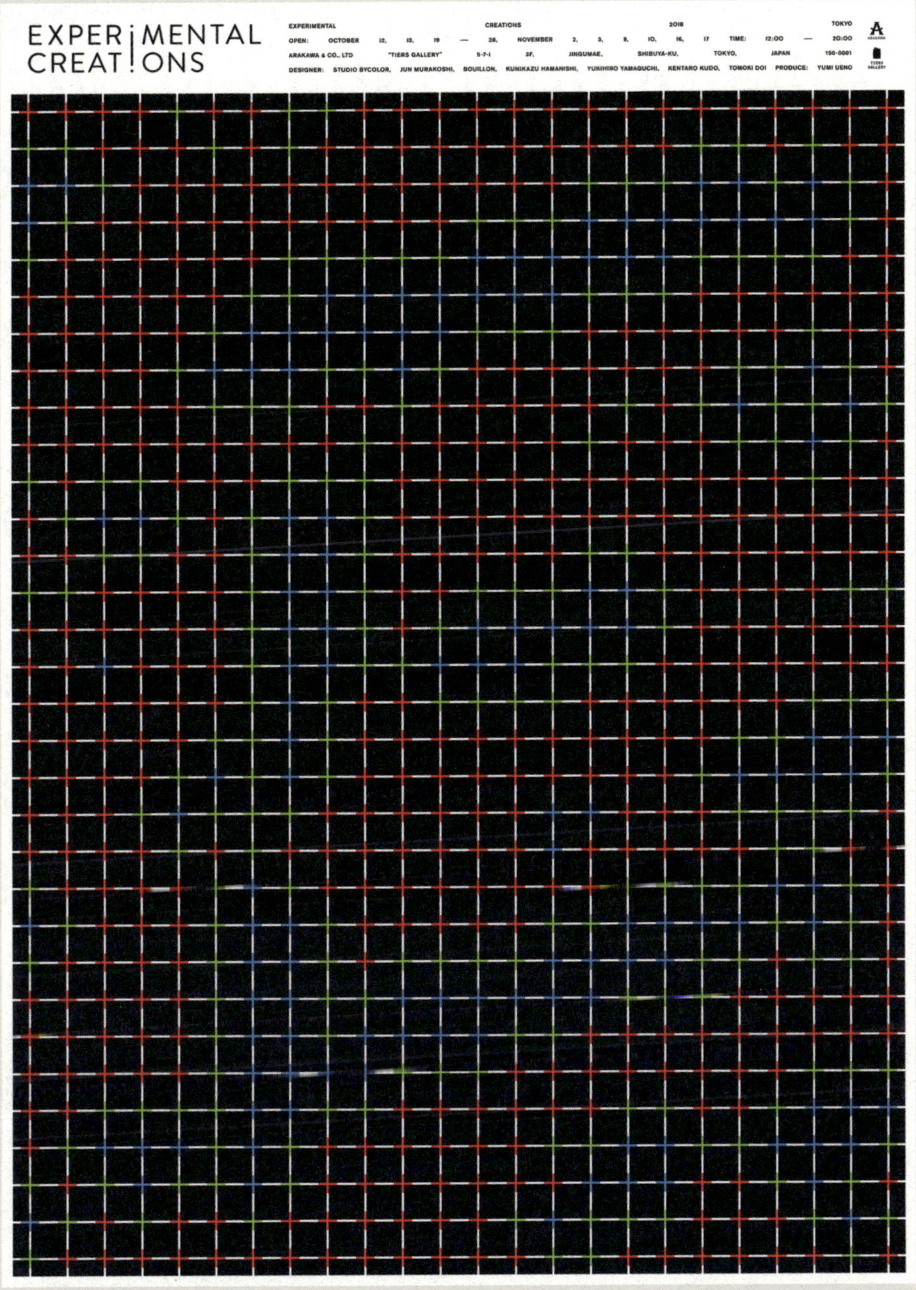

EXPER¡MENTAL
CREAT!ONS
EXPERIMENTAL CREATIONS 2018 TOKYO
OPEN: OCTOBER 12, 13, 19 — 28, NOVEMBER 2, 3, 9, 10, 16, 17 TIME: 12:00 — 20:00
ARAKAWA & CO., LTD "TIERS GALLERY" 5-7-1 3F, JINGUMAE, SHIBUYA-KU, TOKYO, JAPAN 150-0001
DESIGNER: STUDIO BYCOLOR, JUN MURAKOSHI, BOUILLON, KUNIKAZU HAMANISHI, YUKIHIRO YAMAGUCHI, KENTARO KUDO, TOMOKI DOI PRODUCE: YUMI UENO

EMERGE

unconscious
emerge
takahiro yasuda
2021

Laforet
Grand
Bazar
2021
7.17-25

2022
Laforet
Grand
Bazar
1.22-30

Yudai Osawa

Born in 1984, Tama Art University alumnus Yudai Osawa is an art director and graphic designer. Since the mid-2010s, he has been focusing on projects rooted in social issues, through which he constantly searches for ways to contribute to society through design. He is also an active member of the "UNKNOWN ME" ambient unit and "Atoris".

Model
13–28
March
Hoshiki Ara
Exhibition
Model
Hoshiki Ara Exhibition
3.13fri – 28sat. 2020
hpgrp GALLERY TOKYO
hpgrp

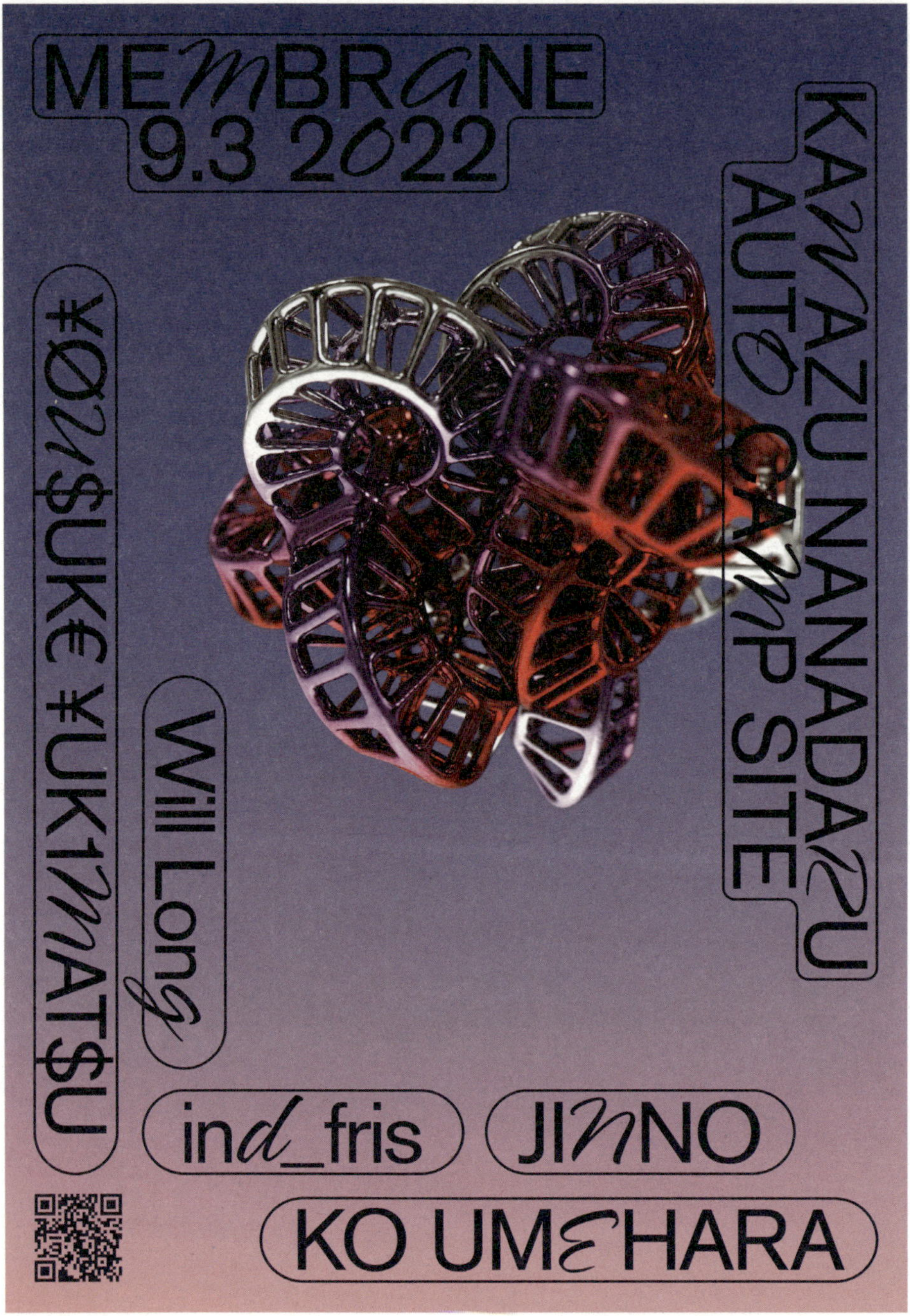
MEMBRANE
9.3 2022
KAWAZU NANADARU
AUTO CAMP SITE
YOUSUKE YUKIMATSU
Will Long
ind_fris
JINNO
KO UMEHARA

CulTech Forum
Japan 2022
文化のDXを考える〜CulTech Forum Japan 2022〜
2022年5月17日(火)13:00〜19:00 竹芝ポートホール
主催=国際大学グローバル・コミュニケーション・センター
#CTFJ2022
5.17tue 13:00–19:00
@Takeshiba Port Hall
Presented by GLOCOM
Culture×DX

PULSE
1.29
2023
蜂
1.29
蜂
PUL
2023

（エン）
2022 11.22 Tue
PGDC-0013
3,000 JPY+Tax
RYUTist
1. 支度
2. 朝の惑星
3. うらぎりもの
4. オーロラ
5. しるし
6. 水硝子
7. たったいま、さっきまで
8. PASSPort
9. 逃避行

HUMAN
SON/C

SON/C
SONIC Agency Inc.
Shinjuku-ku, Tokyo 161-0034, Japan
www.sonic-agency.com

95年からDJを開始。川崎工場地帯の某工場屋上にて行われているインダストリアル・レイブ・パーティー“DK SOUND”で、k404とのTraks BoysとしてレジデントDJを務める。バンド(((さらうんど)))、Jintana & Emeraldsのメンバーとしても活動中。2020年5月に最新アルバム“Aburelu”を自らのレーベル“Cizima”よりリリース。

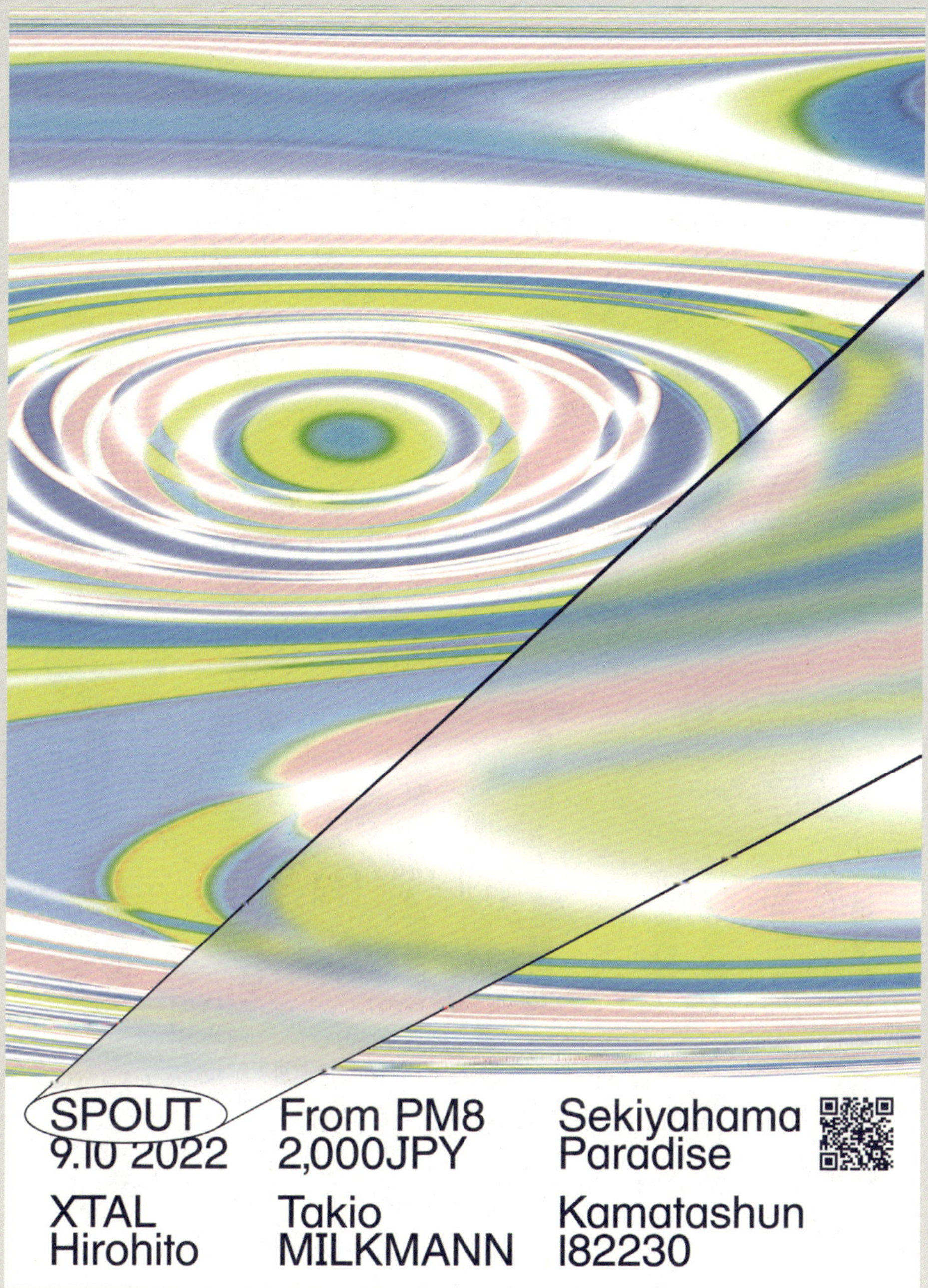
SPOUT
9.10 2022
From PM8
2,000JPY
Sekiyahama
Paradise
XTAL
Hirohito
Takio
MILKMANN
Kamatashun
182230

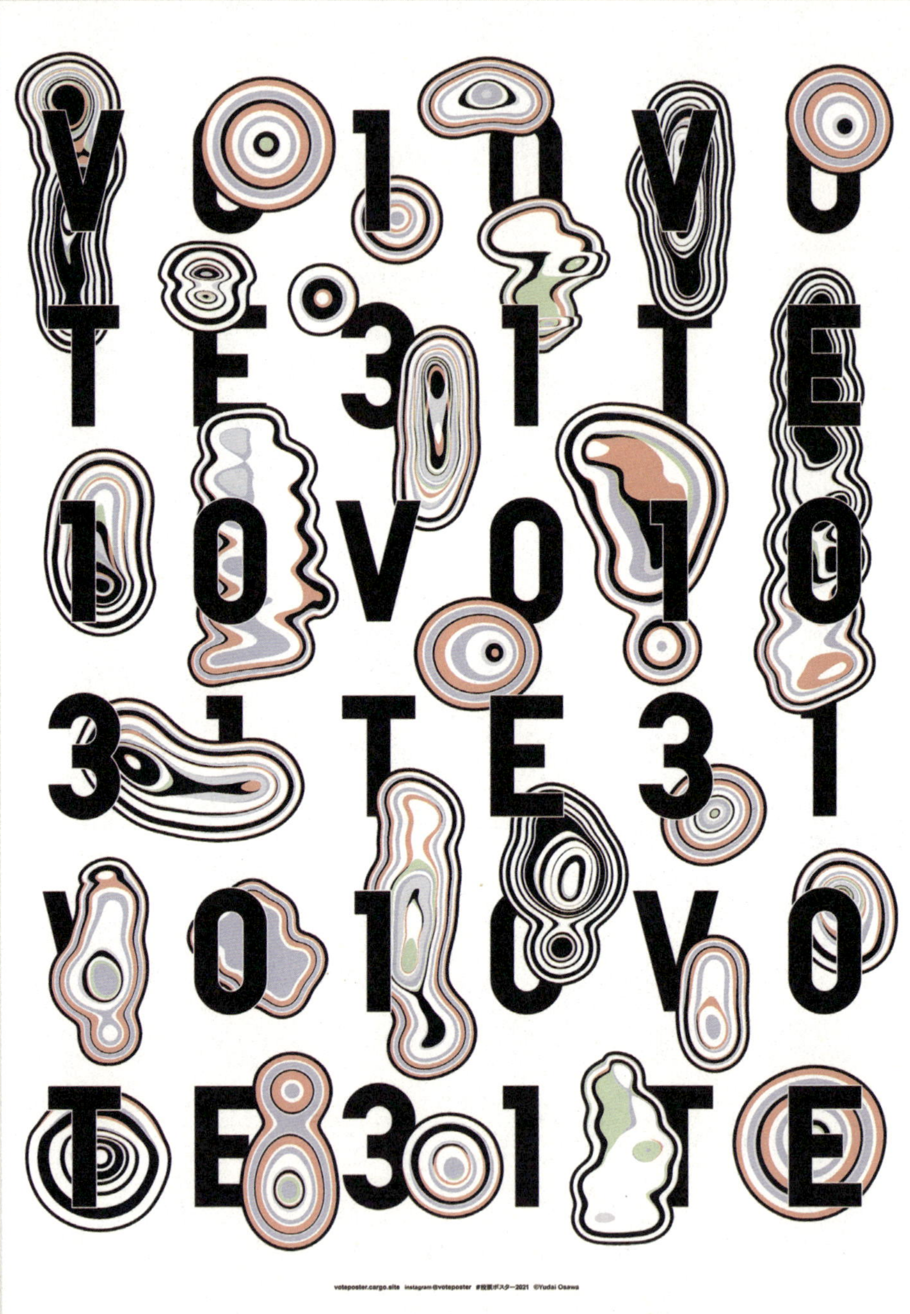
VO10VO
TE31TE
10VO10
31TE31
VO10VO
TE31TE
voteposter.cargo.site instagram @voteposter #投票ポスター2021 ©Yudai Osawa

Yuta Miura

Upon graduating from Tokyo Zokei University in 2017, Yuta Miura began working as an art director at an advertising agency in the same year. On top of graphic design, he also works on advertising as well character planning and design projects. His work has won many accolades, including an Asahi Advertising Award, Tokyo TDC Prize, Japan Typography Annual feature, and D&AD Shortlist. He is also a member of the Japan Graphic Designers Association.

Bloom

Branch

Fall

hello
summer

Kouzushima island
神集島

リトー/イン/トーキョー
MIURA YUTA SOLO EXHIBITION
2020.3.25(WED)~4.5(SUN) PARK GALLERY

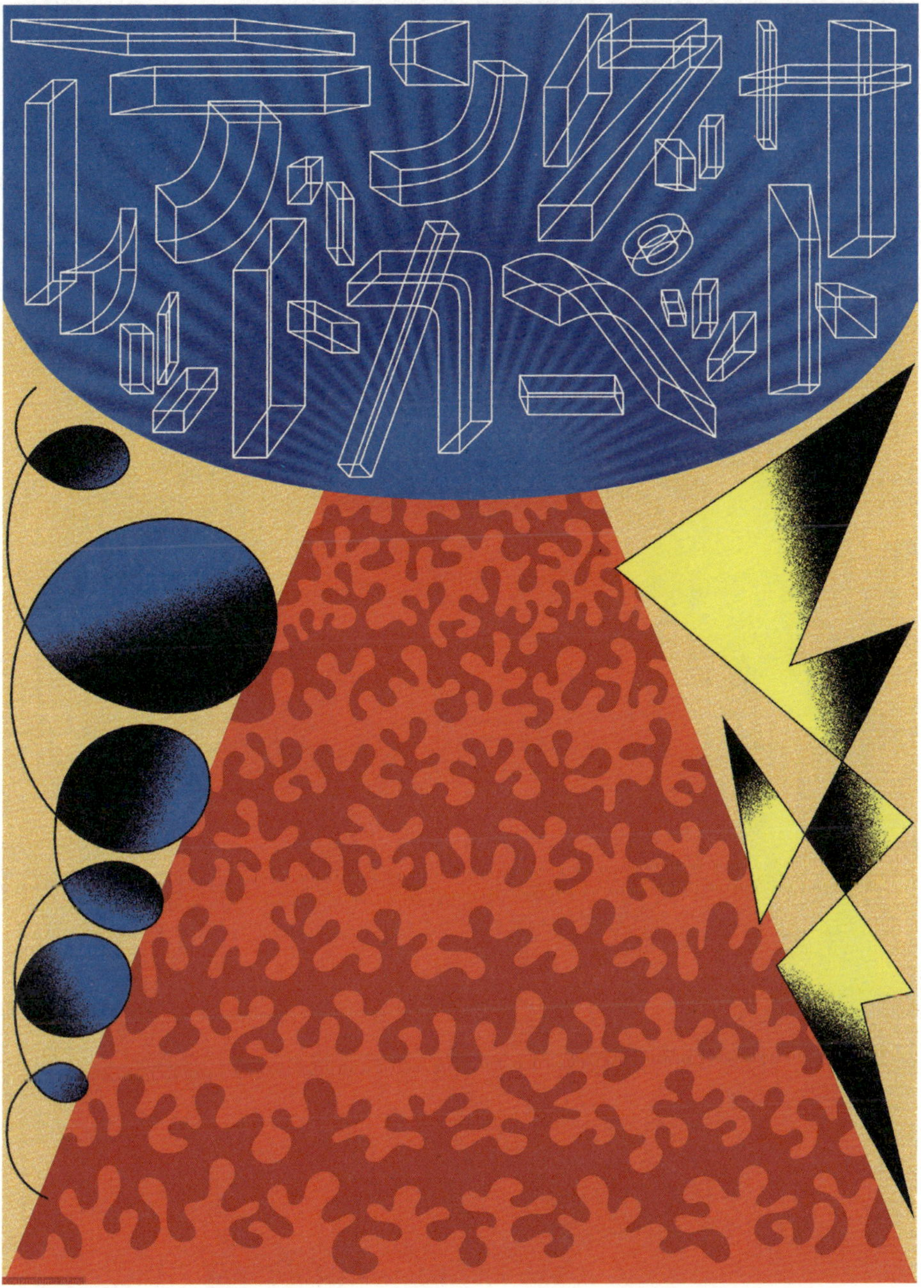

Now Sailing

The Gate
of Wind.

Toshima island

Oshima island

voteposter.cargo.site instagram @voteposter #投票ポスター2022 ©Yuta Miura
VOTE 7.10

Yuuka Kubo

Born in 1995, Tokyo-based Yuuka Kubo's work explores optimal compositions of colours, shapes, and materials. She designs publicity materials based on her art and graphics for given themes. She also produces personal work that embodies her own ideas as concepts and main themes.

imprint
2022.
3.11㊎-
3.27㊐
定休日
火
水
open
12:00-
18:00
ryousuke
aruse
企画
keshik.jp
会場
offsait studio
京都市下京区
西新屋敷揚屋町46-3

スーパーマーケット
“アルター”市場
vol.2
入場無料
会場：
BnA Alter Museum
1F/2F
会期中無休
2021.
2.27-
3.14
参加アーティスト：
TYM344
金田金太郎
時吉あきな
WORKSHOPトレードマーク
西舘朋央
伊佐治雄悟
長谷川由貴
高橋美衣
星拳五
西原彩香
澤あも愛紅
参加ディレクター：
吉田山 (FL田SH)／佐久間磨 (Rondade)
黒田純平 (keshik.jp)／筒井一隆 (BnA Alter Museum)
BnA Alter Museum

Graphic Design: Yuuka Kubo

Meta MALL
2022.
3.5 sat - 3.27 sun
"アルター"市場 vol.03
@BnA Alter Museum
SCG / 1F / 2F
入場無料／会期中無休
参加ディレクター
吉田山 (FL田SH)
武部敬俊 (LIVERARY)
佐久間磨 (Rondade)
黒田純平 (keshik.jp)
筒井一隆 (BnA Alter Museum)
参加アーティスト
金田金太郎
菊池和晃
時吉あきな
vug
大橋裕之
HOME ECONOMICS EXPERIMENT
on-demand System of Culture
サカイケイタ
清水美於奈
高橋美衣
野田ジャスミン
beewaa
中田有美
松田将英
BnA Alter Museum

集合／開放
2nd Anniversary BnA Alter Museum
集合 展覧会
2021.4.24㊏-5.16㊐（1期）
2021.5.22㊏-6.13㊐（2期）
開放 アートルーム
2021.5.9㊐/5.30㊐
BnA Alter Museum

明日はまた別の1日
Tomorrow was another day
2022
12.3 SAT -12.25 SUN
11:00-20:00
会場：BnA Alter Museum 1F
会期中無休・入場無料
企画協力：黒田純平　グラフィック：久保悠香
霜田哲也
水越智三
Ato1snow
The TOMODACHI !
WAN_TAN
BnA Alter Museum

Yuuri Mikami

Yuuri Mikami is a graphic designer who graduated from Musashino Art University's Department of Visual Communication Design in 2008 before working at Denstu Tec and Taku Satoh Design Office Inc. She established her own design office in 2017.

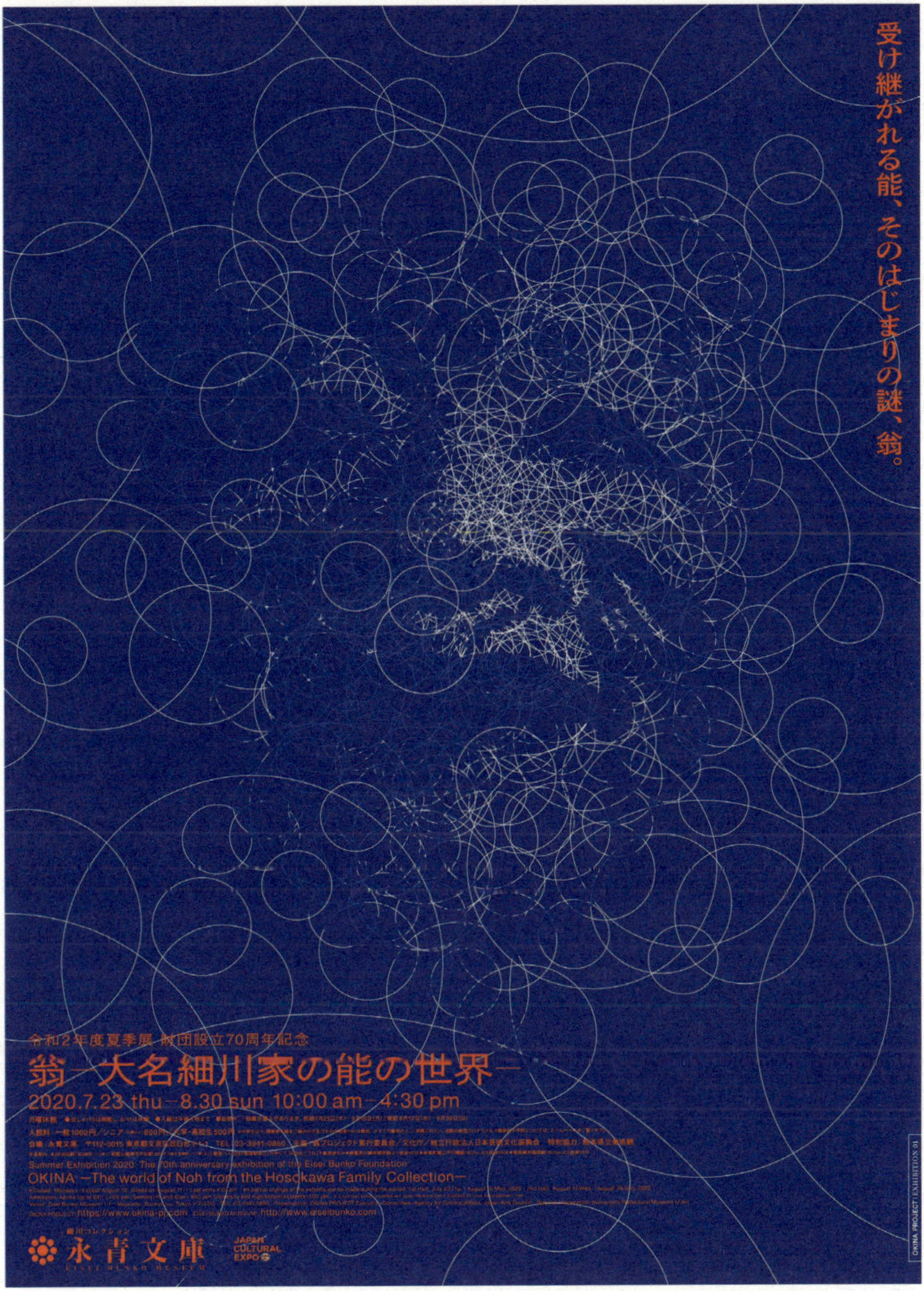
受け継がれる能、そのはじまりの謎、翁。
令和2年度夏季展 財団設立70周年記念
翁―大名細川家の能の世界―
2020.7.23 thu―8.30 sun 10:00 am―4:30 pm
Summer Exhibition 2020: The 70th anniversary exhibition of the Eisei Bunko Foundation
OKINA ―The world of Noh from the Hosokawa Family Collection―
https://www.okina-pj.com
http://www.eiseibunko.com
永青文庫
EISEI BUNKO MUSEUM
JAPAN CULTURAL EXPO
OKINA PROJECT | EXHIBITION 01

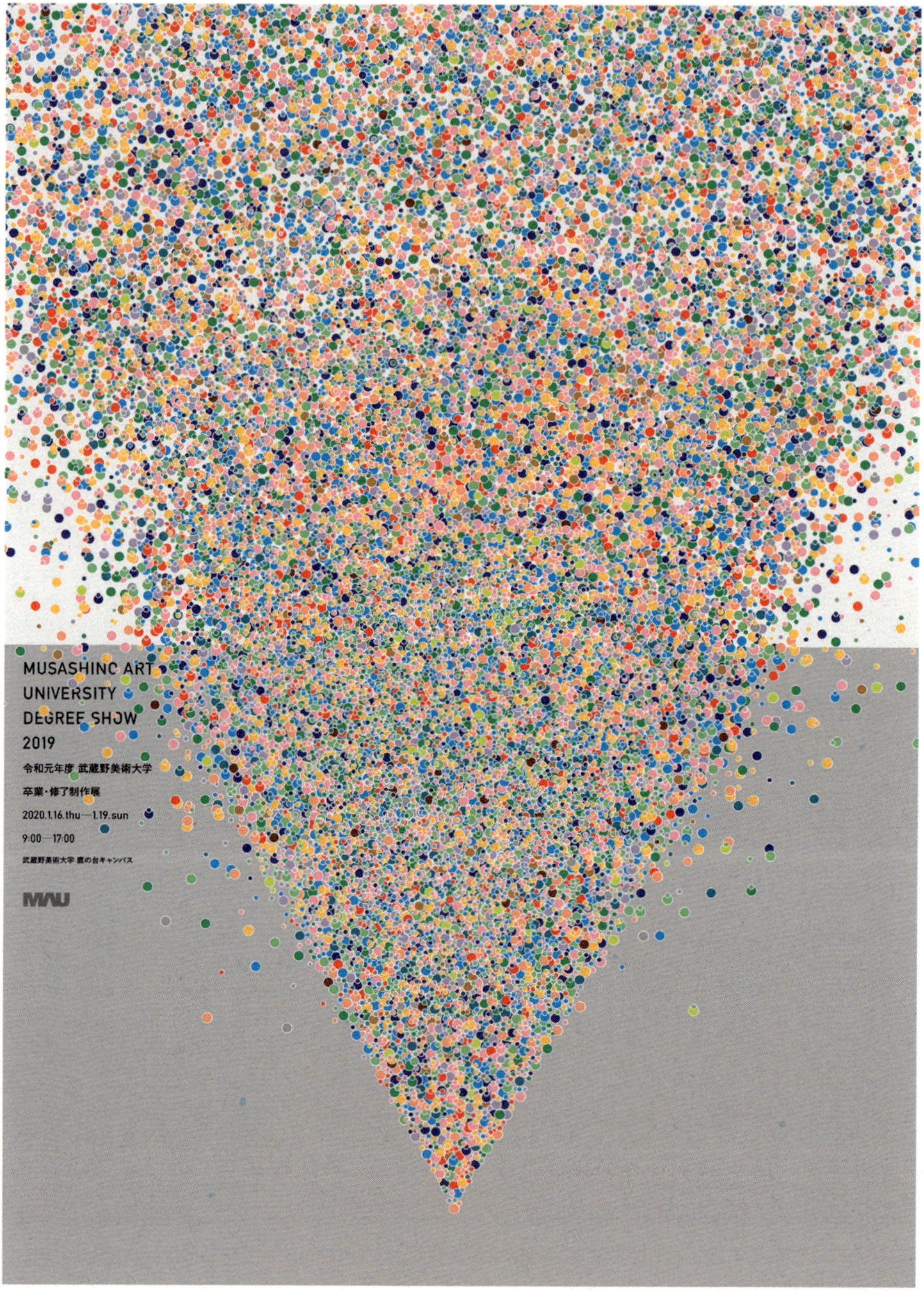
MUSASHINO ART
UNIVERSITY
DEGREE SHOW
2019
令和元年度 武蔵野美術大学
卒業・修了制作展
2020.1.16.thu—1.19.sun
9:00—17:00
武蔵野美術大学 鷹の台キャンパス

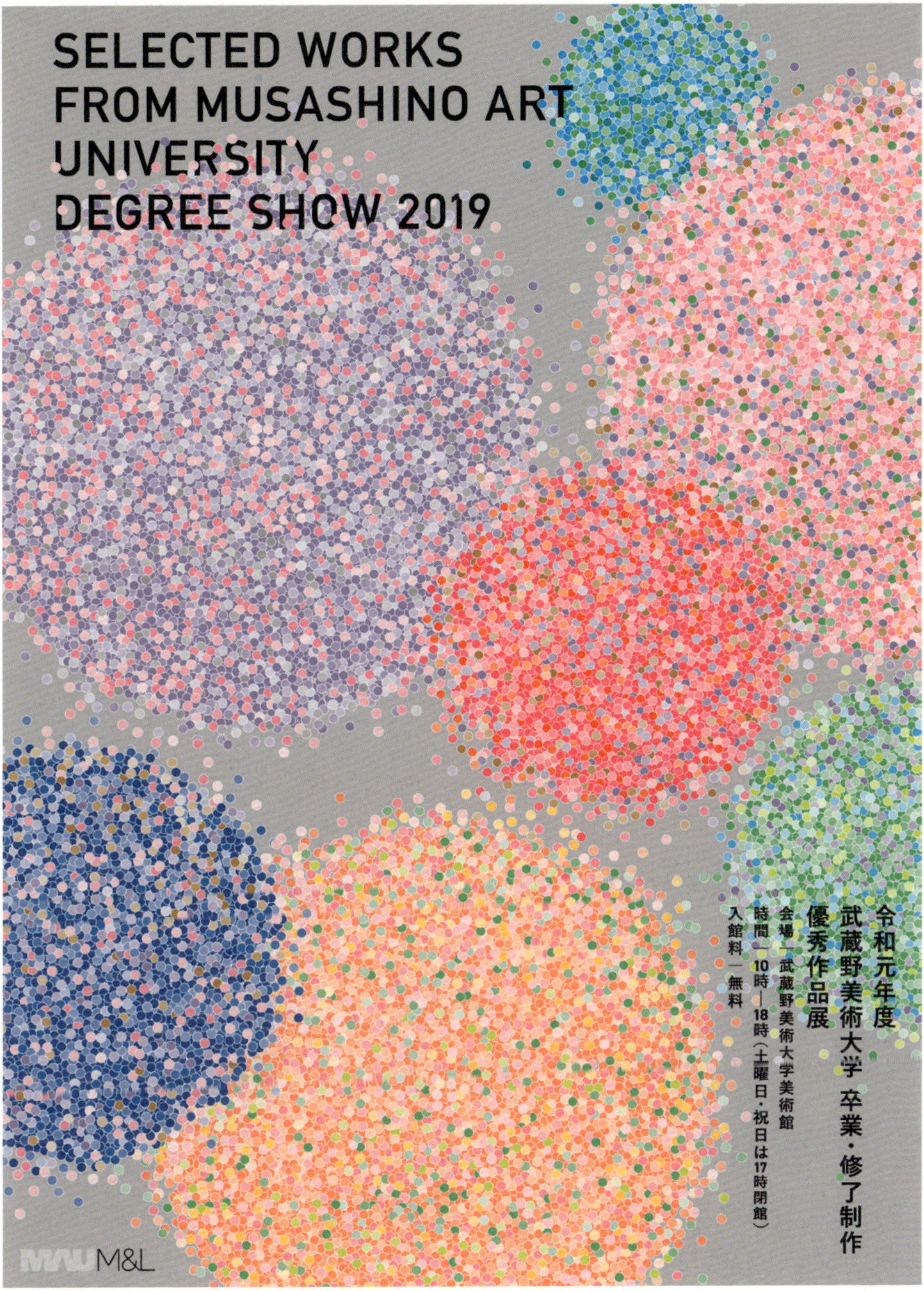
SELECTED WORKS
FROM MUSASHINO ART
UNIVERSITY
DEGREE SHOW 2019
令和元年度
武蔵野美術大学 卒業・修了制作
優秀作品展
会場ー武蔵野美術大学美術館
時間ー10時ー18時（土曜日・祝日は17時閉館）
入館料ー無料
MAU M&L

Index

AFFORDANCE inc.

P. 009
sazae do

P. 010
SLEEPING LIFE WTH ART

P. 011
POSTER Tama Art University graphic design

P. 012
NIHON NO ME

P. 013
Undying Life

P. 014
HOMETOWN

P. 015
TOTONOERU

P. 016–017
OTOKOTACHI

Aiko Koike

P. 019
New Documentary Movie by Takashi Homma "First, jay comes."
Photography: Takashi Homma

P. 020
"PARCO Ai to aimai"

P. 021
"Masahiro Hasunuma "Especially Impossible Fantasies, Kobe art village center."

P. 022
Contact Gonzo "untitled session"

P. 023–025
KYOTO EXPERIMENT Kyoto International Performing Arts Festival

Arata Kubota

P. 027–029
Slice of Heartland
Illustration: Ryuto Miyake

P. 030–031
New wave, new wind.

P. 032–034
Cho Do S.
Illustration: Shigeki Yuriko Yamane

P. 035
Tokyo Copywriters Club Exhibition 2018

P. 036
JOC JUNIOR OLYMPIC CUP

P. 037
POCARI SWEAT

P. 038–039
Japanese sake "ui"

asianvoice

P. 041
Zero Poster Exhibition 2020

P. 042
Zero Poster Exhibition 2022

P. 043
NUIT BLANCHE KYOTO 2022

P. 044
FUROSHIKI Exhibition 2021

P. 045
NY TDC

P. 046
Kodomo Jakuchu

P. 047
Zero Poster Exhibition 2019

P. 048
International Osaka Poster Fest 2021

P. 049
In Praise of Shadows in Tokyo 2020

Asuka Watanabe

P. 051
FUNKDEMIC, March 2022

P. 052
FUNKDEMIC Open Air, October 2022

P. 053
Solar Pot 2021

P. 054
BONNA POT 2021

P. 055
BONNA POT 2022

Atsushi Ishiguro

P. 057–059
NECO ASU

P. 060–063
DELUSION TO HEDI SLIMANE POSTER

P. 064–065
BUNKITSU

P. 066–067
best smoking movies exhibition

P. 068–069
FU-TO UDON

collé

P. 071–073
MILKHALL SOLDES
Client: MILKHALL

P. 074–077
shopping exhibition

P. 078–081
FAMILY

P. 082–083
face myself

coton design

P. 085
TRADITIONAL WAY & FRESH IDEA
Client: Senshu

P. 086
control
Client: horobite

P. 087
poroporo ni
Client: horobite

P. 088
CREEK
Client: CREEK

P. 089
harimazaka marche
Client: harimazaka marche

P. 090
LIVING WITH FARMING

P. 091
Nae wo Ueru
Client: horobite

P. 092
Ikebana Ryusei Exhibition 2020
Client: Ikebana Ryuseiha

P. 093
Ikebana Ryusei Exhibition 2021
Client: Ikebana Ryuseiha

P. 094
kohaku
Client: horobite

P. 095
border
Client: horobite

DENTSU

P. 097–101
1CRP
Art Direction: Aya Yagi
Photography: Shoheil Takenaka, Mariko Ohya, Katsutoshi Sawachika, Yoichi Onoda, Keita Goto

P. 102–105
THE STONE CITY
Creative Direction: Hiroyasu Wakabayashi
Art Direction: Aya Yagi
Copywriting: Ikumi Tonosaki
Design: Kumiko Shiraki, Ruriko Kasai
Illustration: Heisuke Kitazawa
Photography: Kenshu Shintsubo, Tenten

P. 106–109
STONE FACES
Creative Direction: Hiroyasu Wakabayashi
Art Direction: Aya Yagi
Copywriting: Ikumi Tonosaki
Production: Nobu Miyazaki
Design: Kai Kawanishi, Yiwen Kao
Art: tupera tupera
Photography: Fumihito Katamura
Photo Production: Yusuke Shimura

emuni Inc.

P. 111
Tokyo Festival 2022

P. 112
Mintpedia

P. 113
Museum of the people,
by the people, for the people

P. 114–121
VENT NOUVEAU DIGITAL
Photography: Shinya Sato
Retouching: Mariko Yoshitake

Eri Ishihara

P. 123–127
fiore soffitta "SPRING HAS COME."

P. 128–129
Suna to mizutama "landscape"

P. 130–131
Suna to mizutama "blue bird, black hole"

P. 132–133
Suna to mizutama "Tatoeba no Fukei"

Harajuku DESIGN Inc.

P. 135–137
musubi A

P. 138–139
musubi B

P. 140–141
Ohagi3

P. 142–143
tanabesou

P. 144–145
Sado Shima

Haro, Inc.

P. 147
stop-underagedrinking

P. 148–149
Kanji camo series

P. 150–151
Waseda Weekly Special issue

P. 152–155
Tsuru-To-Kame "BATHLIFE"
Photography: Naohiro Kobayashi

P. 156–157
PASOCOM MUSIC CLUB "See-Voice"
Release one man live

Hiroki Fujimaki

P. 159–161
one day

P. 162–163
Seikatsu

P. 164–165
ON Body

P. 166
She in the flower

P. 167
a normal situation

P. 168–169
Invisible but visible

P. 170–171
Scene of Kutani

Hirotoshi Shiki

P. 173–175
LOOK, LOOK! LOOKS EXHIBITION
Art Direction & Design: Keita Asaoka, Hirotoshi Shiki
Copywriting: Kyoko Kita
Organisation: Yowami wo nigiru sushiya

P. 176–177
CURRY GEOGRAPHY

P. 178–179
LIKE BEER

P. 180–181
MOON

P. 182–183
Print of Pudding

P. 184–187
RARE FRUIT

P. 188–189
SaLaDa

homesickdesign

P. 191
Design examination 2018 by Iwate Art Directors Club
Client: Iwate Art Directors Club

P. 192–194
ARTS LIVE IWATE 2022
Client: Iwate Art Support Center

P. 195
The special exhibition of Morioka History and Culture Museum "To Edo"
Client: Morioka History and Culture Museum
Special Credit: Kawaguchi

P. 196–197
Tohoku Portfolio Exhibition 2023
Client: Cyg

P. 198–199
The exhibition of Morioka History and Culture Museum "SHIGEKI"
Client: Morioka History and Culture Museum
Special Credit: Kawaguchi

P. 200–201
The exhibition of Morioka History and Culture Museum "Our Precious Collection"
Client: Morioka History and Culture Museum
Special Credit: Kawaguchi

Kango Shimizu

P. 203–205
Denier

P. 206–209
Karaoke bar manhattan

P. 210–211
PEACEFUL GOOOOD HOLIDAY

P. 212–213
Type family

Keita Asaoka

P. 215–217
RUFFLOG

P. 218–219
Birds

P. 220–221
AKO OYSTER PRODUCTS

P. 222–223
DISTANCE ZANMAI EXHIBITION

Kenichi Kuromaru

P. 225
LINK LINK POSTERS 2022

P. 226–227
Exhibited work for posters selection of Japan Graphic Design Association

Maiko Higuchi

P. 229
Waruishibai vol.22&23 "BODO NO ATO, SAMISHII POP NEW WORLD/YASEI NO KOI" (2019)

Writing & Direction: Akira Yamazaki
Organisation: Waruishibai
Photography: Yoshiro Hayakawa

P. 230
Waruishibai vol.28 "ITOSHI NO BOKAN" (2022)

Writing & Direction: Akira Yamazaki
Organisation: Waruishibai
Photography: Kisshomaru Shimamura

P. 231
Office Uwanosora&Team the 27 "Hotaru" (2019)

Writing & Direction: Kosei Fukatani
Organision: Office Uwanosora

P. 232–233
Goethe "What is in us is already overflowing in the world." (2020)

P. 234
Tone In Nature (2021)

Writing: Norihiko Kamaya

P. 235
Generosity (2020)

P. 236–239
KEItoMAI "KEI KOBAYASHI&MAIKO HIGUCHI SUPER MARCKET" (2016–)

Special Credits: KEI to MAI (Kei Kobayashi, Maiko Higuchi)

P. 240–241
UA25th-30th Anniversary (2021)

Marble illustration: UA

P. 242–243
blood&earth (2022)
Project Planning: Kisshomaru Shimamura
Editing: Moe Nishiyama

Mayuka Nanbu

P. 245
flower and a bird
Client: Taste

P. 246–247
O.T.D.P
Client: Communication Design
Association of Korea

P. 248–249
Strange Feeling
Client: Taste

P. 250–253
Growing Living Things
Client: Taste

Moeta Wakamatsu

P. 255
Confusion and Unity

P. 256–257
Takeshi Wakamatou
Posthumous Exhibition

P. 258
BONNOU TAISAN

P. 259
regeneration

P. 260–261
Othello (board game)

P. 262
suzushi-goto

P. 263
tsuyu

MOTOMOTO inc.

P. 265–269
Play Rule
Design: Kenichi Matsumoto

P. 271
hugcoffee seasonal posters
Art Direction: Kenichi Matsumoto
Design: Kenichi Matsumoto, Chihiro Sato

P. 272–273
hugcoffee
Art Direction: Kenichi Matsumoto
Design: Kenichi Matsumoto, Chihiro Sato

P. 274–275
Jewelry Week 2020
Art Direction: Kenichi Matsumoto
Design: Kenichi Matsumoto, Naomi Sakamoto,
Chihiro Sato

Mu Design Room

P. 277–279
TOKYO FUDOKI for graphic designers
Client: MU DESIGN ROOM, group of he

P. 280
Legend of beautiful things
Client: SHINGEKI theater companies exchange project
Illustration: Hashiguchi Goyō

P. 281
SEINENZA THEATER COMPANY "NOKORIBI (= embers)"
Client: SEINENZA THEATER COMPANY

P. 282
Typojanchi 2017
Client: Korean Society of Typography / Typojanchi 2017

P. 283
"ME" (me = eyes)

N.G.inc.

P. 285–287
HITOTOYO SHICHIHENGE
Client: UNIVERSAL MUSIC JAPAN

P. 288–291
JABARA
Client: CHOSHI GA YOKUNARU CLUB

P. 292
"I'M POSSIBLE" The Third Japan Graphic Design Exhibition
Client: At Design

P. 293
The 101st Sogetsu Annual Exhibition
Client: Sogetsu Foundation

Nanaya Shinbayashi

P. 295
HAND

P. 296–297
Banana

P. 298
JAGDA HOKKAIDO POSTER EXHIBITION 2022 Exhibited Posters
Special Credit: JAGDAHOKKAIDO

P. 299
SOLO EXHIBITION "MYAKU(Pulse)"

P. 300–301
Snake

P. 302
Meteor shower

P. 303
ICC Catch Copy & Poster Design Competition
Special Credit: Inter x cross Creative Center

P. 304
JAGDA HOKKAIDO POSTER EXHIBITION 2022
Special Credit: JAGDA HOKKAIDO

P. 305
TOWN

Naonori Yago

P. 307–309
casa tree

P. 310–311
Itsumademo SHISHIDO KAVKA

P. 312–313
HAKUHODO DY GROUP GLOBAL PURPOSE OPEN BRIEF

Polarno

P. 315–319
Tokyo kougei univesity
Art Direction: Sagara Kentaro
Design: Chiba Rikuya

P. 320–323
miyamoto jyuoumujin
Art Direction: Sagara Kentaro
Design: Shimizu Kango
Painting: Sanuki Ayaka
Photography: Kasai Kenichi

P. 324–327
king of modern light
Art Direction: Sagara Kentaro
Design: Shimizu Kango
Handwriting: Kasai Kenichi
Photography: Okimura Norihiko

REFLECTA, Inc.

P. 329
FORMULA
Photography: Go Itami
Styling: Koji Oyamada
Makeup: Yuka Toyama

P. 330–331
Pipilotti Rist: Your Eye Is My Island
Collage: Pipilotti Rist's video stills

P. 332
Interdiffusion a tribute to Yoshi Wada

P. 333
Syntactic Forest

P. 334
Belevitch Implementation of the 1 0 - Port Ideal Conference Network
Photography: Takuro Ogawa

P. 335
LANDSCAPE GOES DOMESTIC

Ryotaro Hirosaki

P. 337
She is beautiful.

P. 338
Same color, different shape.

P. 339
FLOWERS-One stroke

P. 340
Vase and Flower

P. 341
The Japanese flower

P. 342–343
FLOWERS-Line and Surface

Ryuichi Kawajiri

P. 345–347
Paper Flower Vase
Special Credit: Hokkaishikohsha, HACOYA

P. 348
Cut out the map

P. 349
Jagda New Designer Award Exhibition 2020 & 2021 in Osaka

P. 350
Fruits Report “Apple”

P. 351
Fruits Report “Cherry”

P. 353
GoriNikki “G”

P. 354–355
GoriNikki “Shi”

P. 356–357
GoriNikki “Megane”

Sato Design

P. 359
Boundaries of the ‘natural’ and ‘supernatural’
Client: National Institutes for the Humanities

P. 360–363
Document and References on Art and Life of Sadamasa MOTONAGA—Riding on a time machine—
Client: Takarazuka Arts Center

P. 365–367
REGNUM IMAGINARIUM: Realm of the Marvelous and Uncanny
Client: Fukuoka City Museum
Photography: Yukiyo Daido

P. 368–371
mujara
Client: mujara

Satomi Okubo

P. 373–377
Personal Fuel
Client: Nikkei Inc.

P. 378–381
MIXCITING!
Client: ad:tech tokyo
Production: Satomi Okubo, J.C.SPARK

Shoichi Maehara

P. 383–385
Hanaike Battle
Doll Design: Hiroka Osada

P. 386–389
Yamabiko.inc / Yamabiko magazine
Creative Direction: Shinsaku Watanabe
Production: Go Matsumoto
Photography: Keisuke Ono
Interview: Akifumi Kumai

P. 390–391
TOKYO MIDTOWN DESIGN HUB / KIDS WORKSHOP 2022
Photography: Megumi Oyama

P. 392–393
Photo studio higashi to nishi
Photography: Megumi Oyama

P. 394–395
çà et là / sorakasa kit
Creative Direction: Shinsaku Watanabe
Production: Go Matsumoto
Photography: Megumi Oyama

Shunsuke Suzuki

P. 397–399
On the clumsiness of people

P. 400–401
I don't know myself yet.

P. 402
Fight, man.

P. 403
Be greedy

P. 404–405
figure of a tree

Sitoh inc.

P. 407–411
TRAILS

P. 412–413
shatter

P. 414–415
Strange of Japan

P. 416
för ägg
Production: LABORATORIAN

P. 417
I'M POSSIBLE
Client: At Design

P. 418–419
Designs for Travel
Art: Nitto Soubi
Editing: BNN, Inc.
Photography: Shinya Sato
Retouching: Akio Yamaguchi

P. 420–423
THE GATE
Production: LABORATORIAN
Photography: Shinya Sato
Retouching: Kensaku Uchikoshi

STUDIO WONDER Co.,Ltd.

P. 425
Reservation party for spring goods
Client : Sapporo PARCO

P. 426–427
daughter,MOTHER.

P. 428–429
PARCO CULTURE SUPERMARKET
Client : Sapporo PARCO

P. 430–433
Susukino kissa Purple Dahlia
Client: WONDER CREW Co.,Ltd.
Photography: GAZE fotographica Co.,Ltd.

P. 434–435
The eyes cannot believe one's true thoughts

P. 436–437
Blessings of Living Drift Ice, Okhotsk
Client: Takigen Shoten

STUDY LLC.

P. 439
BETWEEN SYMBOLS & ILLUSTRATIONS

P. 440–447
Para-GRAPH

Tadashi Ueda

P. 449
KANO Poster for Traveling & Hugging
Special Credit: Sentian Dazi
Client: GLAb glab.com.tw

P. 450
Rain, Wind
Client: Korea National University of Arts

P. 451
Shake Hands T & A
Artwork & Client: Alexander Medel Calderón

P. 452
Ishi No Ue Demo Zatsunen
Client: Matsumiya Bunka Labo

P. 453
Rising From A Night's Sleep
Client: Gurafiku

P. 454
SHOKKI exhibition SHOKKI exhibition "Are"
Client: talklein
Photography: SHOKKI

P. 455
LUCK014 Mumumu
Client: EARTH + gallery
Artwork: Seiya Kobayashi, Koyubi, Mikako Mizuuchi

Yamato Kitazono

P. 457
AAC Poster Competition : selected

P. 458–460
INVISIBLE HUMANITY

P. 461
Ordinary days in 2021

Yasuda Takahiro

P. 463
"AFTERGLOWS" Film by Taichi Kimura

P. 464
Daisuke Motogi / DDAA LAB Exhibition "Belt Furniture"

P. 465
DDAA "Hackability of The Stool"
Exhibition Design: DDAA LAB
Exhibition Organiser: B1OCK

P. 466
VOTE Poster 2022

P. 467
FACETASM x CITY COUNTRY CITY
bonjour music circus 2018

P. 468
EXPERIMENTAL CREATIONS 2017 Tokyo

P. 469
EXPERIMENTAL CREATIONS 2018 Tokyo

P. 470
Takahiro Yasuda 3rd Solo Exhibition
"EMERGE"

P. 471
Spirit&Nature Graphic Design Exhibition
of Koichi Sato

P. 472
Laforet Grand Bazar 2021 Summer

P. 473
Laforet Grand Bazar 2022 Winter

Yudai Osawa

P. 475
"Model" Hoshiki Ara Exhibition
Artwork: Hoshiki Ara

P. 476
Membrane
Artwork: Kai Yoshizawa

P. 477
CulTech Forum Japan 2022

P. 478
PULSE

P. 479
"EN" RYUTist

P. 480–481
SONIC Agency

P. 482–483
Spout

P. 484
VOTE1031

Yuta Miura

P. 487–489
FLOWER SKETCH

P. 490–498
RITO IN TOKYO

P. 499
VOTE2022

Yuuka Kubo

P. 501
imprint
Illustration: Ryosuke Aruse

P. 502–503
Supermarket Alternative vol.2
Client: BnA Alter Museum

P. 504
Meta MALL Alternative vol.3
Client: BnA Alter Museum

P. 505

TEMPURA Magazine No.12

Client: TEMPURA

P. 506

Assemble/Open 2nd Anniversary BnA Alter Museum

Client: BnA Alter Museum

P. 507

Tomorrow was another day

Client: BnA Alter Museum

Yuuri Mikami

P. 509

OKINA The world of Noh from the Hosokawa Family Collection

Organisation: OKINA PROJECT Executive Committee, Agency for Cultural Affairs, Japan Arts Council
Creative direction: Takuya Hoda, Yuuri Mikami
Special credits: Kumamoto Prefectural Museum of Art

P. 510

Musashino Art University Degree show 2019

P. 511

Selected works from Musashino Art University Degree show 2019

Acknowledgments

We would like to thank all the designers, studios, and companies who were involved in the production of this book for their significant contribution to its compilation. We would also like to express our gratitude to all the producers involved for their invaluable opinions and assistance, as well as the professionals in the creative industry who were generous with their insights and feedback throughout the entire production process. Last but not least, to those who made specific input behind the scenes but were not credited in this book, we acknowledge and appreciate all your effort and continuous support.

Future Editions

If you wish to participate in viction:ary's future projects and publications, please send your website or portfolio to we@victionary.com